CZARS

400 Years of Imperial Grandeur

WONDERS MEMPHIS

CZARS

400 Years of Imperial Grandeur

Essays By

I.A. Bobrovnitskaya

A.K. Levykin

M.V. Martynova

O.B. Melnikova

T.N. Muntian

V.M. Nikitina

I.I. Vishnevskaya

CATALOGUE EDITOR

A.K. Levykin, Scientific Director of the Kremlin Museum

Presented by

WONDERS ≈ MEMPHIS

The Memphis International Cultural Series

Organized by

The State Historical and Cultural Museum
Preserve of the Moscow Kremlin
in association with
Cultural Exhibitions and Events, Inc.

Copyright © 2002 Wonders
The Memphis International Cultural Series
PO Box 3371 Mamphis, TN 38173-0371 Phone 901-312-9161 or 800-2MEMPHIS
www.wonders.org

Text, object descriptions, and object photographs © 2002 The State Historical and Cultural
Museum and Preserve of the Moscow Kremlin

Printed in the United States of America

Project Manager: Russ Gordon

Catalogue Production:
Curatorial Assistance, Los Angeles, California
Director: Graham Howe
Editor: Patrick Pardo
Catalogue Design: Robert Kranzke
Assistant Designer: Eulogio Dayday
Translator: Lora Wheeler
Editorial Assistant: Viyada Schultz
Production Assistants: Alex Mendoza, Christina Rizkallah, Amy Thomas

Front Cover: original illustration by Yuan Lee
Frontispiece: *Throne and Footstool of Emperor Paul I,* 1790s
Russian Czars Timeline, Romanov Genealogy, and Map of Russia created by Eulogio Dayday

Library of Congress Control Number: 2002104309

ISBN 1-882516-15-X (Hardcover)
ISBN 1-882516-14-1 (Paperback)

First Printing

THE COVER OF THE CATALOGUE IS PRINTED ON INTERNATIONAL PAPER *CAROLINA C1S 15PT.*
THE CATALOGUE PAGES ARE PRINTED ON INTERNATIONAL PAPER *SAVVY GLOSS 80 TEXT.*

TABLE OF CONTENTS

Ken Sossaman
1949-2002

If it was Dick Hackett's vision that established WONDERS, it was Ken Sossaman who delivered our message to the world and made WONDERS a household name. Indeed, it was Ken who coined the term "WONDERS." He brought marketing acumen to what at first seemed a strange notion—bringing the world's great art to Memphis, Tennessee. It is largely through his efforts that over three-and-a-half million visitors have attended WONDERS exhibitions. Ken's presence in the community and with WONDERS will be sorely missed. It is a loss not easily filled.

This exhibition catalogue is fondly dedicated to Ken Sossaman.

WONDERS ❧ MEMPHIS

CZARS: 400 Years of Imperial Grandeur marks a milestone in the history of WONDERS. Ten years ago as mayor of Memphis, I had the pleasure of initiating the WONDERS series with the beautiful exhibition *Catherine the Great*. This wonderful exhibition is remembered fondly by so many Memphians as perhaps a symbol for the perfect WONDERS show. I hope *CZARS* will allow you to recapture the magic of Catherine and will point us toward future successes.

CZARS is the result of the efforts of literally hundreds of individuals both in this country and in Russia. First and foremost I must acknowledge the generosity of the State Historical and Cultural Museum and Preserve of the Moscow Kremlin. In particular I must thank General Director Elena Gagarina, Scientific Director Aleksey Levykin, and Deputy Director to the General Director Olga Mironova. It is due to their knowledge, wisdom, and vision that their initial concept of a historical retrospective of the Romanov dynasty has become the incredible exhibition of Russian treasures displayed so beautifully in *CZARS*.

Other Russian colleagues that I feel must be singled out include V. Mariutina, Head of the International Division, L.A. Puchkova, Head of Inventory, G.N. Khatina, Main Specialist of the Division of Exhibitions, and Z.I. Tregulova, Special Consultant to the Kremlin Museum. They all contributed greatly to the success of the exhibition.

Natalie Goriachkin, our representative in Moscow, deserves special commendation for her many late nights of receiving faxes from afar, keeping her U.S. counterparts on the appointed path, and escorting so many of us around Moscow. Without her assistance we would never have been able to accomplish so much in so little time.

Cultural Exhibitions and Events, Inc. spent many years pursuing this exhibition. It is primarily through their efforts, and in particular Betty Simecka's refusal to give up, that this project has finally come to fruition. This represents CEE's first exhibition and I wish them and the newly formed Kansas International Museum the very best in all their future endeavors.

WONDERS is blessed to be under the leadership of a truly exceptional board of directors. Chaired by Diane Rudner, their wise counsel has often been invaluable in resolving difficult issues. They are the ones who have insured the smooth transition of WONDERS from its former status as a division of city government to its present status as a private not-for-profit. I must specially note Honey Scheidt's personal commitment to WONDERS. Without her support the transition would have been ever so much more difficult.

It is impossible to adequately thank our corporate sponsors for their resources and encouragement. Cricket Comfortable Wireless, our presenting sponsor, under the dynamic leadership of Derek Jett, and Kroger Delta Marketing Area under the tireless leadership of Dick Tillman, have been most generous in supporting *CZARS* and our immediate past exhibition *Eternal Egypt*. The kind donation by Kathy Buckman Davis and Karl Buckman in honor of their grandmother, long time WONDERS patron and philanthropist Mertie Buckman, will insure that every Memphis and Shelby County schoolchild has the opportunity to attend and learn of the culture and history of the world's largest country. Our other principal sponsors include the Assisi Foundation, the Buckman Family, Clear Channel Outdoor, the Hohenberg Family Foundation, the Hyde Family Foundation, International Paper, Memphis Sight & Sound, Northwest Airlines, Peabody Place and The Peabody, Quantum Showroom, the Scheidt Family Foundation, the Wilson Family, and the Plough Foundation, all of whom have joined to help bring this wonderful cultural amenity to Memphis. My deepest expression of appreciation goes to Mayor Herenton and the City Council for continuing to support this unique cultural attraction.

No WONDERS exhibition would ever be possible without the countless hours served by our devoted volunteers, many of whom have participated since our first exhibition *Ramesses the Great*. The WONDERS staff is among the most committed people I have ever worked with. Their loyalty to these projects is without peer.

One particular staff member, Glen Campbell, must be singled out. I dedicate the success of *CZARS* to Glen's commitment. Glen, a longtime friend, has held leadership roles in WONDERS since its inception. It was his task to plan and direct the transition from a City agency to a private not-for-profit organization. It is Glen, along with the support of the Plough Foundation, who has truly insured that WONDERS may never cease.

I am sure I have omitted someone of great importance to the exhibition. If I have, I am sorry. There are still four individuals whom I must not fail to mention: my wife Kathy and our three children, Jason, Mary Shea and William. Without their love and support, I would not be able to devote the time and energy necessary to make *CZARS* a reality.

I hope all our visitors enjoy *CZARS* as much as I have enjoyed working on it.

Sincerely,

Richard C. Hackett
President and CEO
WONDERS

Letter from the General Director of the State Historical and Cultural Museum and Preserve of the Moscow Kremlin

The Moscow Kremlin is the heart of Russia, the symbol of state power of a great land, and the residence of the President of the Russian Federation. This is how millions of people know it throughout various parts of the world. The Moscow Kremlin is also a unique architectural and historical complex which combines the expanse of six centuries. The mighty fortress walls and towers, majestic churches, and luxurious palaces include constructions by both Russian and foreign rulers from the 15th to the 18th century. Here, in the very center of Moscow, is located one of the most famous museums of the world— The State Historical and Cultural Museum and Preserve of the Moscow Kremlin. This historical collection has existed for over 500 years. Experts have long considered the artistic objects preserved in the museum as standards of art, beauty, and craftsmanship.

Many valuable pieces from this unique collection make up the exhibition *CZARS: 400 Years of Imperial Grandeur*. American visitors will see exemplary works of ancient Russian origin: religious icons, armor and weaponry, paintings, as well as decorative and applied art from Russia, Western Europe, and the Far East, from the 16th to the 20th century. Certainly, many of the pieces in the exhibition can be counted as among masterpieces of world art. No less important is the fact that virtually every object is linked to the Russian state and church, and to famous events in Russian history. The amazing royal regalia, church and state vestments, religious icons, ceremonial horse equipage, weapons and orders, and the portraits of the Czars and Czarinas—all of this surrounded the Russian monarchs from the moment of their birth to their ultimate death. Some of these objects were high status symbols of state power and were indispensable for state ceremonies. Other objects were used in daily life. Taken as a group, these objects give visitors the possibility to imagine the centuries of coronations of the Russian monarchs, the luxury of Russian feasts at ceremonial receptions of foreign guests, and ceremonial parades and processions of the leaders to wars, to church services, and on royal hunts.

CZARS: 400 Years of Imperial Grandeur is being presented to a vast American audience as a magnificent combination of art, history, beauty, work, and inspiration. I hope that this exhibition serves to strengthen the cultural bond between the Russian and American people.

E. Iu. Gagarina
General Director
The State Historical and Cultural Museum and Preserve of the Moscow Kremlin

STATE HISTORICAL AND CULTURAL MUSEUM AND PRESERVE OF THE MOSCOW KREMLIN

EXHIBITION COMMITTEE

E.Iu. Gagarina, General Director

Executive Staff
A.K. Levykin, Scientific Director of the Museum
O.I. Mironova, Assistant (Deputy) Director to the General Director
I.V. Mariutina, Head of the International Division
I.K. Larionova, Head of the Section of Exhibits Inventory
L.A. Puchkova, Head of Exhibits Inventory
G.N. Khatina, Main Specialist of the Division of Exhibitions
Z.I. Tregulova, Consultant

Conceptual Authors of the Exhibition
I.A. Bobrovnitskaya, Senior Collaborator and Curator
I.I. Vishnevskaya, Head of Fabric Section
A.K. Levykin, Scientific Director of the Museum
M.V. Martynova, Senior Collaborator and Curator
V.V. Shakurova, Consultant

Working Staff
S.A. Amelekhina, Senior Collaborator and Curator
I.A. Bobrovnitskaya, Senior Collaborator and Curator
I.I. Vishnevskaya, Head of Fabric Section
I.A. Komarov, Head of Weapons and Horse Equipage
M.V. Martynova, Senior Collaborator and Curator
V.M. Roslavskii, Restorer
V.G. Chubinskaya, Senior Collaborator and Curator

Restorers

Iu.A. Osipov	I.M. Kachanova
V.A. Vychuzhanin	S.N. Gorbunov
V.M. Roslavskii	V.S. Shabelnik
N.M. Maresev	L.A. Barbinova
M.N. Kruzhalin	

Jewelry
V.P. Gretskii

WONDERS MEMPHIS

The Memphis International Cultural Series

WONDERS STAFF

ART HANDLING, TRANSPORTATION, AND INSTALLATION

Alexander International
Neely Mallory III, President
W.L. Wadsworth, Executive Vice-President
LeRoy Pettyjohn, Vice-President, Fine Art Handling
Jennifer Scism, Fine Art Supervisor
Bill Ramia, Director of Import Services
John Hearn, Import Services

Nurminen Prima Oy
Igor Filatov, Head, Moscow
Margarita Maslakova, Fine Art Agent, Moscow
Johanna Kailila, Fine Art Agent, Helsinki

Fine Art Installation Team
Larry Anderson
Edna Bomar
Tammy Braitwaite
Judd Childress
Don Harris
Jewel Rosenberg
David White

DESIGN AND CONSTRUCTION

Architectural Design/Team Management
Askew Nixon Ferguson Architects, Inc.
Lee Askew III, FAIA, Principal-in-Charge
Leslie Smith, AIA, Project Architect
Kenneth Parks, Production

Exhibition Design
Design 500
Scott Blake, Exhibit Designer
Henry Swanson, Exhibit Design Coordinator

Graphic Design
K. Design
Kathy Kelly

Illustrator
Kelly Brother, Illustrator
Kelly Brother

Exhibit Lighting
Design 500
Henry Swanson

Graphic Production
Bennett Creative Services
John Bennett

Model Maker
Scale Models Unlimited
Kamran Kiani
Mountmaking
Robert Fuglestadt

Photography
API Photographers
William Carrier III

Exhibition Construction
Wooldridge Construction Company
Jim Wooldridge, President
Kyle Anderson, Estimator and Project Manager
Robert Casper, Job Superintendent

Casework and Specialty Manufacturing
Advance Manufacturing Company
David Craig, President
Roy Koimn, Project Manager
Mike Fry, Project Superintendent
Elisabeth Childress, Faux Artist

CURATION AND EDUCATION

Teachers Guide
Amy Dietrich, Editor
Susan Thompson, Curriculum Coordinator
Heather Baugus, Layout Design

Docent Training
Barbara Belzer-Budgnas, Director of Continuing Education
University of Memphis
The Fogleman Center, University of Memphis

Artifact Assessment
Peter L. Schaffer, A La Vielle Russie

Introductory Video
API cine Memphis
William Carrier III, Director
Dan Conaway, Creative Director

Imagination Station
Elisabeth Childress, Designer

Audio Tour
Antenna Audio, Inc.
Laura Mann, VP of Business Development, North and South America
Dane Towell, Senior Client Services Manager
Alicia Simi, Client Services Manager
Kate Rothrock, Creative Manager
Peter Dunne, Producer
Charna Macfie, Producer

Catalogue Production
Russ Gordon, Project Manager
Graham Howe, Project Supervisor
Patrick Pardo, Editor
Robert Kranzke, Catalogue Designer
Eulogio Dayday, Assistant Designer
Lora Wheeler, Translator
Viyada Schultz, Editorial Assistant
Christina Rizkallah, Production Assistant
Amy Thomas, Production Assistant

SALES, MARKETING, AND PUBLIC RELATIONS

Advertising and Marketing
Sossaman & Associates
Donna Gordy, President
Eric Melkent, Co-Creative Director/Art
Beth Graber, Vice-President Media Services
Randall Hartzog, Director of Production Services
Walter Rose, Associative Creative Director/Interactive
Mike Villanueva, Account Manager/Interactive
Patty Likes, Co-Creative Director/Copy
Kenny Patrick, Art Director
Chris Taylor, Account Manager

Speakers Bureau
Marjorie Gerald, Coordinator

Group Travel
Unique Meetings, Events, Tour, Travel
Dennis Roberts, Owner
John Minervini, Owner
Jay Kirkpatrick, Tour
Kathleen Green, Group Sales
Melodye Ruby, Special Events

Concessions and Catering
Chef's Choice Catering

The Pyramid/SMG
Alan Freeman, General Manager
Chuck Jabbour, Assistant General Manager

Gala Opening
Memphis Cancer Foundation
Sandy Lewis, Co-Chair
Geri McCormack, Co-Chair
Billy Hicks, Co-Chair

Gift Shop
Museum Gift Shop Enterprises
Rifaat Hassan
George Jones
Jane Mitchell
Peggy Mitchell

Ticketing Equipment and Services
Ticketmaster
Charlie Ryan, President

SPONSORS

PRESENTING SPONSOR

MAJOR SPONSOR

PRINCIPAL SPONSORS

THE PLOUGH FOUNDATION

ASSISI FOUNDATION

MEMPHIS SIGHT & SOUND

BUCKMAN FAMILY

NORTHWEST AIRLINES

CLEAR CHANNEL OUTDOOR

PEABODY PLACE & THE PEABODY

HOHENBERG FAMILY FOUNDATION

QUANTUM SHOWROOM

HYDE FAMILY FOUNDATION

SCHEIDT FAMILY FOUNDATION

INTERNATIONAL PAPER

WILSON FAMILY

CITY OF MEMPHIS
DR. WILLIE W. HERENTON, MAYOR

MEMPHIS CITY COUNCIL
Chairman, Ricky Peete
Councilman Joe Brown
Councilman Ed Ford
Councilwoman Janet Hooks
Councilman E.C. Jones
Councilman Myron Lowery
Councilman Tom Marshall
Councilman Jack Sammons
Councilwoman TaJuan Stout-Mitchell
Councilwoman Barbara Swearengen-Holt
Councilman Brent Taylor
Councilwoman Pat Vander Schaaf
Councilman John Vergos

Major Contributors

B. Lee Mallory	Memphis Cancer Foundation
Bell South Advertising	Memphis Marriot Downtown
City of Memphis Division of Police Services Walter Crews, Director	Shelby County Government, Jim Rout, Mayor
First Tennessee	Smith & Nephew, Inc.
Lipscomb & Pitts Insurance, LLC	Saint Francis Hospital
Mednikow Jewelers	The Commercial Appeal
Memphis Arts Council	Time Warner Communications
	World Spice Technologies

Contributors

American Tuxedo	Memphis Convention & Visitors Bureau
A.S. Barboro	Memphis International Airport
The Bogatin Law Firm, LLC	Memphis Magazine
Bonne Terre Country Inn	Metro Memphis Hotel and Lodging Association
Boy Scouts of America	Metro Memphis Attractions Association
Catholic Diocese of Memphis Schools	Mid-South Fair
D. Canale Distributing	National Council of Jewish Women
Chef's Choice Catering	Northwest Airlink
Desoto Times	Olympic Optical
The Downtowner Magazine	Ozark Motor Lines
Girl Scout Council of the Mid-South	The Pyramid
Frank Grisanti's Italian Restaurant	Sarkis Kish Oriental Rugs
Hancock Fabrics	Shelby County Schools
Tom Jones	Sleep Inn at Court Square
Rick Masson	University of Memphis
Memphis Area Transit Authority	WKNO-TV, Channel 10
Memphis Brooks Museum	WMC-TV, Channel 5
Memphis City Schools	WREG-TV, Channel 3

The Romanov Dynasty

The Romanov Dynasty
A Brief History

by A.K. Levykin

THE ROOTS OF THE ROMANOVS

The royal dynasty of the Romanovs ruled Russia from the 17th to the 20th century. The Romanov roots can be traced to Andrei Kobyla, a landowner and nobleman who served at the court of the Muscovy Princes in the mid-14th century. His descendants included not only the Romanovs, but also many of Russia's most prominent noble families. The direct line to the Romanovs was through Feodor Koshkin, Kobyla's youngest son. Feodor had four sons: Ivan Feodorovich, Feodor Goltiai, Alexander Bezzubets, and Mikhail Durnyi. Ivan, the eldest, had four sons of his own: Ivan, Feodor Brekh, Yakov Kazak, and Zakhary; of these, the line continued through the last son, Zakhary.

Zakhary had three sons: Yakov, Yuri, and Vasily Liatsky. From 1487 to 1489 Yuri acted as vice-regent in the political center of Russian Novgorod, and played a leading role in affairs of state. The Romanovs were direct descendants of Yuri's second son, Roman Iurevich. Roman's older brother, Mikhail Iurevich Zakharin, was a *boyar* (nobleman), and held the second most important post in the *Duma* (governing council) of the Great Prince Vasily III. Mikhail's closeness to the Prince led to the choice of Mikhail's niece, Anastasia Romanovna, the daughter of Roman, as the bride for Vasily's son Ivan IV (better known as Ivan the Terrible).

While the Romanovs' ancestry was ancient and noble, this did not make them automatic heirs to the Russian throne; they were, after all, originally boyars and servants to the sovereign. At the turn of the 17th century, however, events took place which radically changed the history of the Russian state. In 1584 Ivan the Terrible died. He had three sons from his first marriage. Dmitry, the eldest, died young, and the second son, Ivan, was pronounced heir to the throne, but he was mortally wounded in a quarrel with his father, whose death was also hastened by the fight. As a result, Feodor Ivanovich, the youngest of the three sons, was crowned Czar. Feodor's reign, however, was short: he died on January 7, 1598, and his death marked the end of the ruling Rurik dynasty, who were descended from the first Muscovy Prince, Daniel, the youngest son of Alexander Nevsky. The country was now faced with the problem of electing a new Czar.

At the beginning of the 17th century, the most eligible contenders to the Russian throne were the Shuisky Princes, descendants of the Rurik family; the scions of the Lithuanian Grand Prince Gedemin, the so-called "Gedeminovichi," who had come to Moscow in the service of the sovereign; and two families of Muscovy boyars who could lay claim to the throne: the Godunovs and the Romanovs, who had greatly increased their influence at court during the reign of Ivan the Terrible. At the time of the succession, both

Russian Czars Timeline

					Nikon appointed Patriarch	
			War with Poland			
					Thirteen Year War begins	
Filaret returns to Russia				Peace with Poland		Schism begins
	Mikhail Feodorovich becomes Czar (1613–1645)					Alexei Mikhailovich becomes Czar (1645–1676)
1605	1610	1615	1620	1625	1630	1635	1640	1645	1650	1655

the Godunovs and the Romanovs were popular in the country, and both were directly linked to the late Czar through the female line. Ivan's first wife had been Anastasia Romanovna, the daughter of Roman Iurevich Zakharin. At the age of sixteen, Ivan, who had come to the throne when only three, declared himself Czar, or Emperor—the first ruler to assume this title. He was crowned on January 16, 1547 and the royal marriage took place later that year on February 3.

The influence of the Romanovs grew by virtue of the fact that Anastasia had borne Ivan the Terrible his three eldest sons. The children of Anastasia's siblings were therefore the closest relatives of the *czareviches* (princes). Even while Ivan the Terrible was alive, the Romanovs were amassing state power. Even after Ivan's second marriage, when he broke with his sons, the Romanovs still controlled the Duma. During the reigns of Ivan the Terrible's sons Ivan and Feodor, the Romanovs became powerful landowners. Most influential among them was Nikita Romanovich Yurev-Zakharin, the "favorite brother-in-law" of Ivan the Terrible. He was appointed guardian to the Czar Feodor and held the most important position in his court.

After Nikita Romanovich died, Boris Godunov became the most influential figure in the state. He had been one of Ivan the Terrible's most loyal allies, and occupied the high rank of Cavalier. His sister Irina was Czar Feodor's wife. Godunov's influence at court was enormous. He was commander-in-chief of the armed forces, received diplomatic missions, conducted negotiations, and was in charge of both domestic and foreign policy: he was, in effect, the ruler of the country.

When Czar Feodor died and the Moscow Rurik dynasty came to an end, a contentious power struggle ensued between the Romanovs and the Godunovs, in which Boris was the victor. Irina was made the official heir to the throne, but declined, preferring instead to enter the Novodevichy Convent. A council was then convened which decisively and solemnly declared Boris Godunov Czar.

TIME OF TROUBLES

Boris Godunov was generally well-liked and admired, but the shortcomings which had been forgiven when Godunov was merely a ruler were not permitted in a Czar. Godunov took harsh measures against his enemies, expelling the Romanovs from Moscow. He was also accused of the murder of Ivan the Terrible's son the Czarevich Dmitry. These events were only the start of the decade known as the "Time of Troubles" when Russia was struck by a series of disasters.

Natural calamities, famine, epidemics, murder, and political intrigue caused great unrest in Russia. At the same time, rumors were spreading that Czarevich Dmitry was not dead after all. One man appeared claiming to be the Czarevich, who had been "saved by a miracle." This "Dmitry" turned out to be a monk named Grigory Otrepev; forced to flee to Poland, the "False Dmitry" gained the support of the Polish king and claimed the Russian throne. In 1604 he and his defenders crossed the Dnieper River into the Russian state. Boris Godunov died soon after, in 1605, and although the Muscovites had sworn allegiance to Boris's son Feodor, Feodor was overthrown and killed by the False Dmitry's men. On June 20, 1605, the pretender entered Moscow, and within a month was crowned Czar Dmitry Ivanovich. Rebellion broke out in Moscow, organized by

Feodor III becomes Czar (1676–1682)

War with Turkey ends
Revolt of the Streltsy
Treaty of Eternal Peace with Poland
Downfall of Regency of Sophia

St. Petersburg founded
War with Turkey

End of Thirteen Year War

Czarevich Alexei dies

Joint Reigns of Sophia Alexeyevna (1682–1689), Ivan Alexeyevich (1682–1696) and Peter Alexeyevich (1682–1725)

| 1670 | 1675 | 1680 | 1685 | 1690 | 1695 | 1700 | 1705 | 1710 | 1715 | 1720 |

Detail of *The Kremlin, or the Moscow Fortress*
Early 1790s

the Shuisky Princes. The False Dmitry was killed. On May 19, 1606 a new ruler was elected, and Prince Vasily Ivanovich Shuisky became Czar of Russia.

The coronation, though, did not end the country's civil war. By this time, forces from Poland and Sweden had now entered the war. All these factors led to a popular uprising, and Vasily was overthrown and deported to Poland in 1610. Power now rested in the hands of a group of boyars headed by the Gedeminovich Prince Feodor Ivanovich Mstislavsky. Seeing the need for a strong central power base, they entered negotiations with the Polish king Sigismund III, with the aim of appointing his son, Prince Vladislav, the new Czar of Russia. The Patriarch Filaret who headed the delegation was none other than Feodor Nikitich Romanov, who was himself once a contender to the Russian throne before being banished to a monastery by Boris Godunov. It was Feodor's son Mikhail who was to become the first Czar of the Romanov dynasty.

At this critical point in Russian history, Moscow was in the hands of the Poles, and the internal struggle ceased being a civil war and became instead a quest for national liberation. The Poles had seized the Russian fortress town of Smolensk. After a siege lasting nearly two years, Sigismund III declared himself Czar. In the north, Novgorod and the surrounding land fell to the Swedes, who were allies of Vasily Shuisky. With Russia threatened with the loss of national independence, resistance to the invaders grew and in the spring of 1611, the first militia was organized in towns across Russia. Initially successful, it eventually collapsed as a result of internal disputes among its leaders. Shortly afterwards, new resistance solidified along the Volga River, and

in August of 1612 Russian forces reached Moscow, and after a long battle, seized control of the town and the Kremlin.

The war, however, did not end there. A united opposition to the Poles was essential, and this could be achieved only through the election of a legitimate monarch. Representatives of local powers—boyars, clergy, landowners, merchants, and local officials—were summoned to Moscow from all over the country. The first and unanimous decision of this council in 1613 was the ensuring that the Russian throne would never pass to a Polish or Swedish king, any of their descendants, or any representative of another state. There were numerous disagreements, however, as to who would assume this power. Many Russian historians believe that the name of Mikhail Feodorovich Romanov was put forward only by chance; others attribute his consideration to his distinguished heritage and connections. Mikhail was a member of one of the most dominant families of boyars; he had support from many different strata of Russian society. His father, Patriarch Filaret, was head of the Russian Orthodox Church. In addition, the Romanovs had married into the families of some of the most noble Russian boyars and princes and could count on their support. Three months after the decision of the council, Mikhail was brought from the Ipatevsky monastery in Kostroma, where he had been living with his mother, ceremonially entered Moscow, and was crowned the first Czar of the Romanov dynasty.

THE FIRST ROMANOV CZAR & HIS HEIRS

The election of Mikhail as Czar stabilized the country, and within a short time domestic strife came to an end. Although Russia had to

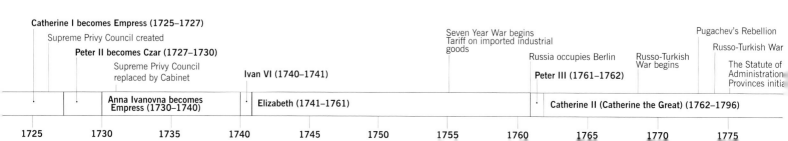

Catherine I becomes Empress (1725–1727)
Supreme Privy Council created
Peter II becomes Czar (1727–1730)
Supreme Privy Council replaced by Cabinet
Ivan VI (1740–1741)
Anna Ivanovna becomes Empress (1730–1740)
Elizabeth (1741–1761)
Seven Year War begins
Tariff on imported industrial goods
Russia occupies Berlin
Russo-Turkish War begins
Peter III (1761–1762)
Pugachev's Rebellion
Russo-Turkish War
The Statute of Administration Provinces initia
Catherine II (Catherine the Great) (1762–1796)

1725   1730   1735   1740   1745   1750   1755   1760   1765   1770   1775

give up a number of its territories and towns, Polish and Swedish expansion halted. Old state structures were resurrected and new ones established. The Court of the Sovereign was established once more. Particular attention was paid to the reintroduction of the Royal Treasury and the Royal Regalia, which had fallen into disrepair during the Time of Troubles. Work began again in the workshops of the Kremlin, which included the Armory, the Gold and Silver Halls, and the workshops of the Cavalry Order.

The early stages of the Romanov dynasty in the 17th century were a period of struggle between old and new, when a new culture began to emerge within the old culture of the Middle Ages. Reforms which had begun during the reign of Mikhail Feodorovich continued under his son Alexei Mikhailovich and his grandchildren Feodor, Czarina Sophia, and especially Peter Alexeyevich, who would become Peter the Great.

Peter the Great was born in 1672 to Czar Alexei and his second wife Natalya Kirillovna Naryshkina. In 1682, after the deaths of his father and the succeeding Czar Feodor III, Peter was crowned jointly with his brother Ivan. Immediately he was embroiled in a bitter seven-year struggle with his sister Czarina Sophia, who held the reins of government. Peter was unlike any of his ancestors. He had been a shipwright and knew the value of labor; he was also a fighting Czar, in the thick of it during the Battle of Poltava. He established new institutions, dividing the country into new administrative regions; he reformed the armed forces, and transformed economic and cultural life. Through victory over Sweden, Russia gained access to the Baltic, on whose shore a new capital of Russia was founded: the

city of St. Petersburg. In place of the Muscovy Czardom a new empire was established, and in 1721 Peter became the first Emperor of Russia.

A BREAK IN SUCCESSION

Under Peter's rule, the country took shape as a European state, yet he left a legacy of insecurity which cast a long shadow in Russian history throughout the 18th century. As in the 16th century, so too did Peter's death lead to a break in the line of succession. His eldest son, the Czarevich Alexei, had been executed by his father as a traitor. His sons from his second marriage, Peter and Paul, died in childhood. In accordance with the law of royal succession composed by Peter himself, the heir to the throne was to be nominated at the discretion of the Emperor; before his death, however, Peter the Great managed only to write down the following words: "I leave everything to…"

In the years following Peter's death, the line of succession was in some sense preserved. The throne passed to his widow, Catherine I, and from her to his grandson, Peter II, son of the executed Czarevich Alexei. Thereafter, however, the single line of the Romanov dynasty divided into several branches. After the death of Peter II in 1730, there were no living male heirs. Anna Ivanovna, the daughter of Peter the Great's brother, Ivan Alexeyevich, became Empress. After Anna Ivanovna's death, the throne passed to the child Ivan Antonovich, whose mother was Anna Ivanovna's niece, Anna Leopoldovna of Brunswick. Anna's mother was Catherine Ivanovna, another niece of Peter the Great. Power thereafter returned once more to Peter's direct descendants—to his daughter Elizabeth I and then her nephew, who became Peter III but was eventually deposed by his wife

Detail of *View of Boyars' Square in the Kremlin* Early 19th century

rters to the Nobility to Towns

French Revolution begins

Russo-Swedish War ends

Russo-Turkish War begins

Russo-Turkish War ends

Russo-Swedish War begins

Russia declares War on France

French invasion of Russia

Defeat of France

Decembrist Uprising

Third Section created

2nd Russo-Turkish War begins

2nd Russo-Turkish War ends

Polish Uprising begins

The Straits Convention

Paul (1796–1801)	Alexander I (1801–1825)	Nicholas I (1825–1855)

| 1790 | 1795 | 1800 | 1805 | 1810 | 1815 | 1820 | 1825 | 1830 | 1835 | 1840 |

Catherine II—Catherine the Great. This fragmented heirdom, disrupted by plots and coups, has no parallel in any other country. The thirty-seven years from the death of Peter the Great to the coronation of Catherine is known in Russian history as the "Era of Court Intrigues."

Catherine's long and successful reign stabilized both the country and the ruler's position. After her death the throne passed to her son and legitimate heir, Paul I. Although the beginning of the 19th century saw a new court coup, this was of a political rather than a dynastic nature. Dissatisfaction with Paul's domestic and foreign policy led to a plot against him, and eventually to his murder. His successor was Alexander I, the eldest son from his second marriage to Maria Feodorovna of Württemberg.

Adhering to the law of succession set forth by Paul on April 5, 1797, the throne now passed from the father to the eldest son, with the sole exception of Emperor Nicholas I. In 1825 Alexander I traveled to southern Russia and on November 19 of that year died of typhoid in Taganrog. He had no children, and the throne should have passed to his brother Konstantin. However, Konstantin's second wife was Polish, and his children therefore had no rights of succession. Alexander had nominated his younger brother Nicholas as his heir, although the edict was neither published nor witnessed by the chosen heir himself. When Alexander died, the Grand Prince Nicholas went to Konstantin to swear an oath of allegiance, but it was the other way around: Konstantin swore allegiance to Nicholas. The line of succession then followed its normal course. Nicholas was succeeded by his eldest son, Alexander II. After Alexander II was murdered by a terrorist in

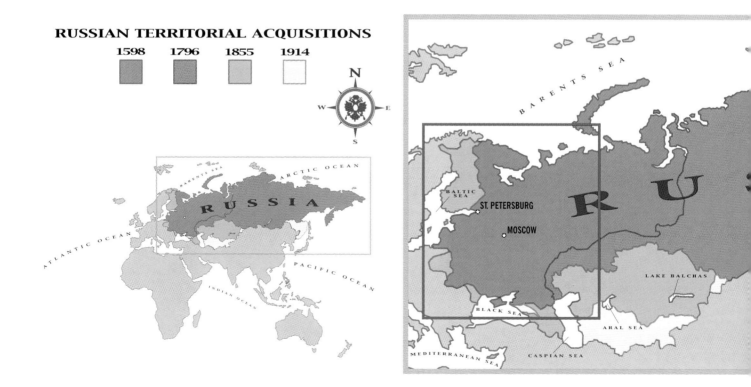

RUSSIAN TERRITORIAL ACQUISITIONS

1598   1796   1855   1914

Start of Russo-Turkish War
   Britain and France
   invade Crimea
    The Kingdom of Sardinia
    declares war on Russia

The Treaty of Paris
ends Crimean War
  Emancipation of Serfs
  Zemstvo Statute
    Alaska sold to the U.S.

Russo-Turkish War begins
Russo-Turkish War ends

Russi
Demo
and L
forme

Alexander II (1855–1881)   Alexander III (1881–1894)   Nicholas II (18

1845   1850   1855   1860   1865   1870   1875   1880   1885   1890   1895

1881, the throne passed to his son Alexander III, father of the last Russian Emperor, Nicholas II.

REVOLUTIONS

In contrast to the orderliness of the succession, the 19th century began with a long and bloody war with France. In 1812 Napoleon's army invaded Russia; Moscow was captured and set ablaze. The century also witnessed the beginning of a revolutionary movement directed against autocratic rule. The first attempt to overthrow the Emperor came in 1825. The revolutionaries were mainly military officers; taking advantage of the confusion after the death of Alexander I, they led a group of soldiers onto the Senate Square in St. Petersburg on December 14, 1825. The uprising was brutally crushed: the leaders were executed and the rest sentenced to hard labor.

The bitter unrest and revolutionary zeal against the rule of the Czar continued throughout the century and into the next.

In 1913 the Russian Empire celebrated the tercentenary of the ruling Romanov dynasty. Celebrations across the country included church services, processions, and the building of new monuments. Yet within four years the monarchy was overthrown. The final and successful revolution began in February 1917. The Emperor Nicholas II was forced to abdicate in favor of his brother Mikhail. Mikhail, in turn, also abdicated the throne. The Romanov family was arrested, and within a year they were shot in Ekaterinburg, the Bolshevik stronghold in the Urals region.

Japanese
gins
so-Japanese
ends
1905 Revolution

Tercentenary of Romanov Dynasty
First World War begins
Nicholas II becomes Commander-in-Chief
Abdication, October Revolution
Murder of Nicholas II and his family

| 1910 | 1915 | 1920 | 1925 | 1930 | 1935 | 1940 | 1945 | 1950 | 1955 | 1960 |

Genealogy of the Romanov Rulers

~ THE FIRST ROMANOV RULERS ~

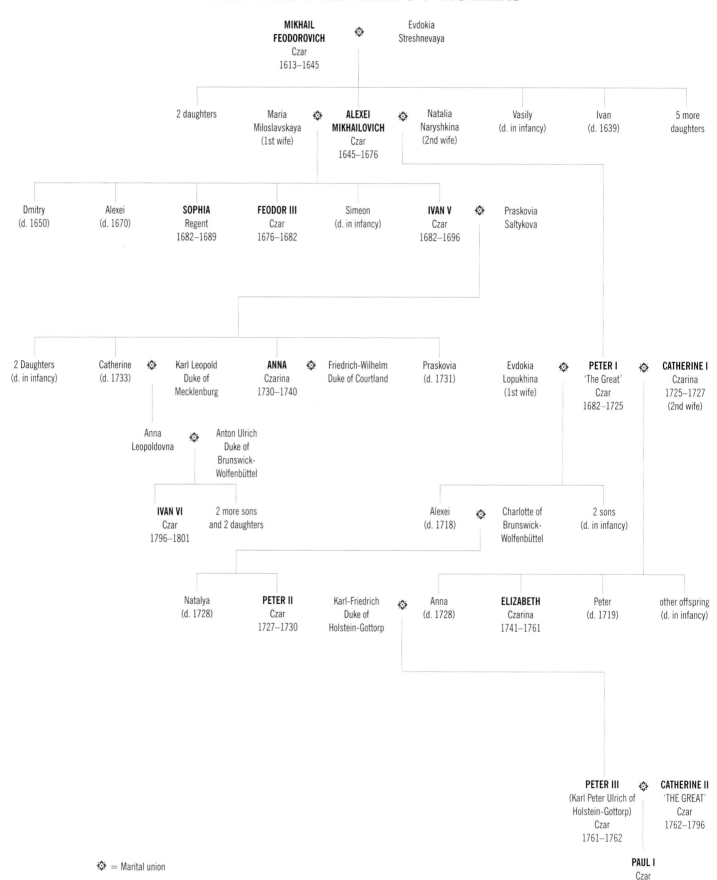

MIKHAIL FEODOROVICH
Czar
1613–1645
✿
Evdokia Streshnevaya

2 daughters

Maria Miloslavskaya (1st wife)
✿
ALEXEI MIKHAILOVICH
Czar
1645–1676
✿
Natalia Naryshkina (2nd wife)

Vasily (d. in infancy)

Ivan (d. 1639)

5 more daughters

Dmitry (d. 1650)

Alexei (d. 1670)

SOPHIA Regent 1682–1689

FEODOR III Czar 1676–1682

Simeon (d. in infancy)

IVAN V Czar 1682–1696
✿
Praskovia Saltykova

2 Daughters (d. in infancy)

Catherine (d. 1733)
✿
Karl Leopold Duke of Mecklenburg

ANNA Czarina 1730–1740
✿
Friedrich-Wilhelm Duke of Courtland

Praskovia (d. 1731)

Evdokia Lopukhina (1st wife)
✿
PETER I 'The Great' Czar 1682–1725
✿
CATHERINE I Czarina 1725–1727 (2nd wife)

Anna Leopoldovna
✿
Anton Ulrich Duke of Brunswick-Wolfenbüttel

IVAN VI Czar 1796–1801

2 more sons and 2 daughters

Alexei (d. 1718)
✿
Charlotte of Brunswick-Wolfenbüttel

2 sons (d. in infancy)

Natalya (d. 1728)

PETER II Czar 1727–1730

Karl-Friedrich Duke of Holstein-Gottorp
✿
Anna (d. 1728)

ELIZABETH Czarina 1741–1761

Peter (d. 1719)

other offspring (d. in infancy)

PETER III (Karl Peter Ulrich of Holstein-Gottorp) Czar 1761–1762
✿
CATHERINE II 'THE GREAT' Czar 1762–1796

PAUL I Czar 1796–1801

✿ = Marital union

❧ THE LAST ROMANOV RULERS ☙

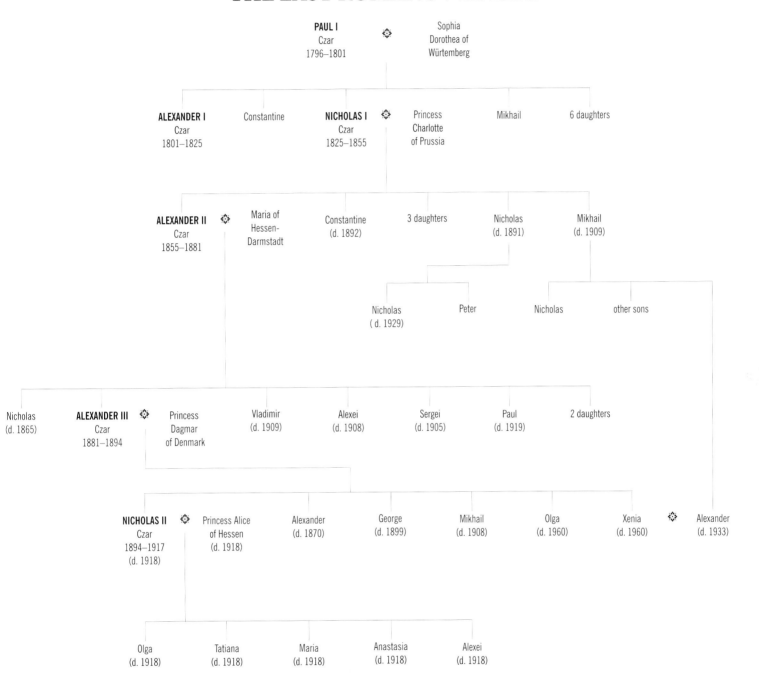

PAUL I
Czar
1796–1801
— Sophia Dorothea of Würtemberg

ALEXANDER I Czar 1801–1825 | Constantine | **NICHOLAS I** Czar 1825–1855 — Princess Charlotte of Prussia | Mikhail | 6 daughters

ALEXANDER II Czar 1855–1881 — Maria of Hessen-Darmstadt | Constantine (d. 1892) | 3 daughters | Nicholas (d. 1891) | Mikhail (d. 1909)

Nicholas (d. 1929) | Peter | Nicholas | other sons

Nicholas (d. 1865) | **ALEXANDER III** Czar 1881–1894 — Princess Dagmar of Denmark | Vladimir (d. 1909) | Alexei (d. 1908) | Sergei (d. 1905) | Paul (d. 1919) | 2 daughters

NICHOLAS II Czar 1894–1917 (d. 1918) — Princess Alice of Hessen (d. 1918) | Alexander (d. 1870) | George (d. 1899) | Mikhail (d. 1908) | Olga (d. 1960) | Xenia (d. 1960) — Alexander (d. 1933)

Olga (d. 1918) | Tatiana (d. 1918) | Maria (d. 1918) | Anastasia (d. 1918) | Alexei (d. 1918)

The Nineteen Romanov Rulers
by A.K. Levykin

MIKHAIL FEODOROVICH ROMANOV

MIKHAIL FEODOROVICH ROMANOV
(B. 1596, D. 1645)
(RULED FROM 1613-1645)

Mikhail Feodorovich Romanov was the founder of the royal dynasty of the Romanovs. He was born on July 18, 1596 to the nobleman Feodor Nikitich Romanov (known subsequently by the ecclesiastical name Filaret) and Isenia Ivanovna Shestovaya (whose ecclesiastical name was Grand Old Martha). He was elected Sovereign of All Russia in Moscow's Red Square by the Assembly of the Land on February 21, 1613, at the age of sixteen, and consecrated Czar on July 11, 1613 in the Assumption Cathedral of the Moscow Kremlin.

During his reign, he established a unified Russian state, ended domestic conflicts, and resumed relations with foreign states. He also made various early reforms, particularly in the Russian army.

He was married twice: first to Maria Vladimirovna Dolgorukaya and then to Evdokia Lukianovna Streshnevaya, with whom he had ten children. Mikhail Feodorovich Romanov died on July 13, 1645 from dropsy.

ALEXEI MIKHAILOVICH

ALEXEI MIKHAILOVICH
(B. 1629, D. 1676)
(RULED FROM 1645-1676)

Born on March 19, 1629, Alexei Mikhailovich was consecrated Czar on July 13, 1645, after the death of his father. One of the most educated men of his time, he wrote and edited many important decrees and documents. He was known as *Tishaishy* ("most quiet one") because of his meek, devout nature.

Alexei's reign was characterized by active domestic and foreign policies. The "Code of the Assembly," a collection of laws, was passed on his personal authority in 1649. He supported Nikon, Patriarch of the Russian Orthodox Church, in ecclesiastical reforms. His greatest foreign policy achievements were the unification of Russia and the Ukraine, and the prevention of an incursion by Crimean Tartars into central regions of the country.

He was married twice: from 1648 to 1669 to Maria Ilinishna Miloslavskaya and from 1671 to 1676 to Natalia Kirillovna Naryshkina. He had a total of twenty-one children from both marriages. He died on January 30, 1676.

FEODOR III (FEODOR ALEXEYEVICH)
(B. 1661, D. 1682)
(RULED FROM 1676-1682)

Son of Czar Alexei Mikhailovich, Feodor Alexeyevich was born on April 30, 1661. Officially declared heir to the throne on September 1, 1674, at the age of twelve, he was consecrated Czar on June 18, 1676 in the Assumption Cathedral, after the death of his father.

Feodor received an excellent education for his time: well-versed in Latin, fluent in Polish, and an able poet. Physically unhealthy, he was cursed with a weak character. During his six-year reign, he was unable to rule with any independence. Power was concentrated in the hands of his maternal relatives, the Miloslavsky Boyars. However, reforms in the organization of the army and the state which began under his grandfather and father continued during his reign. The major foreign policy success of his reign was halting Ottoman expansion into the Ukraine.

He married twice: from 1680 to 1681 to Agafia Semeonovna Grushevskaya and, after her death, to Marfa Matveevna Apraxina. He died on April 27, 1682 without leaving arrangements for his succession.

FEODOR III

IVAN V

IVAN V (IVAN ALEXEYEVICH)
(B. 1666, D. 1696)
(RULED FROM 1682-1696)

Son of Alexei Mikhailovich, he was born on August 27, 1666 from his father's marriage to Maria Miloslavskaya. Although not an official heir to the throne, after the death of Feodor Alexeyevich, as eldest son, he would have succeeded. However, due to Ivan's ill heath, the Boyars' Duma voted Ivan's half-brother the ten-year-old Peter Alexeyevich Czar, on the suggestion of the Patriarch Joachim. But following the insurrection of the Moscow streltsy, Ivan's relatives—the Miloslavsky Boyars—led by Czarevna Sophia, opposed the election of Peter. The Boyars' Duma gave way to these demands and declared Ivan First Czar, Peter Second Czar, and Sofia Alexeyevna Regent. Both Ivan and Peter were consecrated Czars on June 25, 1682.

Ivan V, though, played no role in the affairs of state. He married Praskovia Feodorovna Saltykova and had five children, including the future Empress Anna Ivanovna. He died on January 29, 1696.

SOPHIA ALEXEYEVNA
(B. 1657, D. UNKNOWN)
(RULED FROM 1682-1689)

Born on September 5, 1657, Sophia Alexeyevna was well-educated and noted for her intelligence, energy, and ambition. After the death of Feodor Alexeyevich, she led a group of Miloslavsky Boyars in a struggle for power. On May 29, 1682 she became Regent to Ivan and Peter, and thus effectively the ruler of Russia.

Sophia was extremely active in domestic and foreign policy. Russia concluded "The Eternal Peace" with Poland in 1686, and the Nerchinsky Treaty with China in 1689; there were also two military expeditions to the Crimea. In 1687 the first educational establishment opened in Russia: the Academy of Slavic, Greek, and Latin Studies.

In 1689 Sophia was overthrown by supporters of Peter I and exiled to the Novodevichy Monastery. In 1698 she was forced to take the veil under the name of Susanna, and there is little documentation of her demise.

PETER I (THE GREAT) (PETER ALEXEYEVICH)
(B. 1672, D. 1725)
(RULED FROM 1682-1725)

Peter the Great, the fourteenth child of Alexei Mikhailovich, was born on May 30, 1672 from Alexei's second marriage to Natalia Kirillovna Naryshkina. After the death of his half-brother Feodor Alexeyevich, Peter was not the official heir to the throne. However, after an insurrection of the *streltsy*, inspired by relatives of Alexei Mikhailovich—the Miloslavsky Boyars—the Boyars' Duma confirmed Peter as Second Czar and Ivan as First Czar.

For seven years, a bitter struggle took place between the Miloslavsky and Naryshkina families for control of the throne. Peter lived with his mother in the village of Preobrazhensky, near Moscow, where he occupied himself playing military games. On September 12, 1689 the Naryshkina group overthrew Sophia, and Peter effectively became ruler. After the death of Ivan V in 1696, he was declared Sovereign of all Russia. In the early years of his reign, Peter the Great astounded everyone with his iron will, inexhaustible energy, and intellectual gifts.

Peter the Great undertook extensive reforms: he created a dedicated army and navy, subjugated the Church to the state, introduced new administrative and territorial divisions in the country, and fundamentally changed the apparatus of the state. He was a skillful diplomat and a talented military leader, leading the Russian army in the Azov campaigns against the Turks in 1695–96. In the Northern War with Sweden from 1700 to 1721, he personally commanded his forces in seizing fortresses; he was also known for his leadership in the famous Battle of Poltava of 1709. Under his rule Russia became a great European nation. In 1721 he proclaimed Russia an Empire and was accorded the title of Emperor of All Russia, Great Father of the Fatherland, and, most simply, "The Great."

He married twice: on January 27, 1689, at the insistence of his mother, to nineteen-year-old Evdokia Feodorovna Lopukhina, who was forced to take the veil in 1698; then in 1712 to the Lithuanian Marfa Skavronskaya, who took the Orthodox name Ekaterina (Catherine) Alexeyevna. From both marriages, Peter had eleven children, many of whom died in infancy. The eldest son from his first marriage, Czarevich Alexei, was convicted of high treason by his father and secretly executed in 1718. Peter died from a chill on January 28, 1725 without nominating an heir.

PETER THE GREAT

CATHERINE I

CATHERINE I (MARFA SKAVRONSKAYA)
(B. 1684, D. 1727)
(RULED FROM 1725-1727)

The first Empress of All Russia was the second wife of Peter the Great. Before converting to the Orthodox faith, she was called Marfa Skavronskaya, and was the daughter of a Lithuanian peasant named Samuel. At seventeen she married a Swedish dragoon. When Marienburg fell to Russian forces, Marfa was captured by Count B. P. Sheremetev and put to work in the regimental laundry. From Sheremetev she was passed on to Prince A. D. Menshikov, a favorite of Peter the Great. In 1703 Peter saw Marfa at Menshikov's home and took her as his mistress. In 1705 she converted to the Orthodox faith, and on February 19, 1712 married Peter.

After the death of Peter, Catherine was placed on the throne by guard regiments. Real power, however, remained in the hands of Menshikov and the Supreme Privy Council. She died on May 6, 1727.

PETER II (PETER ALEXEYEVICH)
(B. 1715, D. 1730)
(RULED FROM 1727-1730)

Grandson of Peter the Great and son of Czarevich Alexei Petrovich from his marriage to Crown Princess Sophia Charlotte of Brunswick-Wolfenbüttel, Peter Alexeyevich was born on October 12, 1715. His mother died three days after his birth, and his father died when Peter was three years old. After the death of Catherine I, he ascended the throne at the age of twelve. By order of Catherine I, the state was to be ruled by the Supreme Privy Council with the participation of Czarevnas Anna Petrovna and Elizabeth Petrovna until the young czar came of age. During the first year of Peter's reign, actual power was in the hands of Prince A. D. Menshikov, the young sovereign's guardian. After his engagement to Menshikov's daughter, however, Peter broke free of his guardianship and exiled him to Siberia. On January 9, 1728 Peter II moved to Moscow with his court and the Supreme Privy Council. It was here that his coronation took place on February 25, 1728 in the Assumption Cathedral.

According to contemporary accounts, the young Emperor was very handsome and well educated, with a good knowledge of Latin, German, and French. He did not, however, participate in affairs of state, spending his time in the pursuit of leisure; a particular passion of his was hunting.

On November 30, 1729 Peter was engaged to the eighteen-year-old Catherine Alexeyevna Dolgorukova. On January 6, 1730, however, he caught a chill during a military review and subsequently contracted smallpox. He died on January 19, 1730, and with him the male line of the Romanov dynasty.

PETER II

ANNA IVANOVNA
(B. 1693, D. 1740)
(RULED FROM 1730-1740)

Born on January 28, 1693, Anna Ivanovna was the daughter of Peter the Great's co-ruler, Ivan V, and Praskovia Feodorovna Saltykova. At seventeen she married Friedrich-Wilhelm Duke of Courland, who died suddenly on a journey from Russia to Germany. For nineteen years the widowed countess lived in Mitava. After the death of Emperor Peter II, she was elected to the Russian throne by the Supreme Privy Council which rigidly controlled her power. On March 4, 1730 Anna Ivanovna rejected their conditions, dissolved the council, and on April 28, 1730 crowned herself Empress in the Assumption Cathedral.

Historians have conflicting opinions of her reign. On the one hand, the Empress herself spent little time on affairs of state; real power belonged to the favored Count Biron. On the other hand, her rule marked a period of domestic stability and successful foreign policy. Anna Ivanovna died of kidney disease at the age of forty-seven and left no heirs.

IVAN VI (IVAN ANTONOVICH)
(B. 1740, D. 1764)
(RULED FROM 1740-1741)

Ivan VI was the son of Princess Anna Leopoildovna of Mecklenburg (the niece of Empress Anna Ivanovna) and Duke Anton Ulrich of Brunswick-Wolfenbüttel. He was born on August 12, 1740 and was officially declared heir to the throne by Anna Ivanovna on October 5 the same year. After her death, he became Emperor of Russia at the age of two months. Count Biron, the favorite of the late Empress, remained Regent. However, on November 9 Biron was arrested and sent to Siberia, and the child Emperor's mother was declared Regent.

The reigns of Ivan VI and Anna Leopoldovna were extremely short. On November 25, 1741 the Emperor was overthrown by the Imperial Guard led by Elizabeth Petrovna, daughter of Peter the Great. The child and his family were exiled first to Riga, then to Rannenborg Castle, and finally in 1744 to Kholmogory where, on March 7, 1746, Anna Leopoldovna died. At the beginning of 1756, Ivan Antonovich was taken to the Schlisselborg Fortress where he was kept in extreme secrecy and under strict guard. On the night of July 5, 1764, the twenty-four-year-old Ivan was killed by his guards when his lieutenant, V. I. Mirovich, attempted to free him.

ELIZABETH PETROVNA
(B. 1709, D. 1761)
(RULED FROM 1741-1761)

Daughter of Emperor Peter the Great, Elizabeth Petrovna was born on December 18, 1709 before her father's official marriage to Catherine I.

On the dramatic night of November 25, 1741, Elizabeth went to the barracks of the Preobrazhensky regiment and persuaded the soldiers to follow her. The Brunswick-Wolfenbüttel clan and a number of senior officials were arrested, and the thirty-two-year-old Elizabeth was proclaimed Empress. On April 25, 1742 Elizabeth was crowned in the Assumption Cathedral.

Elizabeth Petrovna was no conventional autocrat. She was beautiful, intelligent, and capable. During her reign, significant advances were made economically and culturally. In foreign policy, Russia assumed a powerful role, and numerous states vied with one another to make treaties. One of Elizabeth's most important decrees was made on May 7, 1744: the abolition of capital punishment. During her reign, not a single person was executed.

At the end of 1742, Elizabeth Petrovna secretly married Alexei Grigorievich. She died on December 25, 1761 at the age of fifty-three, leaving no heir.

PETER III
(KARL PETER ULRICH OF HOLSTEIN-GOTTORP)
(B. 1728, D. 1762)
(RULED FROM 1761-1762)

The son of Count Karl Friedrich of Holstein-Gotorpsk and Anna Petrovna, Peter III was born on February 10, 1728 in Kila and christened Karl Peter Ulrich. Until the age of fourteen, he lived and was educated at the court of Holstein. He was proclaimed official heir to the Russian throne on November 7, 1741 by his aunt, Elizabeth Petrovna.

On August 21, 1745 Peter Feodorovich married Princess Sophia Augusta Frederica of Anhalt-Zerbst, who was christened into the Orthodox faith as Ekaterina Alexeyevna (the future Catherine the Great). Peter ascended the Russian throne on December 25, 1761, the day Empress Elizabeth Petrovna died.

His first action was an amnesty for state figures arrested by Elizabeth after her accession. During his short reign he introduced various reforms, banned the persecution of dissenters, dissolved the Privy Council, and, by special decree, released the gentry from compulsory state service.

On June 28, 1762 he was overthrown by a court coup led by his wife Catherine Alexeyevna (Catherine the Great). He was imprisoned in Ropshinsky Castle, where on July 7, 1762 he was killed by Count Alexei Orlov, presumably at Catherine's behest. He had two children from his marriage with Catherine: a son who would become Czar Paul I, and a daughter who died in infancy.

CATHERINE II (THE GREAT)
(SOPHIA AUGUSTA FREDERICKA OF ANHALT-ZERBST)
(B. 1729, D. 1796)
(RULED FROM 1762-1796)

Born on April 21, 1729 in Poland, into the family of Prince Christian August of Anhalt-Zerbst, Catherine the Great was first christened Sophia Augusta Fredericka. On February 9, 1744, at the age of fifteen, she came to Russia at the invitation of Empress Elizabeth Petrovna as the bride of the heir to the throne, Peter Feodorovich. The marriage took place in St. Petersburg on August 21, 1745, and she was christened into the Orthodox Church as Ekaterina Alexeyevna. Industrious, highly intelligent and strong-willed, she quickly mastered the Russian language.

On July 28, 1762, with the support of the Imperial Guard, she overthrew her husband Peter III. She was crowned Empress of All Russia on September 22, 1762 in the Assumption Cathedral.

Her rule was one of the most prosperous periods of the Russian Empire. She undertook a wide range of internal political reforms, waged two successful wars against the Ottoman Empire, and occupied vast territories on Russia's southern boundaries, eventually advancing the country's border to the Black Sea. She died on November 6, 1796.

ELIZABETH PETROVNA

CATHERINE THE GREAT

PAUL I

ALEXANDER I

NICHOLAS I

PAUL I (PAUL PETROVICH)
(B. 1754, D. 1801)
(RULED FROM 1796-1801)

The son of Peter III and Catherine the Great, Paul I was born on September 20, 1754 and brought up at the court of his grandmother, Empress Elizabeth Petrovna, who intended to appoint him her heir rather than his father, Peter Feodorovich. After Peter III was overthrown, he lived with his family in Gatchina Palace, given to him by his mother and where he had his own court and a small army. On the day of Catherine the Great's death, the forty-two-year-old Paul Petrovich declared himself Emperor.

His coronation signaled a break in the stability of Catherine's reign. Paul I freed those imprisoned by the Privy Council, liberated the Poles, abolished conscription, and limited the power of landowners over serfs. On April 5, 1797 he issued a decree on the rights of succession, establishing procedures for the transfer of power from one monarch to next. In foreign policy he brought about an abrupt reversal, choosing to unite with France instead of warring with it. On the night of March 12, 1801 he was murdered by conspirators.

Paul I was married twice: on September 29, 1773 to Princess Wilhelmina of Hessen-Darmstadt (Natalia Alexeyevna) who died three years later during childbirth; and in 1776 to Princess Sophia Dorothea of Württemberg (Maria Feodorovna), with whom he had ten children.

ALEXANDER I (ALEXANDER PAVLOVICH)
(B. 1777, D. 1825)
(RULED FROM 1801-1825)

The eldest son of Emperor Paul I, Alexander I was born in St. Petersburg on December 12, 1777. From childhood he was greatly influenced by Catherine the Great, who brought him up and considered him her successor.

He came to the throne after the murder of his father Paul I on March 12, 1801, and was crowned in the Assumption Cathedral on September 15 the same year. The young emperor was extremely popular among all levels of society.

The first half of his reign was marked by a liberal domestic policy; his various reforms included a restructuring of the country and an attempt to codify Russian legislation. Alexander was active in foreign policy as well, both in his dealings in the south with Turkey and in the west with France. Beginning in 1812, he led an anti-French coalition, and on March 31, 1814 entered Paris at the head of the allied forces.

In 1793, at the insistence of Catherine the Great, he married Princess Louisa of Baden (Elizabeth Alexeevna). Two daughters died in infancy, so the throne passed to his brother Nicholas Pavlovich. Alexander died on November 19, 1825 in Taganrog.

NICHOLAS I (NICHOLAS PAVLOVICH)
(B. 1796-1855)
(RULED FROM 1825-1855)

Nicholas I was born on May 25, 1796 in Gatchina, near St. Petersburg, the third son of Emperor Paul I. Nicholas received an education in military engineering and was not considered a serious candidate to succeed the throne. In the 1820s, he held the post of Inspector-General of the army's engineers.

Nicholas I came to throne after the death of his elder brother Alexander I and after the refusal of his second brother, Grand Prince Konstantin, to accept sovereignty. He was crowned on August 22, 1826 in the Assumption Cathedral. His first measure as Emperor was the execution of the participants in the uprising of December 14, 1825.

Nicholas's reign saw the flourishing of absolute monarchy in both military and civil areas. He strengthened and centralized government to an unprecedented degree. Harsh and despotic by nature, he had little time for abstract ideas.

Nicholas married Frederica Louisa Charlotte Wilhelmina (Alexandra Feodorovna), daughter of King Friedrich Wilhelm III of Prussia; they had seven children. Nicholas died on February 18, 1855.

ALEXANDER II (ALEXANDER NIKOLAIEVICH)
(B. 1818, D. 1881)
(RULED FROM 1855-1881)

The eldest son of Emperor Nicholas I, Alexander II was born in Moscow on April 17, 1818 and came to the throne on February 19, 1855 after the death of his father. He was crowned in the Assumption Cathedral on August 26, 1856.

On attaining his majority, Alexander Nikolaievich made a tour of Russia. In 1837, he was the first Romanov to visit Siberia. He distinguished himself when ambushed by mountain dwellers in the Caucasus, and was given a military award, the Order of St. George, Fourth Class. After his accession to the throne, Alexander II implemented important reforms, notably the abolition of serfdom, as well as changes in national, military, and municipal organization. In 1867, he sold Alaska and the Aleutian Islands to the United States of America. His greatest foreign-policy achievement was the successful war of 1877–78 against the Ottoman Empire, resulting in the liberation of Bulgaria and the annulment of the conditions of the Treaty of Paris of 1856, imposed after Russia's defeat in the Crimean War.

In 1841 Alexander II married Maria of Hessen-Darmstadt (Maria Alexandrovna). The marriage produced seven children. On March 1, 1881 in St. Petersburg he was mortally wounded by a bomb thrown by a student, I. Grinevitsky, a member of the revolutionary organization "The National Will." The Cathedral of the Resurrection on Blood was erected on the site of the murder.

ALEXANDER III (ALEXANDER ALEXANDROVICH)
(B. 1845, D. 1894)
(RULED FROM 1881-1894)

The second son of Alexander II, born in St. Petersburg on February 26, 1845, Alexander III became the official heir to the throne after the death of his elder brother Nicholas in 1865. He ascended the throne on March 1, 1881, at the age of 36, after the assassination of his father, and was crowned on May 15, 1883 in the Assumption Cathedral.

Alexander Alexandrovich grew up in a military environment and referred to himself as a regimental commander; he was enormously energetic and had unusual physical strength.

His reign coincided with both an industrial revolution in Russia and the spread of capitalism. His domestic policy was particularly harsh, directed against not only revolutionaries but also other liberal movements. Fearing an attempt on his life, he refused to live in the Winter Palace; instead, he lived away from St. Petersburg in Gatchina, the palace of his great-grandfather Paul I, which was designed like a medieval fortress surrounded by moats and watchtowers.

He married the Danish Princess Dagmar (Maria Feodorovna) with whom he had six children. Alexander III died on October 20, 1894 in Livadia, Crimea.

NICHOLAS II (NICHOLAS ALEXANDROVICH)
(B. 1868, D. 1918)
(RULED FROM 1894-1917)

The last Russian Emperor was the eldest son of Alexander III, born on May 6, 1868 in St. Petersburg. He received a fine private education and was fluent in French, English, and German.

He ascended the throne after the death of his father on October 20, 1894, and was crowned on May 14, 1896 in Moscow, but the ceremony was overshadowed by a catastrophe at Khodynka, a suburb of Moscow, where more than a thousand spectators were crushed to death.

He married the daughter of Grand Duke Ludwig of Hessen, Alice Victoria Eleanor Louisa Beatrice (Alexandra Feodorovna) with whom he had five children. There were four daughters: Olga, Tatiana, Maria, and Anastasia. The only boy, Alexei, suffered from hemophilia and was a permanent invalid.

A stubborn supporter of the right of the sovereign despite growing pressure for revolution, Nicholas II did not give way on a single issue, even when unusual and dire circumstances demanded it. He struggled desperately to hold on to power during both the 1905 and 1917 revolutions.

In foreign policy, Nicholas II took steps to stabilize the international front, initiating two peace congresses at The Hague. During his reign, Russia was involved in two wars. In 1904-05 the country suffered a heavy defeat by Japan; some 400,000 men were killed, wounded or captured, and material losses were valued at 2.5 billion gold rubles. Even greater losses, however, were suffered in the First World War which Russia entered on the Allied side on August 1, 1914.

Loss of territory, massive casualties, and confusion at home were the main reasons for the Second Russian Revolution in February 1917. On March 2, 1917 Nicholas II abdicated.

After the abdication, the royal family remained first in Czarskoe Selo (the royal residence), then, by decision of the interim government, were transported to Tobolsk in Siberia. In April 1918, the Bolshevik government decided to move the Imperial family to Ekaterinburg in the Urals, where all were subsequently shot on July 17, 1918.

ALEXANDER II

NICHOLAS II

The Kremlin

View of the Kremlin from across the Moscow River

The Assumption Cathedral

The Annunciation Cathedral

THE MOSCOW KREMLIN

The famous Kremlin—whose name derives from *kreml*, the Russian word for fortress—marked the entry into the ancient city of Moscow. The strategic walls and towers of the Kremlin were built on Borovitsky Hill above the steep banks of the Moscow (*Moskva*) River. The walls encircling the hill and the buildings of the Kremlin run for 1.4 miles, and were primarily constructed in the 1480s to the 1490s during the reign of Ivan III (the Great). Ivan the Great, who ruled from 1462 to 1505, commissioned a complex but beautiful design for the Kremlin from a group of talented Italian architects and initiated the construction of many of the structures.

The Kremlin functioned much like a small city and contained the national seat of government, the cathedrals and churches central to the Russian Orthodox Church, the royal palaces, ceremonial halls, and tombs of the Czars and their families. The Kremlin played a key role in Russian church and state affairs under the Romanovs, and even after Peter the Great moved the capital from Moscow to St. Petersburg in 1712, the Kremlin still retained its spiritual and historical grandeur.

SAVIOR TOWER
One of the most beautiful Kremlin towers is the Savior (*Spasskaya*) Tower, which was featured in the most stately royal processions of the Czars into the Kremlin and on Russian Orthodox feast days. The tower was built in 1491 by the Milanese architect Pietro Antonio Solari. The tower has ten levels and is decorated with white stone carving. It is more than 219 feet high.

CATHEDRAL SQUARE
Cathedral Square is The Kremlin's main square and one of the oldest in Moscow. It is surrounded by some of the most exemplary monuments of medieval architecture. The Assumption, Annunciation, and Archangel

Cathedrals, the Church of the Deposition of the Robe, the Bell Tower of Ivan the Great, the Faceted Hall, and the Patriarchal Palace compose a stunning architectural ensemble.

ASSUMPTION CATHEDRAL
The Assumption (*Uspensky*) Cathedral is the main cathedral church and the heart of the Russian Orthodox Church. It was entrusted to the celebrated Italian architect and engineer Aristotele Fioravanti and was erected on the site of the then-dilapidated original stone Assumption Cathedral structure from 1327. The new cathedral was completed in 1479. The cathedral served as the burial site for the heads of the Russian Church, who were called Metropolitans and Patriarchs. All coronations were held here from 1498 to 1896, and it was here that the Metropolitans and Patriarchs were instated, and important state edicts proclaimed.

ARCHANGEL CATHEDRAL
The Archangel (*Archangelsky*) Cathedral was designed and built by the Italian architect Alevis Novy and was made in 1508. Until the late 17th century, the cathedral was the burial site of the Moscow ruling dynasty. It contains 45 tombs, two memorial slabs, and two burials in shrines. From Peter the Great onwards, the Russian Czars were buried in the Peter and Paul Cathedral in St. Petersburg, with the sole exception of Peter II who died in Moscow and was buried in the Archangel Cathedral in 1730.

ANNUNCIATION CATHEDRAL
Next to the Great Kremlin Palace sits the gold-domed Annunciation (*Blagoveshchensky*) Cathedral. The structure was initially a small single-domed stone church, but was later reconstructed and annexed until there was a total of nine domes. The Annunciation Cathedral, built by masters from the city of Pskov from 1484 to 1489, was the private church of the Russian grand princes and czars until the Church of Our Savior

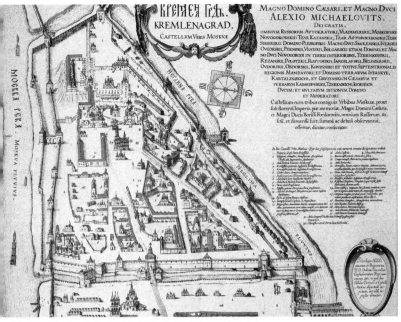

An Early Plan of the Kremlin Rendered During the Reign of Alexei Mikhailovich

The Bell Tower of Ivan the Great (at right) and the Belfry of the Assumption Cathedral (at left)

Behind-the-Golden-Trellis was built in the czar's private residences. Royal weddings and christenings traditionally took place in the Annunciation Cathedral.

CHURCH OF THE DEPOSITION OF THE ROBE

The Church of the Deposition of the Robe was the private church of the Metropolitans and Patriarchs, originally built in 1450. After it was destroyed by fire in 1479, the Pskov masters constructed the present one on the site in 1484-1485 with the same name. When Patriarch Nikon rebuilt the Patriarchal Palace with a new private church in the mid-17th century, the Deposition of the Robe became the private church of the czarinas and czarevnas.

PATRIARCHAL PALACE

The three-story Patriarchal Palace and the adjoining five-domed Church of the Twelve Apostles were the result of a rebuilding in 1655 of the former Metropolitan's Court undertaken in the mid-17th century under Patriarch Nikon. The architects were Alexei Korolkov and Ivan Semenov.

THE BELL TOWER OF IVAN THE GREAT

Located on the east side of Cathedral Square is the Bell Tower of Ivan the Great with the adjoining Assumption Belfry and Filaret Annex. The bell tower was erected in 1505-1508 by the Italian architect Bon Friazin and acquired further tiers on the orders of Czar Boris Godunov in 1600, reaching a final height of 265 feet.

GREAT KREMLIN PALACE

The Great Kremlin Palace was built from 1838 to 1849 (the Armory wing was completed in 1851) from a design by the architect Konstantin Ton in collaboration with the Moscow architects F.F. Richter, N.I. Chichagov, V.A. Bakarev, P.A. Gerasimov, the artist F.G. Solntsev, and others. Emperor Nicholas I supervised the work in person, approving each page of the design for his Moscow residence. Today the Great Kremlin Palace is used for holding official state receptions, high-level negotiations, and the signing of international treaties.

FACETED PALACE

The year 1480, when the army of Ivan III of Moscow forced the Golden Horde invaders to retreat, marked the liberation of Russia from Mongol-Tartar rule. To enhance the prestige of the young state, a grand building program began in Moscow with the assistance of the finest Russian and foreign masters. To this end, Ivan III invited the Italian architects Alevisio Fryazin, Marco Fryazin, and Pietro Antonio Solari to create and build the Faceted (*Granovitaya*) Palace: a large and sumptuous palace, which was constructed between 1487 and 1508 and frequently rebuilt thereafter. Only the official Throne Room of this old palace has survived— the Hall of Facets. Its main façade, which looks onto Cathedral Square, is is covered with blocks of four-faced white stone, from which its name derives.

TEREM PALACE

Terem Palace was erected on the orders of Czar Mikhail Feodorovich Romanov in 1635-1636 by the Russian builders Bazhen Ogurtsov, Antip Konstantinov, Trefil Sharutin, and Larion Ushakov. The uppermost floors of the Terem Palace contained the royal private chambers, where, during the 17th century, the female members of the Romanov family lived in seclusion, enveloped by elaborate protocol. The palace was, for the most part, a kind of gilded cage for the royal female line, until the time of Peter the Great and his grand reforms.

The Church of the Deposition of the Robe

The Faceted Palace

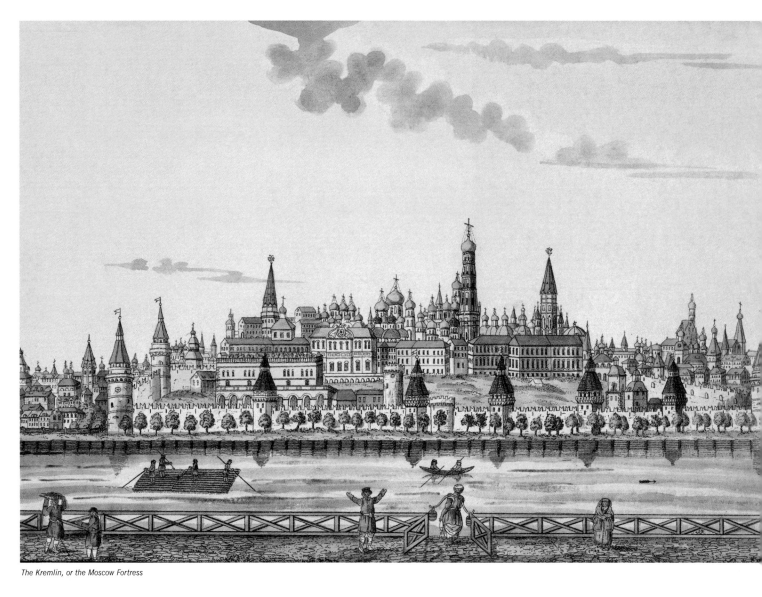

The Kremlin, or the Moscow Fortress

The Kremlin, or the Moscow Fortress
Early 1790s
Fredrick Durfeldt
Russia/Germany
10.6 x 15 inches (26.9 cm x 38 cm)
Engraving (hand-colored with watercolor)
GR-3616

THE KREMLIN, OR THE MOSCOW FORTRESS

This colored engraving is a view of the Kremlin from a
series of ten engravings of Moscow done by the German
engraver Fredrick Durfeldt (1756-1827) who visited the
capital in the early 1790s. In the series there are two
views dedicated to the Kremlin which replicate the
perspective of his peer the well-known Russian artist
M.I. Makhaev. Durfeldt's versions, however, accent the
"exoticism of Russia" and lend the Kremlin a fanciful
fairytale-like feeling.

This engraving shows the panorama of the Kremlin from
the southern side; this view is one of the most
widespread representations of the Kremlin. The Winter
Palace, Cathedral Square, the Bell Tower of Ivan the
Great, and many of the Kremlin's churches are visible
from behind the Kremlin's walls and towers.

Under the engraving to the left is inscribed in French:
"Durfeldt in Moscow"; written in German on the lower
edge is: "The Kremlin, or the Moscow Fortress."

VIEW OF THE KREMLIN FROM THE BANK OF THE MOSCOW RIVER

In this painting of the Kremlin, the artist chose the view from the south bank of the Moscow River, which reveals the main façades of the Kremlin's architectural wonders.

Visible are the Kremlin's main walls and towers situated on Borovitsky Hill above the steep banks of the Moscow River. The panorama includes: the Old Armory (built in 1844-1851); the Great Kremlin Palace, the Czar's residence (1833-1850); the Annunciation Cathedral, the private church of Moscow Grand Princes and Czars (1484-89); the Archangel Cathedral (1505-08); and the Belfry and Bell Tower of Ivan the Great (1505-08).

View of the Kremlin from the Bank of the Moscow River
Mid-19th century
N. I. Podkliuchnikov
Russia
Oil on canvas
40.6 x 63.3 inches (103 cm x 160.7 cm)
Zh-1988

View of the Kremlin from the Bank of the Moscow River

19

View of Boyars' Square in the Kremlin

View of Boyars' Square in the Kremlin
Early 19th century
F. Ia. Alexeyev
Russia
Oil on canvas
34.3 x 46.5 inches (87 cm x 118 cm)
Zh-1930

VIEW OF BOYARS' SQUARE IN THE KREMLIN

This picture preserves for posterity a portion of the Kremlin that no longer exists. The multi-tiered gallery with tall roofs, open terraces, promenades and the improbable geometry of the churches were Russian architectural forms that were never again repeated. The Boyars' Square was the inner courtyard of the Czar's Palace, where high-ranking officials awaited reception or, when commanded, the royal issuing of decrees. On the left of the square is the Terem Palace built during the reign of Czar Mikhail Feodorovich. The Gold Staircase, flanked by two golden lions, leads up to the entrance on the second tier, where the palace living quarters and the Upper Cathedral of Our Savior are located. The upper terrace's staircase is gated by a gilded railing. Behind the staircase, to the right, is a vast unified architectural structure with eleven cupolas covering five churches. Three of these churches are dedicated to Christ, and two of them to the Orthodox Saints Catherine and John. To the right of the palace is the vestibule of the ceremonial hall of the Faceted Palace, and behind that façade looms the main church of Russia—The Assumption Cathedral—and a partial view of the Bell Tower of Ivan the Great. In the foreground of the composition on the left side is a corner of the Palace of Empress Elizabeth Petrovna, which no longer exists.

THE OLD CZAR'S PALACE IN THE MOSCOW KREMLIN

This colored engraving is a view of the Old Czar's Palace inside the Kremlin. In the center of the composition is the three-story Terem Palace, built in 1635-1636 for the children of Czar Mikhail Feodorovich. The Bedchamber Staircase and the Gold Staircase led to the upper living chambers of the Terem Palace from the Boyars' Square. On the left of the square is the Faceted Palace, shown from the courtyard side. Beyond the Terem Palace is the Assumption Cathedral and the Terem Church. The Church of the Nativity of the Virgin is located on the right of the Terem Palace.

The Old Czar's Palace in the Moscow Kremlin
Early 1790s
Fredrick Durfeldt
Russia/Germany
Engraving (hand-colored with watercolor)
10.6 x 15 inches (26.9 cm x 38 cm)
GR-3617

The Old Czar's Palace in the Moscow Kremlin

21

**View of the Kremlin from the Kammeny
Bridge Side**
Early 19th century
Russia
Attributed to F. Ia. Alexeyev
Oil on canvas
32.7 x 44.5 inches (83 cm x 113 cm)
Zh-1941

View of Ivanov Square in the Kremlin
Early 19th century
F. Ia. Alexeyev
Russia
Oil on canvas
33.1 x 43.9 inches (84 cm x 111.5 cm)
Zh-1940

View of the Kremlin from the Kammeny Bridge Side

View of Ivanov Square in the Kremlin

VIEW OF THE KREMLIN FROM THE KAMMENY BRIDGE SIDE

This painting belongs to F. Ia. Alexeyev's mature period, when his style had reached its apex. This Kremlin landscape has been reproduced countless times and is perhaps the most popular of Alexeyev's pictures. The present-day Kremlin was built with stone walls and towers by the Muscovy Prince Ivan III, from 1485 to 1499. Depicted on the left of the composition, on the western side of the fortress, is The Trinity Tower, erected in 1495-1499. The next tower, also an entry tower, is the Bodrovitzky Tower.

In the center of the composition is the Kremlin wall running along the Moscow River and ending in the circular Vodovzvodny Tower. Next to this tower along the river is the Annunciation Tower. The perspective is dominated by the gold cupolas of the grand Bell Tower of Ivan the Great. In front of the Bell Tower is the Archangel Cathedral. To the right of the cathedral in the distance is the top of the Savior Tower which faces out into Red Square. The gates of the tower functioned as the main entrance for the Kremlin.

Running through the center of the painting is the Stone Bridge constructed from the 1640s to 1680s. The Kammeny (Stone) Bridge stood in this location until 1857. In the foreground, small private homes can been seen on the banks of the Moscow River.

✦

VIEW OF IVANOV SQUARE IN THE KREMLIN

This painting of the Moscow Kremlin was also created by F. Ia. Alexeyev, the respected founder of Russian cityscape painting. His depictions of the Kremlin are of great historical value for their faithful representation of both the landscape and architecture of the time. This view shows Ivanov Square, which was the second-most important of the Kremlin's plazas. In contrast to the more ceremonial Cathedral Square, Ivanov Square was the civic center of the capital and the conjunction of all the city's main streets. In the 17th and 18th centuries, royal decrees were pronounced here, and in later centuries it was the site of military parades.

The closed architectural ensemble of Ivanov Square includes the Bell Tower of Ivan the Great, seen on the left. The first tier of the Bell Tower contains the Church of St. John Climacus. In the background on the left sits the Cathedral of the Twelve Apostles, part of the palace complex of the Patriarch Nikon. In the middle of the composition is the façade of the Chudov Monastery, with its Gothic-influenced portico. Behind this, to the right, is the five-domed monastery church of St. Alexei. The right side of the square is enclosed by the palace of Metropolitan Platon.

✦

BELL TOWER OF IVAN THE GREAT IN THE KREMLIN

During the 1840s and 1850s, lithography greatly increased the possibilities for artistic reproductions. Giuseppe Daziaro (1805-1865) was the most popular producer of lithographic views of Moscow. He later opened a workshop and store in St. Petersburg at the end of the 1840s. The Paris lithographic firm Lemercier filled the orders beginning in 1855. The prints were created from drawings commissioned by the publisher in Russia. After the lithographs were finished, the prints returned to Moscow and St. Petersburg and sold in Daziaro's stores.

Depicted on this lithograph is the Bell Tower of Ivan the Great, as seen from the perspective of Ivanov Square. The Bell Tower is framed by adjacent buildings: the Kremlin Belfry, the Faceted Palace, the Assumption Cathedral, and the old Kremlin Armory.

In the lower left corner is the signature of the lithographer: J. B. Arnout. On the bottom right corner is the name of the printer: Lemercier. On the lower left is the title: "The View of the Bell Tower of Ivan the Great in Moscow" (in Russian), which is also printed in French. On the bottom left is the publisher's name (in French): "Mr. G. Daziaro in Moscow and St. Petersburg."

Bell Tower of Ivan the Great in the Kremlin
Mid-19th century
J. B. Arnout (from a drawing by D. Gachen)
Published by G. Daziaro in Moscow and St. Petersburg
Russia
Lithograph (hand-colored with watercolor, whitewash, bronze paint, and lacquer)
21.7 x 14.8 inches (55 cm x 37.5 cm)
GR-3440

Bell Tower of Ivan the Great in the Kremlin

Fabergé Imperial Easter Egg
1916
Master Henrik Wigstrem
Painter: V.I. Zuev
Firm of Carl Fabergé
St. Petersburg, Russia
Egg: Gold, steel, jade, ivory, enamel,
casting, embossing
6.5 inches (16.7 cm) height (with base),
3.5 inches (9 cm) width of base; 2.1
pounds (954 grams) total weight
Painting: watercolor on bone
2 x 2.2 inches (5 cm x 5.5 cm)
Easel: steel, gold
2. 6 inches (6.5 cm) height
MR-6521/1-3

Fabergé Imperial Easter Egg

Miniature Painting from Fabergé Imperial Easter Egg

Miniature Painting from Fabergé Imperial Easter Egg
1916
Master Henrik Wigstrem
Painter: V.I. Zuev
Firm of Carl Fabergé
St. Petersburg, Russia
Painting: watercolor on bone
2 x 2.2 inches (5 cm x 5.5 cm)
Easel: steel, gold
2. 6 inches (6.5 cm) height
MR-6521/1-3

Fabergé Seal with Russian State Emblem
1896-1903
Master Henrik Wigstrem
Firm of Carl Fabergé
St. Petersburg, Russia
Gold, jade, cornelian, rubies, casting, embossing, carving, enamel
3.3 inches (8.3 cm) height, 1.2 inches (3 cm) diameter
OM-2518

FABERGÉ IMPERIAL EASTER EGG

This egg was produced during World War I, which made it one of the very last in the Fabergé collection of the Kremlin Armory. It was originally given as an Easter gift to Emperor Nicholas II by his wife Alexandra Feodorovna in 1916.

The egg and stand are constructed from steel and overlaid in gold with an Imperial crown on top, the crest of the Russian Empire, the seal of Saint George, the year "1916," and the monogram of Alexandra Feodorovna. Emperor Nicholas II was presented this egg in honor of his receipt of the Order of Saint George. The egg contained a wonderful surprise inside—a miniature painting on an easel. The miniature scene was painted on bone with watercolor and depicted the events of 1915 when Emperor Nicholas II and his son Czarevich Alexei Nikolaievich visited the soldiers on the Southern and Western Fronts. The exact moment depicted is a conversation between the Emperor, his son, and the commanding staff of the Army. The miniature is presented in a gold frame, topped with a tiny Imperial crown, and decorated with a ribbon and cross of the Order of Saint George.

FABERGÉ SEAL WITH RUSSIAN STATE EMBLEM

This seal was created for the Russian Imperial Czar by Henrik Wigstrem, one of the leading masters of the firm of Fabergé. The seal is made of cornelian in a gold setting holding a rubber imprint of the Lesser Russian State Seal. The seal's handle is jade, and the base of the handle is covered in white enamel and decorated with garlands of gold and rubies.

Fabergé Seal with Russian State Emblem

Fabergé Easter Egg

FABERGÉ EASTER EGG
THREE CENTURIES OF THE HOUSE OF ROMANOV

Easter is the most important and festive Christian holiday in the Orthodox Church. In Russia it is customary to mark this day by exchanging painted eggs. The Easter eggs that members of the royal family gave to each other were vastly unlike the traditional painted varieties. These one-of-a-kind eggs were made of gold and silver, and decorated with enamel, rare stones, miniature paintings, and whimsical details. Particularly splendid were the Easter eggs commissioned from the firm of Carl Fabergé, the leading maker of Russian jewels.

This opulent custom was begun by Alexander III in 1885. Every year, he commissioned an egg from his court jeweler, Peter Carl Fabergé, as a gift for his wife, the Empress Maria Feodorovna. In all, fifty-six of these masterpieces were produced between 1885 and 1917.

Fabergé masters worked on each Easter egg for nearly a year. Designers, gold and silversmiths, jewelers, stone carvers, painters, and sculptors took part in the preparation and creation. The final touch, however, was always provided by Fabergé himself—"an incomparable genius," in the words of Maria Feodorovna. Eggs by Fabergé were astounding creations which often included delicate mechanisms. They were equally remarkable for their design, precise execution, detail, and the use of the most precious materials.

During the reign of Nicholas II, the 300th anniversary of the rule of the Romanov dynasty was celebrated with great fanfare. The Easter egg of 1913 presented to Empress Alexandra Feodorovna commemorated this event. It was designed and created under the direction of Master Henrik Wigstrem, in whose workshop nearly all the Easter eggs produced after 1903 were made.

The decoration richly symbolized the glory of the Russian state. The gold egg, faced with white enamel, is adorned with stamped two-headed eagles, royal crowns and wreaths, and eighteen miniature portraits of all the representative members of the House of Romanov. These are set into diamond frames, painted in watercolor by the artist V. I. Zuev. The egg rests upon a threefold heraldic eagle, which in turn stands on a circular base of red, in imitation of the state shield.

Traditionally, the egg contained a hidden surprise, made visible when the hinged lid was opened. In this example, a rotating globe is attached to the inside of the egg; the globe has a sea-blue patina, and the land depicted around it is rendered in gold of varying hues. The globe consists of two northern hemispheres. One half shows the territory of Russia at the end of 1613, the date of accession to the throne of the first Romanov Czar, Mikhail Feodorovich. The other half shows the territory of the Russian Empire in 1913, under Nicholas II.

Medal (front view)

MEDAL COMMEMORATING THE THREE-HUNDREDTH ANNIVERSARY OF THE HOUSE OF ROMANOV

On February 21, 1913 Russia celebrated the three-hundred-year reign of the House of Romanov. The event was marked by the issuance of a wide range of medals, medallions, and badges, produced by the Royal Mint and a variety of private firms and workshops in St. Petersburg and Moscow.

Official commemorative medals, struck at the St. Petersburg Mint, were distributed by the Ceremonial Office of the Ministry of the Imperial Court during the celebrations and given to ceremonial participants and honored guests. Members of the royal family were given a set of three copies of this medal, in gold, silver, and bronze.

The front side of the medal shows dual half-length portraits of Czar Mikhail Romanov wearing the Cap of Monomach, and Emperor Nicholas II. Both look to the left, with Mikhail placed in front of Nicholas. Beneath are the dates "1613-1913."

On the reverse side of the medal is a depiction of Mikhail Feodorovich Romanov's election to czardom. The young

Medal (back view)

czar-to-be stands on a platform in the center, with a staff in his hand. Beneath the portrait is the inscription "IN THE YEAR 1613 IN THE MONTH OF MARCH ON THE FIRST DAY." To the right of the portrait, the name of the engraver, August Zhakar, runs along the rim of the medal. Zhakar was a noted engraver who ran his own workshop.

CHAPTER I

The Consecration of the Czar

The Consecration of the Czar

by M.V. Martynova

Detail of *Procession with Regalia to the Assumption Cathedral,* 1642-1643
Miniature from the book *Coronation of Czar Mikhail Feodorovich* (Moscow, Armory Palace)

THE CONSECRATION OF THE FIRST ROMANOV CZAR

The holy ritual that established the sovereignty of the Russian czar was elegant and elaborate, and contained within it the historical and religious foundation of the Russian state. The consecration of the czar was highly symbolic and yet transferred an inordinate amount of duty, wealth, and power to one person. The first Romanov to be elected czar was sixteen-year-old Mikhail Feodorovich Romanov. Historical accounts recorded the splendor and pomp of his consecration.

The date was July 11, 1613, and the setting was the Moscow Kremlin, the ancient residence of the Russian sovereigns. This was the beginning of four centuries of Romanov rule, and young Mikhail—as the first member of the new ruling dynasty—was probably both nervous and excited to accept the crown and the title of "Czar of Russia."

On the morning of Mikhail's consecration, brightly dressed crowds filled the streets and squares of the Kremlin in order to witness the procession. At midday Mikhail made his way to the Golden Chamber, one of the most regal halls of the royal residence. Here his retinue put on their golden robes. Then he summoned his closest boyars to await the moment when he would receive the blessing of the Church and become the ruler of the mighty Orthodox state.

Preparations for the ceremony took place in the gold-domed Assumption Cathedral, the most important religious structure in Russia. The main walkway was laid with broadcloth and red velvet. A lectern draped in rich cloth stood in the center of the cathedral for the royal regalia. On a dais next to the lectern was a throne, faced with gold and studded with precious stones, which had been presented to Czar Boris Godunov by Sheikh Abbas of Persia. The chair of the Metropolitan—the head of the Orthodox church—was placed nearby, and two benches for the clergy flanked the dais.

The first to enter the cathedral were senior clerics in heavy vestments. The Metropolitan, arrayed in his most sacred robes, approached the altar to make preparations for the solemn act. A second group of holy men proceeded slowly to the Royal Treasury and collected the royal regalia. They, too, were attired in luxurious robes embroidered with pearls. The procession was led by the Czar's confessor, supported on either side by two deacons. The post of confessor was traditionally held by the senior priest of the Annunciation (*Blagoveshchensky*) Cathedral, the private church of the royal family. On his head he wore a golden *paten* (Eucharistic plate) draped with rich cloth, and containing the Cross of Life, the crown, and the *barmy* (regalia collar). Behind him, holding the jeweled scepter, came Prince Dmitry Mikhailovich Pozharsky, who had recently led the Russian people in their struggle against foreign oppressors. He was

Detail of *Procession with Regalia to the Assumption Cathedral,1642-1643* Miniature from the book *Coronation of Czar Mikhail Feodorovich* (Moscow, Armory Palace)

followed by boyars bearing the orb and other articles of the royal regalia, which were placed in the Assumption Cathedral on the lectern and then covered with a rich cloth.

On the square outside, orderly columns of *streltsy* (royal guards) cleared a path through the crowd from the royal residence to the cathedral. The air was filled with the ringing of the Kremlin bells as the Czar and his retinue emerged from the Golden Chamber and moved slowly towards the cathedral. As he entered the cathedral, Mikhail kissed the ancient icons and the tombs of the saints. Solemn prayers were said to the Holy Trinity and the Mother of God. These were followed by a prayer to St. Peter, the first Moscow Metropolitan, who in 1325 had moved to Moscow from the ancient Russian town of Vladimir. He had supported the claims of the Muscovy Princes to be rulers of the lands of Russia. From that time, the saint was considered the defender of the Muscovy state; the consecration ceremony began with an appeal to him for protection and patronage.

After the prayers, Mikhail mounted the dais. The people listened reverently to the words of the young Czar. He spoke of the sanctity and inviolability of the Russian throne, which had been occupied by his ancestors, the Kiev Prince Vladimir and the Muscovy Great Princes. In accordance with the ancient custom of all ruling dynasties, Mikhail asserted the legitimacy of his sacred right to the throne. He reminded the people of his

hereditary links with the family of Ivan the Terrible and that, as the nephew of the childless Czar Feodor Ivanovich, he had been elected to the throne "by a nephew's rights."

The Czar's words were followed by those of the Metropolitan, who affirmed the legitimacy of the election of Mikhail Feodorovich Romanov. With anguish in his voice, the Metropolitan spoke of the recent desecration of Russian soil by the enemy, and the destruction of the Royal Treasury, which had contained royal articles acquired from ancient times by the sovereigns of Russia. Turning to the young Mikhail, the Metropolitan called on him to defend the Christian faith and to be "pure and steadfast" in his rule, to love and respect his brothers, and to be "gracious, welcoming and candid towards his subjects."

The sacred ceremony of the consecration now began. It was, in the words of the young Czar, to be conducted "according to our royal rank and property"—that is, according to ancient custom. The ritual dated to the end of the 15th century, the time of the Great Prince Ivan III (1462–1505), whose long reign had seen the final liberation of Russia from the yoke of the Mongol Tartars. The unification of the Russian lands around Moscow, which had begun at the end of the 14th century, was now completed with the formation of a single state. Moscow's claim of supremacy over all the lands of Russia was reflected in the title of Ivan III, who named himself "Sovereign of All Russia." In this way, he underlined that he was not only the eldest brother of the rightful princes but also their ruler.

EARLIER PRECEDENTS

The 15th century had also witnessed another important historical event that influenced the young Russian state. In 1453 Byzantium fell to the Turks, and Russia declared itself the direct and legitimate inheritor of the Byzantine Empire. This claim was strengthened when, in 1472, Ivan III married Sophia Palaeologus, the niece of the last Byzantine Emperor. In 1497 the Byzantine emblem of the two-headed eagle was added to the seal of the Great Prince. This remained the emblem of the Russian state for more than 400 years.

The ceremony of the consecration followed the Byzantine model, which itself had its roots in the ceremony of the accession to the throne of the Roman Emperors. The coronation of the Byzantine Emperors had undergone a significant change in the middle of the 5th century, when the Patriarch began to participate in the ceremony; later, from the 10th century on, it became a purely religious ceremony. The first celebration in Russia took place in 1498 under Ivan III when the Great Prince, who had lost his eldest son from his first marriage, declared his grandson Dmitry his heir. In order to secure Dmitry's succession, Ivan deposed Prince Vasily, son of Sophia Palaeologus. Dmitry, however, was soon removed from real power and two years later, together with his mother, was put in prison, where he remained until his death. Despite the inauspicious end to his reign, the consecration of Dmitry remained significant as the first of its kind in Russian history.

Dmitry's consecration ceremony was conducted by the Metropolitan in the Assumption Cathedral of the Moscow Kremlin. Having made the sign of the cross

over Dmitry, he handed the crown and barmy to Ivan III, who placed them on Dmitry. From then on, these precious objects came to symbolize supreme power to the Muscovy state. According to the literature of the time, the items were reputed to be gifts from the Byzantine Emperor Constantine Monomachus to his grandson, the Kiev Prince Vladimir Monomach, as a reward for a successful campaign in Thrace.

The ceremony of the consecration of the Czar developed over subsequent centuries without any significant changes. During the 1547 consecration of Ivan the Terrible—the first designated Russian Czar—the Czar was presented with a cross, also said to be Constantine's, and a golden chain in addition to the *barmy* and the Cap of Monomach. Thereafter, the scepter became part of the royal regalia, and under Boris Godunov the regalia was also supplemented by the orb.

CZAR OF IMPERIAL RUSSIA

The consecration rite of Czar Mikhail Feodorovich continued when the Cross of Life was placed around his neck. During the reading of the prayers, the Czar was adorned with the *barmy*, which was made of large badges with portraits of the saints; the Cap of Monomach was placed on his head, the scepter in his right hand, and the orb in his left. During the ceremony, Mikhail wore full royal costume. In accordance with Russian tradition, the royal attire always consisted of several pieces of clothing worn one on top of the other. The garments were made of brocade, velvet, and satin, and were richly encrusted with pearls and other precious stones.

During his passage from the *Granovitaya* Palace (known in English as the Faceted

Palace, or the Granite Palace) to the Assumption Cathedral, Mikhail wore a tall fur cap and a cloak with sleeves stretching to the ground over his shoulders. The cloak was made of light silver brocade with gold braid, decorated with emerald buttons, and bordered and hemmed with rows of pearls. A caftan of rich gold silk, decorated with red satin and embroidered with pearls, was visible beneath the cloak. The sleeves of the caftan were short and broad, bordered with pearls and gold badges set with diamonds, rubies, and emeralds. A coat of snow-white taffeta was worn beneath the caftan. Diamonds in gold mounts decorated the borders of its long, narrow sleeves. The silver and gold cloth of the Czar's trousers matched the brocade of the cloak. The ensemble was completed with boots of bright red velvet decorated with pearls and studs containing diamonds, rubies, and emeralds. Once inside the Assumption Cathedral, the Czar wore a *platno*, or state robe, of orange velvet with flowers in high relief instead of a cloak; this was also decorated with pearls and precious stones. In place of the fur cap the Czar wore a golden crown set with diamonds, rubies, emeralds, and pearls.

The effect was, in short, opulent. In describing the attire of the Russian Czar during the ceremony, one foreign guest wrote, "One small part of this magnificence would have been enough to adorn ten sovereigns." As could be imagined, the ceremonial attire of the Czar was remarkable for its immense weight. Attendants had to physically support the sovereign as he made his way into the cathedral.

The ceremony concluded with the anointing, which signified the holy patronage of the new Czar and the sacred nature of his power. After the consecration, Mikhail emerged onto the square and walked towards the Archangel

Feast in the Faceted Palace on the Occasion of the Coronation of Czar Mikhail Feodorovich, 1642-1643
Miniature from the book *Coronation of Czar Mikhail Feodorovich* (Moscow, Armory Palace)

Cathedral, the necropolis of the Russian Great Princes and Czars. Here he kissed the graves of his ancestors, vowing to protect the ancient foundations of the Russian land. He then visited his private church, the Annunciation Cathedral, and was showered with golden coins by his loyal subjects as he passed.

The young Mikhail Feodorovich was now the official Czar—and the patriarch of a family who would rule Russia for nearly four centuries.

The Anointing of Czar Mikhail Feodorovich
Made before 1828
Master S. Grigoriev (after a painting by G. I. Ugriumov)
St. Petersburg Tapestry Manufactory
St. Petersburg, Russia
Woven silk and wool tapestry
108.7 x 139.8 inches (276 cm x 355 cm)
TK-2970

THE ANOINTING OF CZAR MIKHAIL FEODOROVICH

This magnificent work is one of the finest examples of Russian tapestry weaving. Gregory Ivanovich Ugriumov (1764-1823) was a leading Russian historical painter. The original picture was painted in 1799-1800 by order of Paul I for the Mikhailovsky Fortress in St. Petersburg. The artist painted the sixteen-year-old Mikhail in the center of the composition, inside a church with the iconostasis in the background. Mikhail's mother, Maria Ivanovna, stands beside him, and the Archbishop Feodorit of Riazan faces him, dressed in sacred robes. In the foreground are the historical figures who persuaded the unwilling Mikhail to become Czar: F. I. Sheremetev, on his knees, presenting the Cap of Monomach, the scepter, and the gold cross to the Czar; and Prince V. I. Bekhtiarov-Rostovsky, who carries the orb. The Archimandrite Avramy of the Chudov Monastery in a mitre and chasuble, and the Abbot Avramy Palitsyn of the Troitse-Sergiev Monastery, preside on the right of the composition. On the left side of the tapestry stands a group of varying rank, in clothes of classical style to which the artist has introduced elements of 17th-century Russian national dress.

Tapestry weaving in Russia dates from 1715-16, when master craftsmen from the Gobelins tapestry workshops in Paris came to St. Petersburg. Established in 1717 by Peter I, the St. Petersburg Tapestry Manufactory was also a school for Russian apprentices, and by 1730 all the work there—which included descriptive and ornamental tapestries, portraits, emblems, fire screens, and covers for furniture—was done by Russian weavers.

This tapestry was made in St. Petersburg by Stepan Grigoriev during the years of patriotic fervor which followed the victory over Napoleon in 1812. At this time themes from Russian history and images of the unity of the Czar and his people were particularly popular. In 1831 it was sent to Moscow as decoration for the interior of the Petrovsky Fortress. There is a copy of this tapestry in the Württemberg Museum in Germany.

The Anointing of Czar Mikhail Feodorovich

Procession of Czar Mikhail Feodorovich with Regalia to the Ceremony of Consecration from the Golden Hall to the Assumption Cathedral

Procession of Czar Mikhail Feodorovich with Regalia to the Ceremony of Consecration from the Golden Hall to the Assumption Cathedral
From the book *Illustrations from the Book of the Election of Czar Mikhail Feodorovich*
1856
Colored in 1898 by A. A. Potanov
Lithographer: V. Kudinov
Moscow, Russia
Lithograph (hand-colored with watercolor, gold, and silver)
29.9 x 25.2 inches (76 cm x 64 cm)
Kn-250/1

Consecration of Czar Mikhail Feodorovich in the Assumption Cathedral
From the book *Illustrations from the Book of the Election of Czar Mikhail Feodorovich*
1856
Colored in 1898 by A. A. Potanov
Lithographer: V. Kudinov
Moscow, Russia
Lithograph (hand-colored with watercolor, gold, and silver)
29.9 x 25.2 inches (76 cm x 64 cm)
Kn-250/2

PROCESSION OF CZAR MIKHAIL FEODOROVICH WITH REGALIA TO THE CEREMONY OF CONSECRATION FROM THE GOLDEN HALL TO ASSUMPTION CATHEDRAL

The book *Illustrations from the Book of the Election of Czar Mikhail Feodorovich* was published in 1856 by the State Commission of Official Documents and Contracts in Moscow. There were twenty-one illustrations, taken from the original book and transferred onto a printable medium.

The original, illustrated with colorful miniatures, was created in the Kremlin Armory in 1672-1673. The scene in the miniature was of the ceremonial procession to the Cathedral Square of the Kremlin during the election of the Czar to the throne. The procession is seen accompanying the future Czar Mikhail Romanov, who walks alongside the archpriest Cyril of the Assumption Cathedral. Surrounding them are boyars, priests, and other clerical servants. The procession is headed from the Golden Halls of the Czar's Palace across the gallery of the Czar's private church, the Annunciation Cathedral, to the Assumption Cathedral. Before the ceremony, the official state regalia was transferred to the Assumption Cathedral.

✝

CONSECRATION OF CZAR MIKHAIL FEODOROVICH IN THE ASSUMPTION CATHEDRAL

The scene featured on this miniature depicts the consecration of Czar Mikhail Feodorovich in the Assumption Cathedral. The interior of the church is shown from the south wall in the center where Czar Mikhail Feodorovich can be seen on a raised throne surrounded by clergy and relatives. Next to the Czar is Kazan's Metropolitan Efrim, who, during the service and before the liturgy, blessed Mikhail Feodorovich with a holy cross and placed the crown on his head.

Consecration of Czar Mikhail Feodorovich in the Assumption Cathedral

Portrait of Czar Alexei Mikhailovich
18th century
Unknown Artist
Russia
Oil on canvas
36.2 x 29.1 inches (92 cm x 74 cm)
Zh-1961

Portrait of Czar Mikhail Feodorovich
18th century
Unknown Artist
Russia
Oil on canvas
33.9 x 27.6 inches (86 cm x 70 cm)
Zh-1960

PORTRAITS OF CZARS MIKHAIL FEODOROVICH AND ALEXEI MIKHAILOVICH

The first Czar of the Romanovs did not inherit the intense energy and dynamism of his parents, Patriarch Filaret and Maria Ivanovna. His passivity was remarked upon by many of his contemporaries. The Englishman S. Collins, who served as the court physician, wrote: "Mikhail is a leader of extraordinary kindness, he has always lived in peace and in friendship with all Christian nations. He loves foreigners and is very pious."

This image of Czar Mikhail Feodorovich is nearly identical to the portrait of his son, Alexei Mikhailovich; both are dressed in robes (*platno*) with regalia collars (*barmy*), and both hold scepters and orbs in their hands. Both paintings were completed in the mid-18th century.

Portraits of this type, which first appeared at the court of the early Romanovs, are known in Russian art history by the term *parsuna* (a corruption of the Latin *persona*). The style of these two *parsuny* can be linked directly to icon painting. In the depictions of Mikhail and Alexei, the poses are static and flat, the palette is muted, and line dominates over modeling—qualities illustrative of icon

Portrait of Czar Alexei Mikhailovich

paintings. However, the work of the icon painter was geared towards the spiritual world and in portraying religious images of Christian saints. The unknown painter of these portraits was, by contrast, representing a living person, and so, wanted to capture a true likeness. This change in approach was brought about by the numerous commissions for parsuny from members of the royal court and high-ranking boyars.

The grand royal portrait also glorified its subject and helped to show generational links and resemblances. The commemorative nature of these portraits upheld the idea of the supremacy of the rule of the Russian sovereigns; they also formed a political chronicle "in faces," adding a personal touch to the history of the state.

In Russian history, Czar Alexei Mikhailovich is referred to as "the Quiet One." However, this title refers more to the ideal of the Orthodox Czardom than to the actual personality of Alexei Mikhailovich. In reality, Alexei was neither quiet nor calm. He was both energetic and active and involved in all areas of government. He made diplomatic treaties, took part in military expeditions in Lithuania and Poland, wrote his own orders and decrees, and authored a book about the war with Poland. Alexei was also the initiator of many reforms in the area of Russian life. During his reign, the Moscow Court acquainted itself with foreign literature and art, and Czar Alexei started the first court theater in 1672.

Portrait of Czar Mikhail Feodorovich

music for the church. Wanting to increase the educational opportunities in Russia, he helped found the Slavo-Greek and Latin Academy.

The Czar was known for his spiritual qualities, which were expressed not only through his philanthropy, but also through his active patronage in building monasteries and churches.

Portrait of Czar Ivan Alexeyevich
17th-18th century
Unknown Artist
Russia
Oil on canvas
22.7 x 18.2 inches (57.6 cm x 46.2 cm)
Zh-1963

Portrait of Czar Feodor Alexeyevich
19th century
Unknown Artist
Russia
Oil on canvas
64.2 x 46.5 inches (163 cm x 118 cm)
Zh-1946

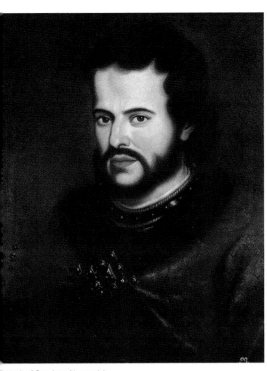

Portrait of Czar Ivan Alexeyevich

PORTRAIT OF CZAR IVAN ALEXEYEVICH

Czar Ivan Alexeyevich was elected to the throne at the same time as his younger brother Peter, an event which inaugurated the Petersburg Imperial period in Russian history. During this era, art took on a host of characteristics from traditions begun in the Middle Ages. As such, the sacred images of Ivan and Peter Alexeyevich were done in the style of religious icons.

As a result of his early death and his slight historical role, there are very few portraits of Czar Ivan Alexeyevich. In this portrait he is shown in a Western European knight's pose with his coat thrown over him and a clasp pinned to his chest. This well-known portrait is most likely the only oil painting done of the Czar, probably by a European artist of the 17th or 18th century.

PORTRAIT OF CZAR FEODOR ALEXEYEVICH

This 19th-century portrait of Czar Feodor Alexeyevich recalls the painting style popular in the late 17th century. The portrait does not portray a realistic view of the young Czar, but rather the characteristic peculiarity of his attire. The anonymous artist was most likely aware of the prominent works of Russian art at the end of the 17th century. The most well-known portrait of Czar Feodor in this style was done posthumously in 1686 by an artist in the Kremlin Armory and placed on his coffin in the burial vault of the Archangel Cathedral.

Despite poor health, Feodor Alexeyevich (who died at age twenty-one) was able to prepare himself well for his ascension to the throne. He received an excellent education under the guidance of the court poet, Simon Polotsky. Feodor Alexeyevich studied Latin and Polish, translated holy books, wrote poems, and composed

Portrait of Czar Feodor Alexeyevich

Pectoral Cross of Czar Mikhail Feodorovich
1619-1633
Kremlin Workshops
Moscow, Russia
Gold, precious stones, pearls, embossing,
carving, niello
4.7 x 3.4 inches (12 cm x 8 cm)
TK-2696

Staff of Czar Mikhail Feodorovich
First quarter of the 17th century
Kremlin Workshops
Moscow, Russia
Silver, precious stones, wood, casting,
embossing, flat chasing, gilding
53.9 inches (137 cm) length of rod, 7.1
inches (18 cm) length of crutch
MR-5789

STAFF OF CZAR MIKHAIL FEODOROVICH

In the 16th and 17th centuries the staff was regarded as an essential component of court ceremonies. In 1613 Mikhail Feodorovich Romanov signaled his acceptance of the Russian throne by taking the royal staff from the hands of the Archbishop Feodorit of Riazan in the church at the Ipatievsky Monastery.

During the coronation of the Czar, a staff was given to the monarch on his passage from the Granovitaya Palace to the Assumption Cathedral, and again when he visited the Annunciation and Archangel Cathedrals after donning the royal regalia. Numerous royal staffs were kept in the Kremlin Treasury, among the articles of "ancient royal rank." This staff belonged to that group. It is made of silver gilt, decorated with fine sapphires and trefoils flat-chased on a smooth ground. The artistic integrity of the staff is typical of Russian jewelry of the first half of the 17th century. It is thought that the staff's first owner was Czar Mikhail Feodorovich.

Pectoral Cross of Czar Mikhail Feodorovich

PECTORAL CROSS OF CZAR MIKHAIL FEODOROVICH

As explained by the inscription on its reverse side, this cross was the very same one used by the Patriarch Filaret to bless his son, Czar Mikhail Feodorovich. Feodor Nikitich Romanov, the future Patriarch, was the cousin of Czar Feodor Ivanovich, the last ruler of the Rurik dynasty. When Boris Godunov—who was chosen as Czar in 1598 thanks to some deft maneuvering on his part and who had no hereditary claim to power—assumed the throne, he quickly sent Feodor Nikitich to a monastery where he took the name Filaret in 1601. At the end of the Time of Troubles (1605-1613), Filaret was sent to Poland on a diplomatic mission, but was imprisoned and then returned to Russia in 1619, six years after his son became Czar. It may be at this time that he gave his son this cross. Like many Russian pectoral crosses, this cross is a reliquary. Contained inside the cross are pieces of relics from John the Baptist, Deacon Stephen, and other Greek holy figures. The aesthetic form of the cross, the combination of gold, pearls, and bright faceted rocks in a smooth cast are characteristic of wares produced in Moscow in the 17th century.

Staff of Czar Mikhail Feodorovich

Dish (Stoianetz)

Dish (*Stoianetz*)
Second half of the 17th century
Kremlin Workshops
Moscow, Russia
Silver, embossing, carving, gilding
5 inches (12.7 cm) height, 7.7 inches
(19.5 cm) diameter of cup, 5.2 inches
(13.3 cm) diameter of base
MR-4207

Pectoral Cross
1662
Kremlin Workshops
Moscow, Russia
Gold, precious stones, casting,
embossing, carving, enamel
2.2 inches (5.6 cm) height, 4.2 inches
(10.7 cm) width
R-13/1-2

DISH (STOIANETZ)

Descriptions of such dishes are well-documented by 17th-century clergymen who gave florid accounts of the luxurious holdings of the Moscow sovereigns. This dish was used during the ceremonial meetings held in the Granovitaya Palace—the Parade Hall of the Czar's Palace. During one of these court ceremonies, an attendee observed that "the dish of gilded ambassadorial silver sat on the window-sill filled with an apple (the word for "orb" in old Russian) and with precious stones."

PECTORAL CROSS

In the 17th century the pectoral cross was an integral element of the royal dress worn during the czar's coronation and at state ceremonies. The face of this highly detailed cross is decorated with tiny images of Christian feast days as well as with fine diamonds in mounts, made from strikingly colored translucent enamel. The cool luster of the diamonds set in the monogram of Christ and the frame of the cross are brought out by the wide range of colors in the enamel. These features combine to create a sparkling mosaic-like effect. Enamel compositions can also be found beneath the diamond cross. In the middle of these is an inscription bearing the year 1662, the date the cross was created. On the reverse side of the cross is a figure of St. Theodore the Recruit, the patron saint of Czar Feodor Alexeyevich, set in an enamel design. This portrait was supposedly added to the cross during Feodor's reign.

Of particular interest is the fact that inscriptions in the cross are in both Russian and Greek, which is evidence of

the participation of foreign craftsmen in its making. Documents show that in the 1660s, Greek jewelers were invited to Moscow from Istanbul. They worked in the Kremlin workshops for several years, undertaking commissions from the royal court.

Pectoral Cross

Chain
17th century
Kremlin Workshops
Moscow, Russia
Gold, embossing, carving, niello, flat chasing
1 inch (3.6 cm) diameter of ring (88 rings total)
R-23

Vestment (Sakkos) of the Patriarch Filaret
First quarter of the 17th century
Looped Brocade: 17th century, Italy
Embroidery: First half of the 17th century, Kremlin Workshops
Gold, silver, velvet, satin, gold thread, pearls, weaving, embroidery, niello, brocade, 11 niello gold buttons, 2 silver bells
52.8 inches (134 cm) length
TK-18

CHAIN

In the Middle Ages, long gold chains were an essential part of the parade attire for princes and czars. According to Russian legend, the first royal chain was brought to Russia by the Byzantine Emperor Constantine Monomachus and presented to the Russian sovereign along with other regalia. Ancient ecclesiastical writings and wills made by the Princes of the Rurik dynasty document that by the beginning of the 14th century gold chains were cherished family items passed on to the oldest son. In the 16th and 17th centuries, chains composed part of the "Grand Regalia"—the ceremonial articles used at the consecration of the czar and at other historic state ceremonies.

Surviving 17th-century chains consist of great flat rings, often decorated with niello (a black metallic material),

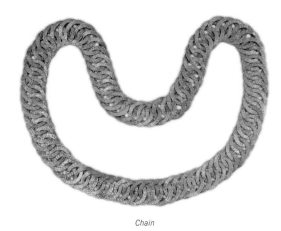

Chain

filigree (intricate wire-work), and enamel. The gold chain shown here of Czar Mikhail Feodorovich is perhaps the most interesting among them. His title—first member of the Romanov dynasty—and the date of his accession to the throne are engraved on each of its eighty-eight rings.

VESTMENT (SAKKOS) OF THE PATRIARCH FILARET

The Patriarch Filaret was a figure of particular importance among the leading members of the Russian clergy, since he was not only the head of the Russian Orthodox Church under Czar Mikhail Feodorovich, but also the Czar's natural father. After he assumed the office of Patriarch in 1619, Filaret became co-ruler with his son, the young Czar. He took an active role in the decisions of both domestic and foreign policy of the Russian state. The supreme decrees and resolutions of this time were issued jointly by the Czar and the Patriarch, and both carried the title of "Great Sovereign." Business concerning state affairs was addressed by both the Czar and the Patriarch, who sat at the right hand of the Czar during state receptions. The Patriarch Filaret possessed great political experience, and was also a gifted statesman. He was largely responsible for his son becoming head of the Russian state. It is possible that one of the ways in which the Czar expressed his gratitude to his father was through the creation of a range of church vestments, produced in the Czarina's Workshops especially for the Patriarch by royal decree. This sakkos, or dalmatic, was part of this collection from 1631, as is indicated by the inscription woven in small pearls along the upper rim of the shoulder piece.

Later, during the renovation of the Patriarch's vestry initiated by the Patriarch Nikon in the 1650s, the pearl embroidery which adorned the shoulders, armlets, sides and hem of the dalmatic was reapplied to new cloth. This new cloth was gilt looped brocade, with a rich design of stylized acanthus leaves and stems with flowers.

Vestment (Sakkos) of the Patriarch Filaret

Two-headed Eagle Pendant

Two-headed Eagle Pendant
17th century
Kremlin Workshops
Moscow, Russia
Gold, precious stones, embossing,
carving, enamel
4.3 x 3.7 inches (11 cm x 9.5 cm)
4.7 ounces (134 grams) weight
MR-2456

TWO-HEADED EAGLE PENDANT

This gold pendant is in the form of a two-headed eagle—the emblem of Russia—wearing a coronation crown. The front is decorated with emeralds and rubies, and the plumage on the reverse side is made of white and black enamel. Gold rings are soldered onto the heads of the eagle, showing that it was hung on a chain over the ceremonial robes.

Several features suggest that this is the work of Kremlin jewelers of the second half of the 17th century. These include the combination of green and red semi-precious stones, the use of painted enamel along with translucent colored enamel, and the manner in which the stones are mounted. There are no other surviving pendants from the 17th century or, remarkably, even from the preceding or following centuries. The unique nature of the object and the richness of its artistry and materials suggest that it belonged to a member of the royal family.

The Byzantine two-headed eagle, first used as a Russian state emblem at the end of the 15th century, underwent several changes before being adopted by Russia: the position of its wings was altered; the number of crowns above the heads increased from one to three; and the addition of an orb and scepter in its claws, and a shield with the figure of St. George, the emblem of Moscow, on its breast.

In 1856 the emblem underwent significant reworking, and from that time until 1917 the representation of the eagle was strictly regulated. The transitional government which came to power after the February Revolution of 1917 and the abdication of Nicholas II continued to use the two-headed eagle as the state emblem, but the symbols of monarchy – the crowns, orb and specter – were removed. After the October Bolshevik Revolution of 1917, the eagle was abolished until 1993, when it became, once again, the emblem of Russia.

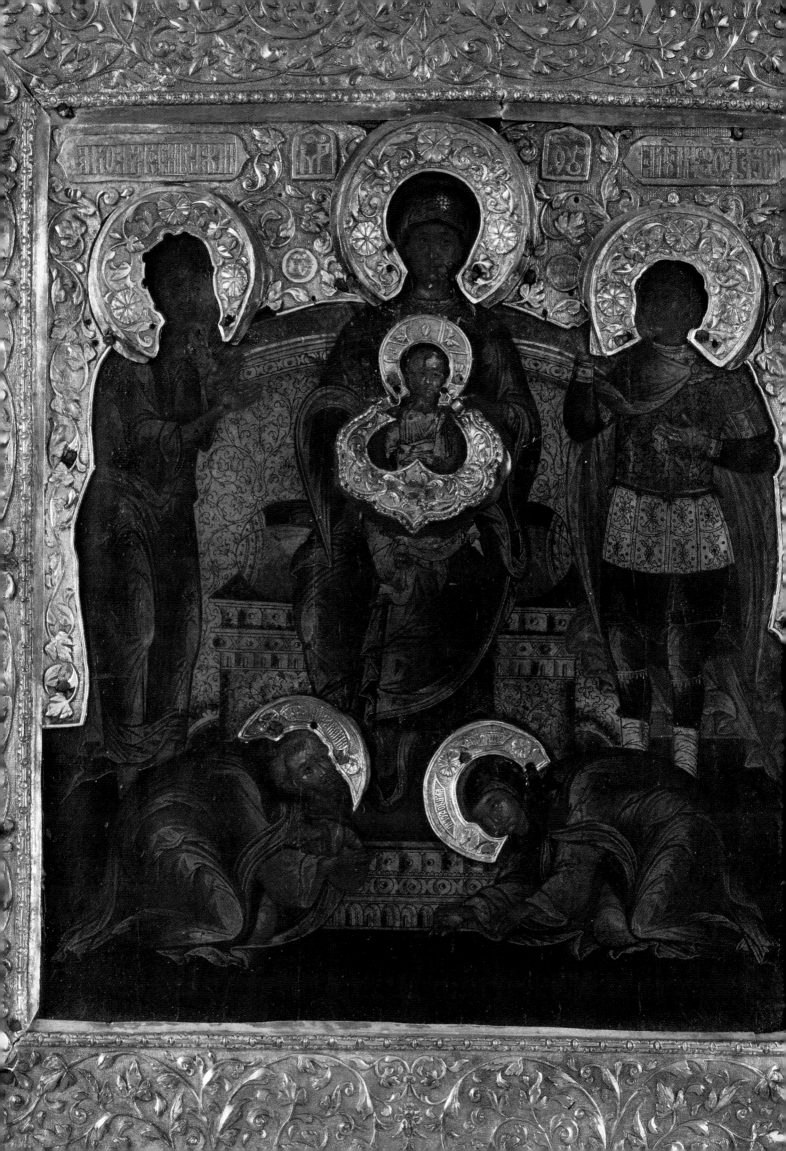

CHAPTER II

The Royal Court and the Orthodox Church

in the 17th Century

The Royal Court and the Orthodox Church

in the 17ᵗʰ Century

by I.I. Vishnevskaya

View of the Interior of the Assumption Cathedral

THE CZAR AND THE PATRIARCH

At the turn of the 17th century and shortly before the accession to the throne of the first Czar of the Romanov dynasty, a significant event took place in the history of the Russian Orthodox Church: the establishment of the Patriarchate. The Russian Orthodox Church had been effectively independent since the middle of the 15th century (after the fall of Constantinople to the Turks in 1453 and the Florentine Union). Now, however, the Church became fully separated from the Constantinople Patriarchate.

The proposal to establish a Patriarchate was first put forward by Czar Feodor Ivanovich, the last of Ivan Kalita's descendants to rule in Moscow. After permission had been granted by all the hierarchies of the Eastern Church, Feodor Ivanovich ratified the election of a new head of the Russian Church. Alongside the Czar, who was the leader of secular life, the Patriarch assumed the new role as leader of ecclesiastical life. This established an inextricable link between the two supreme political powers in Russia, the monarchy and the Church.

The principle of the "Two chosen by God"— that is, the indivisible union of Church and state—was adopted by Russia from Byzantium along with Christianity in the 10th century. Over the course of several centuries, relations between Church and state were sometimes complicated and conflicting, but they were all the while governed by this principle.

The Russian Orthodox Church was instrumental in unifying the disparate lands controlled by Moscow and in gaining political freedom from the yoke of the Golden Horde. The transfer of the center of power from Vladimir to Moscow at the beginning of the 14th century was of particular benefit politically to the ruling Muscovy Princes. By giving its literal blessing to domestic and foreign policy measures, the Church helped the monarchy attain its goals. Any obstinate princes from other lands behaving disobediently or maliciously towards Russia could expect not only military reprisals, but also expulsion from the Church, a punishment no less feared. As Moscow became a political player—and one of Eastern Europe's most potent centralized states—the significance of the Russian Orthodox Church also grew. The voice of the Metropolitan of Russia took on a more vocal tone. After the bloodless struggle with the Turks, and after Byzantium and the Constantinople Patriarch were forced to enter into a union with Catholic Rome, Moscow declared itself the true defender of the Orthodox faith. At the turn of the 16th century, a new political idea arose in the monasteries of Russia: "Moscow, the third Rome." For several centuries this thought endured as the ideological core of the domestic and foreign policies of the ruling Russian autocrats.

As the Russian rulers understood it, however, autocracy meant sole power, and the "Sovereign of All Russia" was unwilling to share this power with anyone—not even with the Church. For this reason, during the political terror released by Ivan the Terrible, not only were innumerable secular victims put to the sword, but many ecclesiastical ones were as well. Only the defeat of the interventionists and the restoration of nationhood after the Time of Troubles resurrected the authority of the Russian Orthodox Church. In the Romanov era, the Patriarchs Filaret and Nikon were both extremely active in overseeing and conducting state policy. It was the Patriarch Filaret—Feodor Nikitich Romanov, the father of the first Czar of the Romanov dynasty—who, according to many historians, was the genuine head of state in the early 17th century. In the middle of the 17th century, the Patriarch Nikon did not simply govern ecclesiastical affairs, but he also governed the state while Czar Alexei Mikhailovich was away on military campaigns. The secular powers, however, bitterly watched the dissolution of their rights until eventually the ecclesiastical council gave way to pressure from Czar Alexei. The once all-powerful Patriarch was deposed and sent to one of the northern monasteries as a lowly monk. Russia was now under the power of a sole ruler. Several more decades passed before Peter the Great issued an official decree officially abolishing the Patriarchate, 150 years after its establishment.

THE COURT OF THE PATRIARCH

The ancient Byzantine tenet of the "Two chosen by God" found a particular symbolic expression in the two residences in the Moscow Kremlin—the Czar's and the Patriarch's. As early as the beginning of the 14th century, Ivan Danilovich Kalita, the founder of the first Moscow royal dynasty, had set aside some land within the Kremlin for the Metropolitan's court, where wooden buildings were to be constructed. In the mid-17th century, by order of the Patriarch Nikon, a new stone Patriarch's Palace was founded, with a private church that has survived to this day. The principal room of the palace was called the "Cross Chamber" and was a large rectangular hall, with a groin-vaulted ceiling with no central support. The Cross Chamber served much the same purpose for the Patriarch as did the Granovitaya Palace for the Czar. Here the Patriarch received the Czar, foreign emissaries, and visiting priests; it was also the place of meetings for the Church Council.

In most respects the customs surrounding the life of the Patriarch were similar to those of the Czar; often, the Patriarch's court matched the royal court in opulence and luxury. The ceremonial processions of the Patriarch on foot and by carriage were reminiscent of the parade processions of the Czar. Thus, during "distant journeys"—which included pilgrimages by the Patriarch to Moscow monasteries—his Holiness was invariably accompanied by *streltsy* (the royal guards). The Patriarchs also had their own staff of attendants, of the same rank as those at the royal court. They had their own *boyars*, *okolnichie* (a rank slightly below a boyar), *stolniki* (lesser nobles), and *deti boiarski* ("boyars' sons"—of inferior rank still).

Like the Czar, the Patriarch had his own

View of the Exterior of the Assumption Cathedral

artistic workshops, where precious utensils and clothes were made. These were kept in the Patriarch's Treasury, along with a variety of foreign treasures. The Patriarch's Treasury consisted of the Secret Treasury, which contained his personal belongings, and the Sacristy, the treasure house of the Russian Orthodox Church. The Sacristy, located in the Uspensky Cathedral, housed splendid ceremonial vestments worn by the Patriarch and made from expensive imported cloth, and embroidered with pearls and precious stones. Also included in the collection were unique church plates, fashioned from gold and silver and decorated with precious stones and intricately stamped designs. When banquets were hosted by the Patriarchs in the Cross Chamber, the ceremonial table service contained an enormous quantity of gold and silver vessels: goblets, *chashi* (bowls), *kovshi* (drinking ladles), *charki* (drinking vessels), and *bratiny* (loving cups).

THE ORTHODOX PLACE OF WORSHIP

In addition to the Patriarch's chambers, the Moscow Kremlin contained the most important place of worship in Russia—the *Uspensky* (Assumption) Cathedral. Founded in 1479 by the Great Prince Ivan III, the Uspensky Cathedral was altered and enriched by nearly all the Romanov Czars and Czarinas, who took great care in its construction and decoration. The Uspensky is a supreme example of the Orthodox place of worship and is in its construction and design a glorious synthesis of architecture, icon and fresco painting, and decorative and applied arts of remarkable variety. Each item in the cathedral has a symbolic significance and is subject to strict rules and canons. Each fresco embodies a theological tenet and occupies a defined space within the cathedral. Collectively, their role is to inspire the devotion of worshippers.

View of the Exterior of the Assumption Cathedral

The most significant images of the Orthodox hierarchy are portrayed in the most important parts of the church: on the ceilings of the cupolas and under the vaults. Prophets and evangelists are portrayed in the drums and small arches of the domes, while the vaults and lower parts of the walls are decorated with scenes from the Gospels. On the western wall, as dictated by tradition, is a portrayal of the Day of Judgment. The columns are covered with portraits of saints and martyrs, who were considered the building's "pillars."

Icons were perhaps the most important element in the Orthodox church, since Orthodox theology considered sculptures of the saints as heathen idols; consequently, sculptures were rare in religious buildings. Icons served as texts for the illiterate, assisting in the spiritual growth and ascent of believers. This distinct symbolic purpose was achieved through the use of artistic techniques characteristic of ancient Russian art, techniques which endured until the end of the 17th century. The symbolic center of the icon was found in the countenance of the saint, portrayed in various spiritual states. The eyes and mouth of the saint were the focus of the spiritual state, along with the gestures of the arms and, in particular, the position of the hands. Figures on icons were usually portrayed full face or three-quarter face. The spirituality of the figures was underlined by the absence of material attributes, and by the way in which they were portrayed on a flat plane without perspective, so that graphic quality predominated over pictorial quality.

Russian icons are unique not only for their distinct artistic language, but also for the way in which they are positioned in the church. Most icons were set in the iconostasis, which was a wall or partition of icons separating the altar from the rest of the cathedral. The iconostasis, which became an essential part of ecclesiastical architecture at the beginning of the 15th century, consisted of several rows. The first row, placed at the same level as the partition referred to as the "royal door" at the center of the iconostasis, contained the "local icon" set amid other icons. The local icon was connected to the specific subject or saint to whom the cathedral was dedicated. Above the royal door were the icons portraying the deesis (the icon of Christ flanked by the Virgin Mary and John the Baptist) and the Archangels Michael and Gabriel in devotional poses. The row above the deesis was the festal row, containing icons illustrating the main Christian feast days. The next highest row featured depictions of the prophets, while the highest row bore icons depicting the Christian patriarchs. The combined effect, with frescoes covering the walls, an abundance of icons, precious vessels, and gold-spun vestments, was one of radiant beauty.

CHURCH SERVICES

The elements of the Orthodox service were orchestrated to equally rich effect: the chanting of prayers and congregational singing, the measured rhythm of the priests' movements, the flicker of the icon lamps, the flames of the candles, and the delicate wisps of incense wafting from the censers (incense burners). The senses of the faithful were overwhelmed with sights, sounds, and fragrances. The purpose was to lead the congregation into a religious state of grace.

In the 17th century the congregation was assembled to church services by the ringing of a bell known as a *blagovest*. On feast days, or when services were held in the Kremlin cathedrals, all the bells rang out. At such times, Moscow would echo with the deep sounds of the Uspensky Cathedral bell, interspersed with the ringing of smaller bells. On major feast days, the distinctive peal from the Bell Tower

of Ivan the Great would ring out, summoning the Moscow clergy to the Cross Chamber of the Patriarch's Palace, where they would convene before being sent out to conduct services in Moscow's cathedrals, monasteries, and parish churches. A special "exit" bell would mark the procession of the Czar to church services.

The Moscow Czars made pilgrimages on every church holiday, and took part in all the rituals and ceremonies that marked the church year. In the eyes of his subjects, the pilgrimages of the Czar were of national significance, for it was believed that the prayers of the Czar would save the state and its people. The piety of the Czar was an expression of the piety of his people. For this reason, the Czars were rigorous in their observance of the full cycle of church services and prayers. They would attend in ceremonial dress, as befitted the head of the Orthodox state.

FEAST DAYS

The ceremonies which marked the principal feast days of the church calendar were modeled on the religious rites of the Byzantine Church. Each feast day had its own particular significance, and all took place in the Kremlin with a great display of solemnity. On Christmas Eve, for example, it was traditional for the Czar, accompanied only by his streltsy and officials of the Privy Council, to make a secret journey to prisons and almshouses, where he distributed alms with his own hands. Later that day, choristers would come to the palace to sing praises to Christ. At the end of the ceremony, the Czar would offer them red and white mead, brought in by one of the courtiers, in gold and silver kovshi.

On Christmas Day, after the early service, when the bells summoned the congregation to the liturgy, the Czar would go to the Dining

View of the Interior of the Assumption Cathedral

47

(Facing Page)
Patriarch Filaret, 1672
Miniature portrait from the book *Portraits, Emblems and Seals of the Great State Book of 1672* (St. Petersburg, 1903)

Chamber of the palace, where he awaited the Patriarch and the clergy. For this occasion the hall was decorated with carpets and broadcloth. The Czar was seated in the Dining Chamber and then commanded his boyars and other nobles to do the same, while junior courtiers remained standing. He then greeted his guests in the vestibule: the Patriarch carrying a cross and holy water and accompanied by high-ranking clergy. After the prayers, the choristers wished the Czar long life, while the Patriarch delivered an official greeting and blessed the Czar. The Patriarch proceeded to greet the Czarina and other members of the royal family, and from there he made his way to the service in the Uspensky Cathedral where, by now, the Czar was already in his place, dressed in all his parade finery. At the end of the service, the Czar returned to his palace, where he prepared for the feast day banquet.

The Patriarch also figured prominently in the New Year festival, celebrated in 17th-century Russia on September 1, calculated from the supposed date of the Creation. A special dais covered with red broadcloth was erected in Kremlin Square between the Archangel Cathedral and the royal palace. On the dais were three richly decorated lecterns. The first of these was for the icon of St. Simeon Stylites, whose feast day was celebrated on September 1; the second was for the Patriarch to read from the Gospels; the third was for the archdeacon. A large goblet of holy water stood on a table behind the lecterns, covered with a parade cloth. Two special places were set opposite the icon: one for the seat of the Czar, on three raised steps, and covered with a canopy of gold cloth; and the other for the seat of the Patriarch, on two raised steps, covered with a colored carpet. As the bells rang out, the Czar, escorted by courtiers, and a procession of the clergy carrying religious images would make their way from the

Uspensky Cathedral. After blessing the water, the Patriarch would make the sign of the cross and sprinkle water over the Czar and the people, before making a welcoming speech. For this occasion more than 20,000 people would gather in Kremlin Square. Many of them held out petitions, which would be collected by the Czar's attendants.

This ceremony was modified by Peter the Great, who moved the New Year festival to the first of January, and decreed that years should be dated from the time of the birth of Christ. Ten days after his decree, on January 1, 1700, a celebratory service was held in the Uspensky Cathedral "for a prosperous start to the year," with the traditional wishing of long life to the Czar. As before, the Kremlin was filled with people. Regiments of soldiers were positioned around the square and, as the church bells pealed, an artillery salute rang out. That evening, Moscow witnessed an unprecedented spectacle: fireworks. A new year and a new century had begun, and with it a new epoch in the history of the Russian state and Church.

Великїй гдрь свтѣйшїй   патрїархъ Филаретъ
                         нїкїтичъ московскїй
                              и всеа русїи

"John the Baptist" Icon with Frame
Painting and frame: 17th century,
Moscow
Gold, precious stones, pearls, wood,
gesso, damask, carving, enamel, tempera
10.9 x 5.3 inches (27.7 cm x 13.5 cm)
Zh-1758/1-2

**"Mother of God at the Altar with
Supplicants" Icon with Frame**
First half of the 17th century
Moscow, Russia
Wood, tempera, silver, embossing,
gilding, cloth
13.7 x 23.7 inches (34.8 cm x 30.3 cm)
Zh-523/1-2

"John the Baptist" Icon with Frame

During the Middle Ages in Russia, almost every building—from a peasant's hut to a civic building—contained an icon. This icon because of its small size belonged not to a church but to a private residence.

John the Baptist was very popular among the Russians. In this icon he is presented in a pose with outstretched wings. In his left hand he holds a scroll and an illuminated vessel containing his own head—a symbol of his sacrificial death. This icon of John the Baptist was probably owned by a high-ranking official, a fact that is reinforced by its expensive frame decorated with rubies, emeralds, and pearls.

✦

"Mother of God at the Altar with Supplicants" Icon with Frame

The holy figures represented in this icon contribute to its unique composition. The Virgin Mary is pictured on a throne in the center with the baby Jesus in her arms. On the left and right of her are holy figures aligned with members of Czar Mikhail Feodorovich's family: Feodor Pergisky—patron saint of the Patriarch Filaret, father of the czar; Mikhail Malein and Evdokia—heavenly

"John the Baptist" Icon with Frame

protectors of the Czar and his wife Evdokia Lukianovna; and a depiction of Alexei Man of God, the patron of their oldest son, future Czar Alexei Mikhailovich.

The selection of holy figures in the composition help to date the icon. Since the patron saint of Czar Mikhail Feodorovich's father is represented, but the patron saint of his mother is not, the date of the icon is probably around 1631 to 1633, the period between the deaths of both parents.

An icon of such personal sentimentality was probably kept at the royal palace, but after the death of one of the Czareviches, the icon was moved to the Archangel Cathedral inside the Kremlin.

"Mother of God at the Altar with Supplicants" Icon with Frame

**Frame (*Oklad*) for the Icon "St. Nicholas
of Zaraisk with Relic"**
1608
Russia
Gold, silver, precious stones, pearls,
turquoise, glass, wood, velvet,
embossing, black enamel, carving,
enamel, flat chasing, gilding
44.3 x 35.6 inches (112.5 cm x 90.5 cm)
MR-10094/1-2

Frame (Oklad) for the Icon "St. Nicholas of Zaraisk with Relic"

FRAME (OKLAD) FOR THE ICON "ST. NICHOLAS OF ZARAISK WITH RELIC"

This precious frame, called an *oklad*, was given to the St. Nicholas Cathedral in the ancient Russian town of Zaraisk by Czar Vasily Shuisky in 1608. It is a magnificent example of the Russian jeweler's art.

This work is closely linked to the history of the Russian state, and dates from the complex epoch of the Time of Troubles. At the beginning of the 17th century, many Russian towns, including Moscow, were sacked and razed to the ground by invading enemies. Most of the gold and silver kept in the Royal Treasury and in the vestries of the largest cathedrals were stolen. The creation of this oklad, for which more than ten pounds (4.5 kg) of gold was used, was a unique event. The uncertain status of the new Moscow sovereign dramatically necessitated the creation of a monument which would immortalize his name in history, as well as pay tribute to St. Nicholas; the saint had been revered as the defender of Russian towns from the time of the Mongol Tartar invasion, and was given the title of "Principal Protector of the Russian Lands."

The icon of St. Nicholas, over which this oklad was placed, dates from the first half of the 16th century.

Altar Cross
1623
Kremlin Workshops
Moscow, Russia
Silver, pearls, carving, embossing, flat
chasing, gilding
14.6 inches (37 cm) height, 3.5 inches
(9 cm) width
MR-4971

Altar Cloth (*Vozdukh*)
17th-18th century
Italy/Russia
Cloth: 17th century, Italy
Embroidery:18th century, Russia
Damask, braid, brocade, lace ribbon,
rope, weaving, embroidery, glass, pearls,
stones, silk moiré,
21.5 x 22.8 inches (54.5 cm x 58 cm)
TK-1711

ALTAR CROSS

The altar cross is the most sacred religious article in the
Orthodox service; the cross is the symbol of the
crucifixion of Christ. Traditional altar crosses depict The
Calvary Mountain with Adam's skull shown under the
feet of Christ on the cross, as per the belief that Christ
was resurrected on the burial spot of the first human.

This Russian Orthodox altar cross has eight corners with
two extra short cross beams—the upper straight beam
and the lower diagonal beam. The lower beam is a
particular feature of the Russian Orthodox cross. The
symbolic explanation of this beam is that it visually
demonstrated to man the road from earth to heaven—
and also to hell.

This cross was made at the request of Czar Mikhail
Feodorovich and his father, Patriarch Filaret.

Altar Cross

Altar Cloth (Vozdukh)

ALTAR CLOTH (VOZDUKH)

The *vozdukh* was the largest of the three cloths used in
the Communion service of the Orthodox church. The
two smaller cloths—one square, the other cross-
shaped—covered the chalice and the Eucharistic plate
(*paten*) and cover (*zvezditsa*) respectively. The
rectangular vozdukh was placed over all three holy items.
The name derives from the way in which the priest
would wave the cloth as he recited the creed, thus stirring
the air, or vozdukh.

The vozdukh seen here was made from two types of
Italian patterned brocade. Imported cloth was utilized
with extreme care, and patterns were chosen to set off the
design of the finished article. In this case the center of the
vozdukh contains a small piece of stitched *aksamit*
(Italian brocade) with fragment of cloth, positioned in
such a way as to form a crown over the Cross of
Golgotha, which is embroidered with pearls and precious
stones in the center of the cloth.

Liturgical Chalice

LITURGICAL CHALICE

The chalice in the Orthodox service is a practical and highly symbolic vessel. It holds the wine and also represents the chalice that Christ shared with his disciples. The Russian Orthodox chalice has retained the same traditional form as in ancient times: a large bowl on a round circular base. Like other liturgical objects, the chalice is made from silver and covered in gild. The decorative design on the chalice reflects the aesthetic taste of the times. Typical of late-17th century craftsmanship, this chalice combines popular carving techniques and the use of niello, a metallic alloy of different elements including silver, lead, and sulphur.

Liturgical Chalice
17th century
Russia
Silver, casting, forging, carving, embossing, niello, gilding
13 inches (33 cm) height, 6.1 inches (15.5 cm) diameter of cup
MR-4430

Eucharistic Plate (*Paten*) and Cover (*Zvezditsa*)
1687
Moscow, Russia
Silver, embossing, carving, niello, gilding
Plate: 4.7 inches (12 cm) height, 10.2 inches (26 cm) diameter of bowl
MR-8982
Cover: 14.6 inches (37 cm) length of arches, 4.9 inches (12.5 cm) height
MR-4502

EUCHARISTIC PLATE (PATEN) AND COVER (ZVEZDITSA)

This *paten* (also known as a *diskos*) and *zvezditsa* are well-crafted liturgical objects—delicately carved and embossed and finely finished. This paten is in the form of a dish, supported by a gold-gild round base. An image of Christ as an infant with an angel on either side of him has been etched into the face of the paten.

The zvezditsa, or cover, consists of two legs, joined together in the center. The name zvezditsa—which means "star" in Russian—is a reference to the star of Bethlehem. The four Metropolitans of the 14th–16th centuries, Peter, Alexei, John and Phillip, are represented in small circles on each of the cover's four arches.

Eucharistic Plate (Paten) and Cover (Zvezditsa)

Communion Spoon (Lzhitsa)

COMMUNION SPOON (LZHITSA)

The *lzhitsa* is a Russian Orthodox liturgical object in the shape of a spoon. During the Orthodox service, the spoon represents the metaphorical relationship between the believer and the church: the church, both literally and figuratively, feeds the soul of the believer.

SACRAMENT COVER (RIPIDA)

Since ancient times, a *ripida*—from the Greek word for "fan"—was used during the Orthodox church service. The presence of the ripida originated in the practical need to keep insects away from the liturgical bread and wine on the altar.

Over time, this pragmatic object took on a symbolic meaning and was stamped with cherubs and seraphs, part of the religious belief that they protected people from evil spirits. Later the ripida was made in the form of a disk attached to a long handle. This ripida came to the Kremlin collection from the Archangel Cathedral.

Sacrament Cover (Ripida)

EUCHARISTIC PLATE (PATEN)

This silver gilded plate with a niello depiction of the Crucifixion of Christ held the Eucharistic bread, eaten in Orthodox services in memory of Christ. The plate is also used during the liturgy to break the bread into smaller parts. On the face of the plate are representations of the angels Michael and Gabriel and nine apostles; garlands and bunches of flowers form a decorative motif.

VESSEL FOR HOLY WATER

This vessel held the holy water used during the Russian Orthodox Church service. The water is a metaphor for spiritual cleansing, while the cup itself is a symbol of the Virgin Mary.

This silver holy-water vessel, which belongs to the Kremlin collection, has a low hemispherical bowl on a stable base. The base of the vessel is intricately embossed in the form of a six-leafed rosette. An intriguing decorative feature of this vessel is the inclusion of a pair of small cast lion's heads on the rim of the bowl; in the mouths of the beasts are rings which serve as handles. The inscription on the crown states that the vessel was made expressly for Czar Mikhail Feodorovich and Czarina Evdokia Lukianovna.

The vessel joined the Kremlin collection in 1918 from the Voznesensky Maiden's Monastery, which was founded by the wife of Prince Dimity Danskoi, a military commander who led a decisive victory over the Mongol Tartars in 1380. The monastery served the czarinas and czarevnas until the end of the 17th century.

Eucharistic Plate (Paten)

Eucharistic Plate (*Paten*)
17th century
Moscow, Russia
Silver, embossing, flat chasing, niello, gilding
10 inches (25.5 cm) diameter; 10.6 ounces (301 grams) weight
MR-4488

Vessel for Holy Water
1645
Moscow, Russia
Silver, embossing, carving, casting, flat chasing, gilding
12.6 inches (32 cm) height, 18.3 inches (46.5 cm) diameter
MR-8991

(Facing Page)
Communion Spoon (*Lzhitsa*)
17th century
Moscow, Russia
Silver, niello, embossing, gilding
8.5 inches (21.5 cm) length
MR-1780

Sacrament Cover (*Ripida*)
17th-19th century
Moscow, Russia
Silver, embossing, carving, gilding
63 inches (160 cm) height, 12.6 inches (32 cm) diameter
MR-9434

Vessel for Holy Water

55

Panagia
Late 17th century
Russia
Gold, silver, precious stones, pearls,
crystal, mother-of-pearl, casting, carving,
embossing, enamel, flat chasing, gilding
6.2 inches (15.8 cm) height, 3.9 inches
(9.8 cm) width
MR-5771/1-2

Candlestick
Late 17th century
Russia
Silver, metal base, embossing, carving,
gilding
51.6 inches (131 cm) height, 6 inches
(15.3 cm) diameter of candle plate
MR-10092

Candlestick

Panagia

PANAGIA

The word "*panagia*" derives from the Greek word for "all holy." It is also one of the prayer names for the Virgin Mary and is invoked during the Orthodox service to refer to the Eucharistic bread in the name of the Virgin Mary. Additionally, this word is used to denote a small box used to hold the bread.

Panagias such as this one were believed to protect a person from misfortune, especially during travels, and was worn on the chest in ancient times. Eventually, the panagia became a sign of the higher Russian clergymen. This panagia is made of gilded silver. In the center is a Calvary Cross with a faceted crystal. Along the sides of the cross are a cane and a kopie, an instrument of torture associated with Christ. Pearls border the edge of the panagia; two delicate gold studs with enamel flowers and stones and an ornamental design at the top lend the piece a decorative elegance.

CANDLESTICK

There were many different light sources used to illuminate and decorate the Russian Orthodox Church in the 17th century. Among them were pots of hot oil and candlesticks like this one, placed in front of the icons. In Orthodox theology, the illumination of an icon is a testament to the believer's faith, and the flame symbolized the believer's love to God and the other holy figures.

This silver gilded candlestick comes from the New Savior Monastery (*Novospassky*), one of the oldest monasteries in Moscow; it was founded in the Kremlin, but in the 15th century moved to a new location on the other side of the Moscow River.

Palitsa

Censer (Kadilo)

PALITSA

The *palitsa* was an integral element of the vestments of the Orthodox clergy. It symbolized God's sword and was worn on the right side of the body. In Russian church ritual, the palitsa was awarded as a mark of excellence and could be bestowed on an ordinary priest, who could wear the palitsa at ceremonial church services.

This palitsa has the traditional rhomboid form, with a gilded silver hook on the outer corner for hanging and gold tassels attached to the other three. The front side of the palitsa is made from scarlet velvet and decorated with embroidery executed in gold thread with colored silk rivets and pearls. In the very center of the cloth is a multi-figured composition, "The Resurrection of Christ," framed within a circle. Also represented in smaller circles bordering the center are images of the twelve apostles. In the four corners are embroidered the symbols of the Four Evangelists—the angel, the lion, the eagle and the calf. Along the edge of the palitsa is a prayer sewn with silver thread.

CENSER (KADILO)

The *kadilo* (also known as a censer in English) is a Russian Orthodox religious object used to burn incense during the church service. In the Russian Orthodox Church this ritual is carried out and gently swung in front of the icons and as attendants enter the church. This ritual celebrates the glory of God and acts also as a symbol of the Holy Spirit descending upon the congregation.

Ancient Russian censers were designed to reflect the church architectural styles, of which this particular kadilo is a grand example. It was designed and constructed to look like a square church with a cupola decorated with a cross. This is a copy of a gold kadilo made in 1676 by the order of Czar Feodor Alexeyevich for the main church in the old Russian city of Suzdal.

Palitsa
Cloth: 17th century, Western Europe
Embroidery: 17th century, Russia
Kremlin Workshops
Moscow, Russia
Satin, gold and silk thread, silver, pearls, weaving, embroidery
16.1 x 15.7 inches (41 cm x 40 cm)
TK-2524

Censer (Kadilo)
17th century
Moscow, Russia
Silver, casting, embossing, carving, gilding
13 inches (33 cm) height, 3.9 inches (10 cm) width; 18.1 inches (46 cm) length of chain
MR-5215

Mantle of Patriarch Adrian
17th century
Kremlin Workshops
Moscow, Russia
Velvet and satin: First half of the 17th
century, Italy
Embroidery: 1690s, Russia
Satin, velvet, braid, ribbon, gold, gold
thread, precious stones, weaving, pearls,
embroidery, gilding
57.9 inches (147 cm) length
TK-2273

Clergyman's Stole (Epitrakhil)
Late 16th century
Kremlin Workshops
Moscow, Russia
Damask, taffeta, satin, gold and silk
thread, ribbon, silver, weaving,
embroidery
53.1 x 11.8 inches (135 cm x 30 cm)
TK-2520

CLERGYMAN'S STOLE (EPITRAKHIL)

The *epitrakhil* was worn by Orthodox clergymen on top of their robes. Most likely, this stole was made for one of the high Russian clergymen of the 16th century, serving in the Assumption Cathedral in the Kremlin. On the dark berry-colored satin of the epitrakhil are eight holy figures. Their positions are not accidental: they are presented in the same order that they are remembered in the liturgy, during the preparations for the Eucharist. All the holy figures are pictured in full vestments. Each is making a blessing with the right hand and clutching a Bible in the left. The faces of the figures are sewn in a flesh-colored silk thread. The gold embroidery on the figures' clothing recalls the gold embossing on the frames of icons.

Clergyman's Stole (Epitrakhil)

Judging by the quality of the embroidery and the richness of the materials used in the stole, it could only have been produced by the masters of the Kremlin Workshops in the second half of the 16th century.

MANTLE OF PATRIARCH ADRIAN

The mantle was the outer garment worn by Russian Patriarchs. It was in the form of a long cloak, fastened at the collar. Stripes, known as *istochniki* (literally "sources"), were sewn horizontally onto the mantle, while two pairs of rectangular shapes, known as *skrizhali* (literally "annals"), were applied along the collar and the hem. The former symbolized the spirit of grace in the wearer, while the latter represented the Old and New

Mantle of Patriarch Adrian

estaments, the foundations of the Orthodox service.
 ocuments show that the Patriarch's mantles in 17th-
 ntury Russia were woven from velvet or dense silk
 oth, in pink, green, blue, or dark crimson.

 he mantle of Adrian, the last Patriarch before the reign
 f Peter the Great, is made of Italian green velvet, with a
 esign of crowns and stylized roses. The istochniki are of
 old braid; the skrizhali are of dark crimson velvet. The
 pper skrizhali are decorated with gold crosses set with
 recious stones, while the lower ones are adorned with
 uds in the shape of rosettes.

 he velvet was produced in the first half of the 17th
 entury, which suggests that the mantle for the Patriarch
 drian was remade from a garment of one of his
 redecessors, most likely the Patriarch Nikon, who at the
 eception of the Antioch Patriarch Makarios in 1655,
 ore a mantle "of green figured cut velvet, with skrizhali
 f red velvet, in the center of which were pictures of
 erubs with gold and pearls."

Pair of Oversleeves (Poruchi)

AIR OF OVERSLEEVES (PORUCHI)

 oruchi were an essential part of the attire of the
 Orthodox priest. They were long cuffs, or oversleeves,
 orn during services.

 he foliate design of the embroidery on these poruchi is
 nriched with images of a stylized flowerpot and
 ornucopias. Such a combination of traditional Russian
 rnamentation with motifs borrowed from Western
 uropean art became fairly widespread in Russian art in
 ne second half of the 17th century. Also typical of the
 me is the sheer variety of materials used by Russian
 mbroiderers. The embroidery of these poruchi required
 earls of differing sizes, large and small precious stones,
 old thread of intricate design, and gold sequins. The
 rincipal details of the design are executed in medium-
 ized pearls; smaller pearls are used for the secondary
 etails, while the smallest pearls are applied to the gold
 equins which make up the background of the
 mbroidery. The center of each poruch bears an oval

silver plate with a carved image of the Virgin Mary on
one, and the Archangel Gabriel on the other; together
they represent the Annunciation, when Gabriel
announced to the Virgin the incarnation of Christ.

SHOULDER PIECE FOR A PRIESTLY VESTMENT

This shoulder-piece was part of a church robe that was
never fully completed. The preservation of fragments of
worn-out clothing was a widespread practice in Russia in
the 17th century. This was done to preserve not only the
exorbitantly expensive materials, but also the excellent
quality of the embroidery. The most frequently recycled
articles of clothing either belonged to members of the
czar's family or had been produced by the Kremlin
Workshops. This piece is thought to have been crafted in
these workshops.

In this unique piece, pearls have been sewn
symmetrically around the neckline, and an intricate
pattern of pearls forms flower-like compositions in the
four corners. Contained in this pattern are two large
sapphires and round silver studs with precious stones.
The background of the embroidery is filled with gilded
silver sequins sewn to the velvet with gold thread.

Pair of Oversleeves (Poruchi)
Cloth: 17th century, Persia
Embroidery: Late 17th century, Russia
Satin, gold thread, silver, precious stones,
glass, pearls, weaving, embroidery,
carving, gilding
8.5 x 11.8 inches (21.5 cm x 30 cm)
TK-157/1-2

Shoulder Piece for a Priestly Vestment
17th century
Velvet: Western Europe
Embroidery and studs: Russia
Satin, gold and silk thread, silver, pearls,
weaving, embroidery
16.5 x 15.6 inches (42 cm x 39.5 cm)
TK-43

Shoulder Piece for a Priestly Vestment

Gospel Book in Cover (front view)

Gospel Book in Cover
Book: 1689
Cover: Late 17th century
Kremlin Workshops
Moscow, Russia
Gold, silver, precious stones, wood,
velvet, silk, paper, embossing, enamel,
gilding
27.8 x 19 inches (70.5 cm x 48.2 cm)
KH-35/1-2

GOSPEL BOOK IN COVER

The altar Gospel Book is a central article in the Orthodox service and during the liturgy signifies Jesus Christ. Traditionally, the deesis—the depiction of Christ flanked by the Virgin Mary and St. John the Baptist—wa on the cover of the book in the center. On this Gospel, however, Christ is alone. The Evangelists, each accompanied by his own symbol, are represented in the four corners.

As with other altar books in covers, the iconic images here appear on the front side. However, towards the end of the 17th century holy renderings were often featured on both the front and back. The other side of this book, for example, has a carefully-worked depiction of a tree with roots and a genealogy of Christ.

This Gospel Book is from the Bogoiavlensky Monastery, one of the oldest in Moscow, founded in 1293 by the Moscow Prince Daniel Alexandrovich.

Gospel Book in Cover (back view)

COFFIN CLOTH FOR THE TOMB OF METROPOLITAN PETER

Coffin cloths with embroidered images of saints were placed on the tomb or shrine of the saint during ceremonial services. This was one of the traditional forms of reverence accorded the saint. In the middle of the 17th century, a set of large coffin cloths were made for the prelates, including the Metropolitans Peter, Alexei, Johann and Philipp. The dedications on the coffin cloths explain that they were specially commissioned by Czar Alexei Mikhailovich and his wife Maria Ilinichna.

This particular cloth features an embroidered full-length portrayal of the Metropolitan Peter. He is dressed in a *chasuble* and *klobuk* (traditional monk's headgear); one hand holds the Gospels, while the other is in a gesture of prayer. Above his head is a small image of the Trinity. His face and hands are embroidered in white and blue silk, while the rest of the cloth is done in gold and silver thread, with colored ornamentation. The outline, details, and inscriptions are threaded with pearls. The halo consists of gold studs set with precious stones, two of which are in the shape of a bow and decorated with black enamel. The embroidery techniques used in the making of this coffin cloth, with the abundance of gold, precious stones, and pearls, recall the most lavish jewelry work.

Peter transferred the seat of the Metropolitan from Vladimir to Moscow and was revered as a miracle worker and as a protector of Moscow.

Coffin Cloth for the Tomb of Metropolitan Peter

The Czar's Gates

Coffin Cloth for the Tomb of Metropolitan Peter
1648-1669
Kremlin Workshops
Moscow, Russia
Cloth: 17th century, Italy
Damask, velvet, gold and silk thread, gold, precious stones, pearls, embroidery, weaving, enamel
86.6 x 36.2 inches (220 cm x 92 cm)
TK-31

The Czar's Gates
Icon: Mid-17th century, Moscow
Frame: 19th century, Moscow
Wood, gesso, tempera, copper, embossing, filigree
Each panel: 65.7 x 15.7 x 1.2 inches (167 cm x 40 cm x 3 cm)
Zh-452/1-4

THE CZAR'S GATES

The Czar's Gates, also referred to as "The Royal Door," were set in the middle of the iconostasis and led to the central part of the altar, where the altar table was situated. During the liturgy, the Gospels and the Eucharistic items symbolizing Christ were brought out through the Royal Door. Compositions of the Annunciation and the Four Evangelists were usually depicted on the door.

The form of this royal door, with its characteristic figured outline, was in wide use in Russia in the 16th and 17th centuries. The artist's signature is hidden beneath the inscription and a dried layer of holy oil. Several elements of the composition, however, suggest that the door was the work of a Moscow icon painter of the first half of the 17th century. These include the lack of perspective in the treatment of the architectural forms; the brown hills with bleached edges; and the heavy build and large heads of the figures.

The stamped metal frame, dating from the 19th century, was installed later; it is decorated with a foliate ornament in the style of 17th-century work.

CHAPTER III

The Private Lives of the Czars

The Private Lives of the Czars

by M. V. Martynova

Detail of a miniature illustration from the book *Description of the Celebration of Feb 5, 1626 at the Wedding of Czar and Great Prince Mikhail Feodorovich and Sovereign Czarina Evdokia Lukianovna*

The private lives of members of the royal household in the 17th century were strictly regimented. Events in the collective life of the royal family were considered of great significance to the state and were accompanied by a ceremonial rigor that had been carefully established in the preceding centuries.

The births of the royal offspring and those of the czareviches—the heirs to the throne—were formal, somber matters. In ancient Russia a woman's principal role was to bear children. There was no greater misfortune for a royal wife than the inability to produce an heir, and in particular, a male heir. Female impotence was considered shameful and sinful, and often brought about personal disaster: czarinas who could not have children were forcibly committed to nunneries.

THE BIRTH & EARLY LIFE OF THE CZAREVICH

According to Russian tradition, immediately after the birth of a czarevich his measurements were taken; an icon of his patron saint was then commissioned in his exact size. This work was normally undertaken by a well known icon painter from the Kremlin Workshops. A few hours after the birth of the czarevich, the whole court, clad in brightly colored clothes suitable for the occasion, gathered to give thanks in the Uspensky Cathedral. The Czar then made a tour of the Kremlin churches and

monasteries to receive congratulations. A few days later, a "Birth Feast" was held in the Granovitaya Palace. This was notable for its abundance of sweet dishes, meats, and vegetables. A stunning degree of imagination and craftsmanship went into the preparation of the feast.

The christening of the Czarevich was also attended by considerable extravagance. There are conflicting accounts as to how many days after the birth this took place. The ceremony normally took place in the church of the Chudov monastery in the Kremlin. The royal children were brought here in a fine sleigh or carriage with seats and cushions bordered with gold brocade. The godparents were the child's nursemaid and either his elder sister or aunt. After the christening, according to Orthodox tradition, a few locks of the baby's hair were wound up in a piece of wax and placed in safekeeping in the Cathedral to protect the newborn from grief and suffering. The christening, like the birth, was marked by a ceremonial feast and the presentation of gifts.

From his first days until the age of seven, the czarevich was surrounded by a retinue of female servants who followed his every step. A wet-nurse was selected from women of different ranks. The wet-nurse lived permanently at court, feeding the child usually until the age of two and a half. In return for this service, the wet-nurse's husband was customarily awarded land and estates.

n the 17th century the life of the young zarevich was one of extreme luxury. Within a month of his birth, clothes of rich fabrics were made for him. As the czarevich grew, he acquired a large number of toys. Among these were wooden toy horses (covered in foal skin), drums, bells, and miniature musical instruments. Tiny carriages were also built for the royal children who traveled through the streets of Russia in them. Artists from the Kremlin drew picture books. The personal taste of the child influenced his selection of toys. Peter I, for example, from an early age, owned many weapons. According to documents of the time, he also had miniature axes, maces, cannons, knives, and bows and arrows. Most of his toys were made in the Kremlin Workshops; others were bought from foreign traders.

At the age of six or seven the czarevich broke off from the women in his life and lived under the guardianship of men, his education and wardship undertaken by intelligent, conscientious boyars; later his teachers included deacons from the ambassadorial office who taught him to read and write. Until the age of fifteen, the czarevich was surrounded only by relatives, royalty, and tutors. He never appeared before the public. Even when the czarevich and czarevna went to church they were hidden from view by a linen cloth. Only when the czarevich reached the age of fifteen was he solemnly "declared," and the people were granted special visits to the capital in order to look upon the future sovereign.

THE ROYAL MARRIAGE

n ancient Russia a man did not reach adulthood by virtue of age, but was accorded those rights only upon marriage. The marriage of the czarevich was therefore all the more important. In addition, the marriage of the heir to the throne had particular political

significance in ancient Russia, since in the 16th and 17th centuries those close to the Czar played an integral role in the governing of the state; frequently these people were relatives of the czarina.

Until the 15th century the Muscovy rulers had traditionally married the daughters of princes, noble boyars, men at arms, or Novgorod vice-regents. When the Muscovy prince declared himself the sovereign of all Russia, such marriages became impossible, since the protocol did not allow marriage to a subject. Ivan III made his second marriage to a Greek princess, married his eldest son to the daughter of a Moldavian warlord, and gave his daughter Elena in marriage to a Lithuanian Grand Prince. He attempted to arrange the marriages of his other children with representatives of European ruling dynasties. This turned out to be far from simple. The difference in faith represented a particular obstacle and, perhaps more importantly, Europe at the time was still unfamiliar with the Muscovy state. Consequently the Muscovy rulers were forced to choose brides from among their subjects.

In such circumstances it would have been natural to marry representatives of noble families. However, this would have led to one family being elevated above the other, which would have created a rival to the royal family. As a result, following the tradition of the Byzantine emperors, the Russian czars began to choose their brides from among the people, selecting from the daughters of landed gentry and paying attention only to the personal qualities of the prospective bride. By entering such a union the sovereign did not diminish his royal dignity; indeed, he placed himself above his subjects since none apart from him was able to choose his bride in this way.

For Czar Alexei Mikhailovich's second

Detail of a miniature illustration, 1626
From the book *Description of the Celebration of Feb 5, 1626 at the Wedding of Czar and Great Prince Mikhail Feodorovich and Sovereign Czarina Evdokia Lukianovna*

marriage, he chose his bride from among twenty young women. The search lasted for more than six months until the Czar conferred his choice upon Natalia Kirillovna Naryshkina, the future mother of Peter the Great. The groom presented the girl who pleased him with a golden ring and a woven cloth which consummated the act of selection. Thereafter, the girl was given the title of "Czarevna" and took her place at court. From this moment she had a special status; even her father did not have the right to call her his daughter.

Marriage ceremonies at the Russian court were remarkable for their opulence; in form they followed national traditions established over many centuries. The role of courtiers in all stages of the ceremony was carefully set out in marriage records of the 17th century. Particular significance was given to the servants of honor at the marriage ceremony, since this position testified to the closeness of the courtier's relationship to the head of state.

THE WEDDING DAY

Before the ceremony, the young couple were solemnly blessed by their parents with icons of the Virgin Mary and Christ. Attendants and noblewomen dressed the bride for the ceremony and placed on her head a golden crown inlaid with precious stones and pearls, a symbol of virginity. The regalia of the bridegroom for the ceremony was no less fine than for a coronation. Czar Mikhail Feodorovich, for example, wore a half-length sable caftan with gold brocade and a sable-lined velvet coat, with panels thrown back over the shoulders; his belt was solid gold. The boyars who accompanied the Czar wore silver fox-fur hats and gold robes with standing or folded collars studded with pearls.

The wedding day was not just a means of continuing the royal line; it was also a time of

Detail of a miniature illustration, 1626
From the book *Description of the Celebration of Feb 5, 1626 at the Wedding of Czar and Great Prince Mikhail Feodorovich and Sovereign Czarina Evdokia Lukianovna*

hope: for a life of love and harmony, particularly since the czar had chosen his bride himself. The staterooms were decorated for the occasion: every wall was hung with icons draped with pearl curtains. The icons contained images of the saints, and the bride and groom prayed to them for a happy marriage. Before the wedding ceremony, the czar and czarevna went to the Granovitaya Palace where, according to Russian tradition, their hair was combed and dipped in honey. The czarevna donned a wedding head-dress, and her face was covered with a veil woven with pearls and precious stones. The young couple were then showered with golden coins in addition to grain and hops, which symbolized fertility.

A special fur-covered seat with a velvet canopy was set up in Granovitaya Palace for the bride and groom. According to folk custom, sitting on fur promised wealth to the young couple. Nearby stood a table with three tablecloths; at given moments during the ceremony, the cloths were removed one by one. Placed on the table were a saltcellar and a special pie offered to the bridegroom and boyars before the ceremony.

A large number of courtiers took part in the marriage ceremony, each with his or her own assigned role. Some were matchmakers, confidants of the bride and groom, wedding sponsors, and the so-called "sitting" boyars and boyarinas who formed a special honorary council in the staterooms. Another group of boyars made up the wedding train and accompanied the bride and groom on their procession. The entourage also included loaf carriers, who held special round bread loaves wrapped in precious cloth on velvet-covered trays; candle bearers, with delicate wedding candles and the heavy candles of the sovereign and his bride, decorated with gilded rings; lamplighters; and assorted others.

The bride was carried to the Assumption

Cathedral in a sleigh, while the Czar rode on a horse of the Argamak breed. After the wedding, the young couple and their guests were entertained in the Granovitaya Palace. The bride and groom sat at a table without eating anything; at the start of the third course, a chicken— a symbol of wedded love—was traditionally placed in front of them. The Czar's witness then wrapped up the chicken in cloth and carried it into the bedroom.

In simple folk tradition, the bridal bed was made of sheaths of rye, wheat, and barley. In the royal palace, however, the sheaths were covered with a carpet and a down quilt; the sheaths foreshadowed wealth in the home. Two thick candles were placed at the head of the bed, one for the sovereign and one for his bride. A tub filled with wheat was placed by the bed, along with a large cross and icons of the birth of Christ and the birth of the Virgin. A guard on horseback rode all night outside the bedchamber with drawn sword to protect the couple from potential harm and evil spells. In the days following the wedding, tables were set up in the chambers of the Czar and the Czarina. Here were displayed the many gifts presented to the couple by their subjects.

THE DEATH OF A CZAR

Unfortunate, though unavoidable, events in the life of the ruling dynasty were also marked by carefully defined rituals. When a member of the royal family passed away, the misfortune was signaled by a slow ringing of the church bells; the tolling of the bells had particular significance for the Russian people and was regarded with extreme reverence. By contrast, joyful ceremonies were accompanied by relentless peals.

When a czar died, his courtiers kissed his hand and bade him farewell. His body was then wrapped in luxurious materials and placed in

a coffin fitted with gold cloth. Those closest to the czar, the "Chamber Boyars," took the coffin away and placed it on a specially prepared sleigh covered with a rich pall and strewn with branches. The coffin was then carried to the burial ground of the Moscow sovereigns at the Archangel Cathedral. Hundreds of monks and priests holding candles lined the funeral route. Clergy walked in front of the coffin carrying crosses and icons. A precious icon was carried on top of the coffin and placed beside the tomb. The icon painted at the time of the czar's birth was brought to the tomb, along with an icon of the czar's patron saint. The latter icon was normally painted after the consecration of the czar and until his death was held in the Annunciation Cathedral, the royal family's private church.

On the third day after the funeral, memorial feasts were held in all the monasteries and churches of Russia. For forty days after the courtiers had stood guard over the czar's tomb day and night, a memorial service was held. The wake for the dead was a custom strictly observed by the Romanovs. Homage was paid to the memory not only of members of the family but also of all past Muscovy rulers. Particular veneration was accorded to the murdered son of Ivan the Terrible, Czarevich Dmitry, who had been canonized by the Russian Orthodox Church.

As dictated by Orthodox tradition, a special dish was prepared for the burial and the wake: a porridge known as *kutia*. In ancient Russia, kutia was made by boiling millet and wheat in sweetened water; in later times, it was made from rice. Kutia was served in a special vessel known as a bratina, several of which were then placed on the deceased Czar's tomb. In general, the bittersweet rituals of burying and commemorating the dead, ordained by Christian law, were strictly observed in ancient Russia.

Detail of a miniature illustration, 1626
From the book *Description of the Celebration of Feb 5, 1626 at the Wedding of Czar and Great Prince Mikhail Feodorovich and Sovereign Czarina Evdokia Lukianovna*

full costume sparkling with precious stones sat on two silver chairs under holy icons. The older brother, pulling his hat over his forehead, stared at the ground, not seeing anyone and sat almost motionless. The younger brother [Peter I] looked everywhere. His face was open and beautiful. When you addressed him, his young blood became even more animated. This unbelievable beauty was striking to all the Moscow dignitaries."

+

CHILD'S ARMOR

This child's armor was probably made for the Czarevich Alexei (later Czar Alexei Mikhailovich), son of Mikhail Feodorovich. Like adult armor, it consists of a helmet, cuirass (torso armor), and a pair each of vambraces (forearm braces), cuisses (thigh armor), and gauntlets (gloves). Its decoration is characteristic of the time, with cast laps of brass, on which is featured a figured ornament in relief. This expensive toy was kept in the Kremlin Armory and may also have been used by the Czar Alexei Mikhailovich's children, including the future Peter the Great.

Portrait of Peter I as a Child

Portrait of Peter I as a Child
First half of the 18th century
Unknown Artist
Russia
Oil on canvas
23.4 x 19.4 inches (59.4 cm x 49.4 cm)
Zh-1966

Child's Armor
Second half of the 17th century
Russia
Iron, leather, forging, embossing, carving, casting, riveting, brass
10.6 inches (27 cm) height of helmet,
12.2 inches (31 cm) height of cuirass
(torso armor)
OR-304/1-10

PORTRAIT OF PETER I AS A CHILD

In the last quarter of the 17th century, the family of the Czar commissioned several portraits of Peter I (Peter Alexeyevich) at a young age. These portraits, based on ancient religious portraiture, featured Peter as the Christ-Emmanuel or the Deacon Stephen. Portraits of Peter were also painted in secular compositions, unencumbered by iconographic strictures. The ten-year-old Peter is often presented wearing his crown and carrying a scepter and orb. The earliest secular portrait of Peter is the miniature in the *Titles Book*, which contained important people and seals produced by the Kremlin Workshops from 1673 to 1677. The miniature of young Peter was ordered by his father, Alexei Mikhailovich, to complete the Romanov Dynasty. This portrait of Peter I, based on the miniature, was received by the Kremlin Armory in 1838.

The Swiss Secretary to the Ambassador Kemfer described Peter I in 1683 as follows: "In the reception hall, covered with Turkish rugs, both Czars dressed in

Child's Armor

QUIVER AND BOW CASE (SAADAK)

From the 15th to 17th century the term *saadak* referred to the complete set of armaments, including a bow in its case, or *naluch*, and the arrow in its case, or *kolchen*. In the 16th century, this was the main weapon of feudal horsemen. However, in the 17th century with the invention of firearms, the saadak was replaced with pistols and carbines, though the saadak continued to play an important role in the ceremonial armament of the Russian czars. They were produced by special order only for the Czar or for the Czar's official heir; the other czareviches were not allowed this privileged weapon. The ceremonial saadaks contained an additional *takhtui*, a cover for the bow case, as well as a cover for the entire saadak set.

In the current collection of the Kremlin Armory, this is the only saadak composed of all three pieces. It was created for the Czarevich Alexei Alexeyevich (1654-1670), the second son of Czar Alexei Mikhailovich who was named heir to the throne after his birth. His older brother Dmitry died as an infant. In May 1654, a few months after his birth, Alexei was listed in documents as having accompanied his father to the battle at Smolensk Fortress.

This saadak was made by three masters of the Kremlin Workshops on the order of Alexei Mikhailovich on February 18, 1667 when his son turned thirteen. It was presented to the Czarevich on April 12, 1667. The saadak is made out of white satin and embroidered with gold and colored silk thread. The ornamental mark on the bow's case is a two-headed eagle under three crowns—the emblem of the Russian State—and a depiction of the Russian Kremlin as seen from Red Square. The takhtui is decorated with the same material and bears the same marks as the saadak.

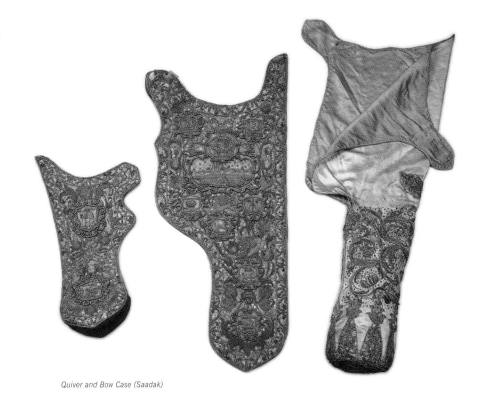

Quiver and Bow Case (Saadak)

Quiver and Bow Case (Saadak)
1667
Masters Dmitry Astafev, P. Ashchreyev, and A. Eliseyev
Kremlin Armory
Moscow, Russia
Gold thread, leather, silver thread, embroidery, gilding, satin
28.5 inches (72.5 cm) length of quiver,
16.5 inches (42 cm) length of bow case;
4.7 inches (12 cm) length of cover
OR-146/1-3

Detail of Bow Case

Child's Saddle and Pair of Stirrups
17th century
Western Europe
Saddle: velvet, wood, silver, copper,
leather, rope, ribbon, weaving, gilding,
embossing, weaving
8.3 inches (21 cm) height of pommel,
6.7 inches (17 cm) height of cantle,
15.4 inches (39 cm) total length
K-739
Stirrups: silver, ribbon, iron, leather,
carving, gilding, weaving
4.1 inches (10.3 cm) height; total weight
12.2 ounces (346.9 grams)
K-740/1-2

**Carbine with Flintlock of Czarevich
Alexei Alexeyevich**
1660
Kremlin Armory
Moscow, Russia
Iron, wood, mother-of-pearl, drop-forging,
silver plating, gilding, inlay work
37.4 inches (95 cm) total length, 25.6
inches (65 cm) length of carbine, 12 mm
caliber
OR-1964

CHILD'S SADDLE AND PAIR OF STIRRUPS

Russian czars learned the art of war and leadership early in life. A fundamental aspect of this education was simply learning to sit in the saddle. The Kremlin Workshops made small saddles for the czareviches to be used on small horses. In 1673 when Czarevich Peter Alexeyevich had barely learned to walk, the workshops had already prepared his saddle. The earliest documentation of children's saddles dates back to 1642, for Czarevich Alexei Mikhailovich. Unfortunately, it is difficult to positively identify the provenance of this particular saddle. The shape of the saddle is typical of Western European saddles of the 17th and 18th centuries.

This exemplary leather saddle was fabricated with great command of materials, care, and skill. The wine-colored velvet seat-cover is decorated with stitching and gold braid, and fastened to the saddle with brass nails. The stirrup rigging is silk with variegated braid. The silver stirrups have narrow arches and an oval form, and the smooth surface is gilded. The outer edges of the arches are decorated with flower motifs, and along the edge is a thin border.

✦

CARBINE WITH FLINTLOCK OF CZAREVICH ALEXEI ALEXEYEVICH

This magnificent carbine was given to Czarevich Alexei Alexeyevich in 1660 by a well-known member of the Russian Court, Stolnik Vasily Nikitich Steshnev. Stolnik was one of the highest Russian court ranks. Officially, Stolniks served the czar, but often they were appointed to higher state and military positions.

The Czarevich's carbine shown here is relatively short and light for a horseman's gun. Usually, a carbine was carried on a strap affixed to a ring on the left side of the stock by means of a metal clip. The masters at the

Kremlin Workshops produced richly decorated carbines especially for the czars' hunting trips. The barrel is decorated with engraved images of women and musical instruments, and tiny renderings of a fox, rabbit, and bird hidden amid stylized plants. The cocking mechanism is decorated with the head of a dog and a custom-designed finger hook.

The selection of the carbine as a gift was not by chance. In 1600 Czarevich Alexei turned six years old. He had already been learning to ride horses and had appeared in parades, but an actual hunting arquebus was too heavy for the child. This light carbine took the place of the Czarevich's toy weapon and allowed him to go on ceremonial hunts with his father.

Carbine with Flintlock

Child's Saddle and Pair of Stirrups

Cradle

Cradle
Late 17th century
Russia
Velvet: mid-17th century, China
Velvet, filigree, wood, iron, weaving,
carving, gilding
62.2 inches (158 cm) length of sticks;
39.8 x 42.5 inches (101 cm x 108 cm)
dimensions of velvet
TK-2840

Rattle
Last quarter of 17th century
Nuremberg, Germany
Silver, embossing, casting, engraving,
gilding
7.5 inches (19 cm) length
MZ-1093

Child's Bag
17th century
Russia
Velvet: 17th century, Turkey
Velvet, taffeta, silk and gold thread,
weaving, rope
3.3 x 2.4 inches (8.5 cm x 6 cm)
TK-645

CRADLE

The Russian cradle, historically, was made from a wooden frame and covered with sturdy cloth. The cradle for an infant of royal birth, however, was made from top quality wood and expensive cloth. In addition, an elegantly decorated blanket and pillow were tailored by the finest masters in the Kremlin Workshop. As custom dictated, the royal cradle was ordered a few days after the birth of the child by the child's godmother. The children slept in these cradles for many years. Czarevich Feodor Alexeyevich, the older brother of Czar Peter I, slept in his cradle until he was twelve years old.

The wooden part of this cradle has been decorated with horses and golden spheres. The cradle's scarlet velvet was imported from China.

RATTLE

Toys for the royal children were made in the Kremlin Workshops or purchased abroad. They entertained the young czareviches and czarevnas and guided their spiritual and aesthetic development, since their toys were often brilliant creations of accomplished jewelers and artists. This silver rattle, the work of a German master, is refined in shape and harmonious in proportion. Its beautifully embossed décor includes baroque motifs characteristic of the time.

CHILD'S BAG

The purse was an essential accessory of ancient Russian fashion. Attached to a belt or worn over the shoulder, it was used instead of a pocket to carry money and objects of daily use. The bag on display here is rectangular and made of Turkish velvet bearing a foliate ornament. It hangs from two woven-silk cords with a fine blue silk tassel affixed to the end.

A bag made of cloth or leather was known as a *moshchnaya* or *kalitaya*. The nickname "Kalita" was given in the 14th century to the Muscovy Prince Ivan Danilovich, who was famed for his parsimony.

Child's Bag

Rattle

71

"Alexei, Man of God" Icon with Frame
Icon: 17th century, Moscow, Russia
Frame (*Oklad*): 1629, Moscow, Russia
Kremlin Workshops
Wood, silk, egg tempera, silver, precious stones, pearls
19 x 5.7 inches (48.3 cm x 14.5 cm);
total weight 4.45 lbs. (2,017 grams)
Zh-549/1-2

"ALEXEI, MAN OF GOD" ICON WITH FRAME (OKLAD)

This icon belongs to a special genre known as measured, or christening, icons. The creation of these icons began directly after the birth of Czarevich Ivan, the second son of Ivan the Terrible. The icon served as a record of the newborn czarevich's size and displayed a painted depiction of the czarevich's patron saint on a small narrow board equivalent to the czarevich's height. This practice originated during the reign of Ivan the Terrible and expressed the belief that the czar's power was indeed sacred. Measured icons became relics after the czarevich's death and were placed in the iconostasis over his tomb in the Archangel Cathedral.

This particular icon was painted in 1629 after the birth of Alexei, the oldest son of Mikhail Feodorovich. The Czarevich's patron saint, St. Alexei, lived during the 5th century. Above the saint is a depiction of the Holy Trinity. The frame has been given a foliate design in the style of Russian jewelry at the turn of the 17th century.

"Alexei, Man of God" Icon with Frame (Oklad)

Towel

Towel
17th century
Moscow, Russia
Linen, gold and silver thread, weaving,
embroidery
126 x 23.6 inches (320 cm x 60 cm)
TK-722

**Mirror of Princess Maria
Romadanovskaya**
17th century
Moscow, Russia
Silver, mirror, gold rope, embossing,
carving, chasing, gilding
6.8 x 6.1 inches (17.3 cm x 15.4 cm)
MR-4201

MIRROR OF PRINCESS MARIA ROMADANOVSKAYA

Glass mirrors first appeared in Europe at the end of the 16th century and became widespread in Russia at that time as well.

This mirror in a silver case belonged to Princess Maria Yurevna Romadanovskaya, a member of an old boyar family; her brother was a close associate of Peter the Great.

The main decorative element of the mirror is the crown and shield inscribed with the name of the owner on the front of the mirror's case. This is usually a personal or family seal. The composition of this design resembles a seal, though it is thought that the image found here is only an imitation of a seal.

Personal seals appeared relatively late in Russia, presented on precious metals only in the second half of the 17th century. Although the Romanovs had their own seal at the end of the 16th century, it was unusual for unmarried women to use them.

OWEL

rnamental towels woven entirely by ladies' hands erved as a kind of calling card for their makers, an xample of their artistic taste and craftsmanship. Female andicrafts had long been highly valued in Russia, and ne ability to embroider, thread pearls, knit, and make ce were considered feminine virtues. Embroidered wels made up an important part of the marriage eremony, since they showed the bride's prowess in aking and decorating articles of daily life. The towel nown here is remarkable for its delicacy and grace of rm. Its creator chose only gold and silver thread and ne purest white linen. Fantastical flowers and branches re spread thickly across the surface and united by a ackground of golden sweet peas. The towel was mbroidered by means of a special two-sided technique hich allows the decoration to appear the same when iewed from either side.

Mirror of Princess Maria Romadanovskaya

Comb with Case
17th century
Turkey
Comb: Tortoise shell, carving, gold,
precious stones
Case: Velvet, gold thread, weaving,
embroidery, gold, precious stones, satin
5.8 x 2.3 inches (14.7 cm x 5.9 cm)
length of comb, 6.5 x 2.9 inches (16.5
cm x 7.4 cm) length of case
DK-1427/1-2

Jewel Box (*Larets*)
Late 17th century
Solvychegodsk, Russia
Silver, mirror, embossing, enamel,
gilding, filigree
3.8 x 2.3 inches (9.7 cm x 5.8 cm)
MR-1231

Comb with Case

COMB WITH CASE

Combs in old Russia were made of various local
materials including wood and animal bone. Special
combs made out of Cyprus wood, walrus tusks, and
tortoise shells were obtained for the Imperial Court.
Combs were often presented to the Russian State as
ambassadorial gifts. In 1930 the Turkish Ambassador,
Foma Cantacuzin, presented Czar Mikhail Feodorovich
with "a comb of horn, covered in jasper, with gold carved
into the jasper and reeds carved into the gold." This
Turkish comb is similar in quality and appearance, but

made from tortoise shell rather than horn. The comb is
accompanied by a velvet case embroidered with gold
thread. On the background are sewn golden studs with
emeralds and rubies. In Turkey such combs were
intended for highly formal bathing ceremonies. In Russia
combs were used for wedding rituals. On the eve of the
wedding, the groom would present his bride with a small
box containing a mirror and comb.

+

JEWEL BOX (LARETS)

The word *larets* in Russia refers to boxes of different
sizes, used for storing jewelry or perfume. This type of
box was rectangular and placed on short spherical legs,
with a hinged lid. A mirror was often installed on the
inside of the box's lid. The boxes were constructed out of
various materials including wood, bone, and metal.

This jewel box is made from gilded silver. Its walls and lid
are decorated with straight long twigs with bunches of
flowers and leaves rendered in painted enamel. It was
made in Solvychegodsk, a city in the European part of
Russia. At the end of the 17th century, the city was a
common trade route through Russia and was praised for
its painted enamel; these pieces were highly sought after
and enjoyed by the Russian czars.

Jewel Box (Larets)

TABLE ORNAMENT IN THE SHAPE OF A SHIP

Ships were one of the most popular motifs and wares made by European goldsmiths, beginning as early as the Middle Ages. Castles and palaces gradually became filled with entire fleets of these decorative ships, which were at times up to three feet high. The bodies were made from a variety of materials: crystals, coconuts, seashells, gold, and, most frequently, silver. Some of these ships doubled as fountains or goblets. The ships also offered a certain element of play for both children and adults dreaming of nautical journeys and new lands. The Russians, however, did not have their own fleet until the time of Peter the Great.

This single-masted ship on wheels functioned as a table decoration. Goldsmiths produced these ships in honor of the fabled English monarchs who were said to have traveled on land by means of such ships. Today, such ships appear very rarely in both private collections and museums. The wide body of the ship is embossed with grape clusters; a tiny figurine of the Greek god Bacchus sits on a keg under the main sail holding a wine glass and a cluster of grapes. Both sails of the ship are decorated with gold laurel wreaths and a gold flag and crown.

✦

TANKARD

As indicated by the inscription on its underside, this silver tankard (shown in the middle) initially belonged to Czarevich Ivan (1554-1581), the son of Czar Ivan the Terrible (1533-1584). Following the ancient traditions observed by the czar and later by the Imperial Court, priceless vessels were presented as gifts at a child's

christening. In the Kremlin Armory there are two such tankards received as part of this Christian sacrament. This tankard was presented to Czarevich Ivan by Feodor Ivanovich Sheremetev, a member of an ancient and powerful family of boyars. Ivan's christening took place in the Chudov Monastery of the Moscow Kremlin on March 22, 1629.

This is one of the few surviving pieces of Southern German work from the second half of the 16th century. In addition, European goldsmith masters rarely worked with filigree, making this piece even more unusual. The Augsburg masters were among the most important silver and gold craftsmen in Germany. Master Abraham I. Lotter used a double-braid filigree technique, inlaying a concentric design of multi-petaled rosettes.

✦

TANKARD

This tankard (on the right) was produced in the mid-17th century in Germany and later obtained in the 19th century by a Russian master who subsequently covered the lid with an embossed medallion and stamped a vignette of the wedding of Czar Alexei Mikhailovich and Czarina Natalia Kirillovna onto the tankard's smooth outer body. In the delicate rendering, the Patriarch holds an open book with his left hand and a ring in his right hand. The bride and groom stand beside him, holding hands.

The addition of this scene was not by chance. The 1812 war with Napoleon greatly increased patriotism in the country, and a fascination with the royal line grew. Alexei Mikhailovich, the father of Peter the Great, received special consideration during this time; he is grandly and nostalgically associated with quintessential Old Russia, before the westernizing reforms of his son.

Table Ornament in the Shape of a Ship
Last quarter of 17th century
Augsburg, Germany
Silver, embossing, casting, engraving, poinçon, gilding
17.5 inches (44.5 cm) height
MZ-345

Tankard (middle)
1565–1575
Master Abraham I. Lotter
Augsburg, Germany
Silver, filigree, etching, gilding, embossing, casting
11 inches (28 cm) height
F-122

Tankard (right)
1635-1662
Master Klaus Sulsen
Hamburg, Germany
Silver, embossing, casting, poinçon, gilding
8.5 inches (21.5 cm) height, 4.3 inches (11 cm) diameter; total weight 1.98 lbs. (897.2 grams)
MZ-1679

Table Ornament

Tankard

Tankard

"The Vladimir Mother of God" Icon with Frame

"The Vladimir Mother of God" Icon with Frame
Icon: 19th century, Russia
Frame: 17th century, Russia
Wood, gesso, filigree, gold, precious
stones, pearls, embossing, enamel,
tempera
12.5 x 10.6 inches (31.7 cm x 27 cm)
Zh-547/1-2

Wedding Crowns for Bride and Groom
17th century
Russia
Silver, forging, embossing, carving,
gilding
7.3 inches (18.5 cm) diameter each
MR-5070, MR-5071

"THE VLADIMIR MOTHER OF GOD" ICON WITH FRAME

In the Orthodox marriage ceremony, the role of the icon
of the Virgin was to protect the couple from wrongdoing,
evil, illness, and other misfortunes. The Vladimir Mother
of God image was one of the most widespread, and was a
copy of the ancient Byzantine icon representing Mary
and the infant Jesus. This icon was sent as a gift to Prince
Yuri Dolgoruky at the beginning of the 12th century by
the Constantinople Patriarch. Yuri's son, Prince Andrei,
brought the icon to the city of Vladimir, the second
largest city after Kiev, the ancient capital. The icon was
named after the city. The Vladimir Mother of God
ultimately became a Russian holy figure, attributed with
performing many miracles. In 1395 the icon was brought
to Moscow.

Following the Byzantine tradition, the icon was covered
in a frame, or *oklad*, made of gold and outlined with
rubies, emeralds, and large sapphires; one gem alone had
25 karats. Most likely, this icon was a relic of the royal
family because of its elegant decoration and the fact that
is was housed in the Archangel Cathedral.

✦

WEDDING CROWNS FOR BRIDE AND GROOM

Russian wedding crowns were usually made of silver gilt
in the shape of a smooth hoop, and were decorated with
surprising restraint. A figured finial rises above the front
of the crown. Along the upper edge runs an undulating
band of chased ornament with carved points. The center
bears carved compositions: on one crown is a half-length
portrait of the deesis—Jesus Christ, the Virgin Mary, and
St. John the Baptist; on the other, the "Znamenie" Virgin
with St. Joachim and St. Anne. Joachim and Anne were
the parents of the Virgin, and were therefore a symbol of
marital fidelity. The soft and gentle carving is particularly
attractive and shows off the assured mastery of Russian
engraving of the 17th century.

Wedding crowns were placed on the heads of the bride
and groom during their betrothal in the church. In form
they reflect ancient models made of silver, bronze, iron,
and wood. The crown was a sign of secret union and of
the blessing of the heavenly powers. In Moscow the
splendid wedding ceremony of members of the royal
family took place in the main cathedral of the Kremlin,
the Assumption Cathedral, from which these two silver
crowns have come.

Wedding Crowns for Bride and Groom

KERCHIEF (SHIRINKA)

The *shirinka*—a small formal kerchief —was a practical element of everyday life in 17th-century Russia. It was also an integral aspect of the parade costume, in which, depending on the ceremony, it had multiple symbolic meanings. *Shirinki* played a valuable role in the marriage ceremony: the groom gave his bride a shirinka (sometimes instead of a ring). Shirinki for royal weddings were made in the Kremlin Workshops, and their design was often undertaken by professional court artists. In 1653, for example, the royal icon painter Ivan Matveev spent "a week and six days" preparing the designs for royal hats and shirinki. The surviving kerchiefs are remarkable for their artistic delicacy and their use of both traditional embroidery and gold pillow lace. For Russian seamstresses, gold lacemaking was less common than artistic embroidery. The art of bobbin lacemaking came to Russia from the West. It was a technique mainly used in Moscow, and for some time, was practiced only at court; in 1625 ten lacemakers were employed in the Kremlin Workshops.

Moscow lace took original forms. A favorite practice of the Kremlin seamstresses was the use of river pearls within gold and silver lace. In this method, either separate pearls were worked into the lace, or small parts of the design were filled in with pearls. The sparkle of the white pearls reflected off the metallic surface of the lace and blended into the white taffeta of the shirinka's central section, creating a bright and glorious patch of light.

Kerchief (Shirinka)

RING (PERSTYEN)

Archaeological excavations show that rings in ancient Russia were made by twisting together pieces of thick metal wire. By the 8th or 9th century, Slavic craftsmen had already begun to make rings of solid gold and silver.

In the 16th and 17th centuries, rings were cast and richly decorated with large semi-precious stones, enamel, and niello. Such rings were known in ancient documents as *perstni*, and were worn by both women and men. Royal personages and courtiers wore several rings on their hands, oftentimes one on each finger.

At court, jeweled perstni served as gifts for christenings, name days, and weddings. It is thought that the heart-shaped gold *perstyen* on display here was a wedding gift that the groom presented to his bride together with the traditional *shirinka*, or kerchief.

Kerchief (*Shirinka*)
17th century
Kremlin Workshops
Moscow, Russia
Taffeta: Italy
Lace: Russia
Taffeta, gold thread, pearls, weaving, braiding
17.7 x 18.1 inches (45 cm x 46 cm)
TK-547

Ring (*Perstyen*)
Late 17th century
Kremlin Workshops
Moscow, Russia
Gold, precious stones, embossing, enamel, carving
.75 inches (1.9 cm) diameter
MR-2672

Ring (Perstyen)

Pendant Earrings

Earrings

Earrings

Pair of Pendant Earrings
16th century
Russia
Silver, pearls, filigree, enamel, gilding,
turquoise
6.7 x 2 inches (17 cm x 5 cm)
MR-5763/1-2

Pair of Earrings (top right)
17th century
Russia
Gold, emeralds, rubies, pearls, agate,
enamel
2.7 x .8 inches (6.8 cm x 2 cm)
MR-2677/1-2

Pair of Earrings (bottom right)
17th century
Russia
Gold, emeralds, rubies, pearls, glass,
casting, enamel, carving
1.9 x .8 inches (4.8 cm x 2 cm)
MR-2644/1-2

PAIR OF PENDANT EARRINGS (RIASNY)

In the 12th through 17th centuries, *riasny*—long
pendants—became increasingly widespread in Russia as
a form of jewelry for women. This tradition may have
come from Byzantine, where riasny are often seen in
paintings from the 6th century. The majority of riasny
from the 14th to 17th centuries consisted of various
braided rows of pearls, mixed in with small pieces of
metal, precious stones, and glass; frequently the material
came from icons on which they were hung as decoration.
These riasny decorated one of the icons at the Pokrovsky
Convent in Suzdal, which housed many treasures of the
Russian rulers.

TWO PAIRS OF EARRINGS

The large number of earrings that remain in Russia from
centuries past attests to the importance of earrings in
everyday life. Documentation about life in old Russia
reveals that earrings were worn by women and men,
though men usually wore only one. Demand for earrings
was great, and they were produced in large quantities in
the 16th and 17th centuries. Their shapes varied. The
simplest earrings were rods on which precious stones,
metal, and glass beads were attached through a tiny
hoop. Other earrings were more complicated in form.
The main part of the earring was often configured in
gold or silver and then mounted with colorful stones.
The jewelers at the Kremlin were extremely innovative
and were known for using a wide range of materials and
forms; these two pairs of earrings showcase the delicacy
and mastery of their makers.

COLLECTION OF THREE STUDS

In the Romanov era, studs were used widely in everyday life. They were sewn onto clothing made out of velvet and satin, attached to hats, belts and shoes, and for other decorative purposes on a host of items. Identical in form, studs sometimes were made into long strands referred to as "metal lace," which adorned both churches and royal garments.

These three gold studs feature rubies and diamonds. In the center of the round stud is a large green thirty-karat emerald; the design suggests not only an Eastern accent, but also, like the other two, a Western European influence as well. Russian masters had close contact with jewelers and designers from other lands and showcased this exchange in their work. These studs from the middle of the 17th century, made most likely for parade vestments, at one time decorated the icon "The Vladimir Mother of God."

COLLECTION OF FIVE BUTTONS

Buttons played an instrumental role in the design of both men's and women's clothing in Russia during the Romanov reign. The demand for buttons at the Imperial Court was so high that the masters at the Kremlin Workshops could barely produce enough. Often, clothing-makers purchased buttons by the pound from button makers at the Moscow silver market. The forms, techniques, and decorative facets for buttons varied considerably. Buttons ranged from the size of a pea to the size of an egg.

The elegant coats of the czars were decorated with buttons made of precious stones and metals. Such buttons stood out not only for their beauty, but also for the expensive materials that sometimes cost more than the coats themselves. This group of five buttons belonged to the czars. One of them is made of raw agate. Two of them are oval-shaped glass beads, in the style of opaque light-blue opal. The two large gold buttons are extremely luxurious and decorated with transparent enamel and inset precious stones.

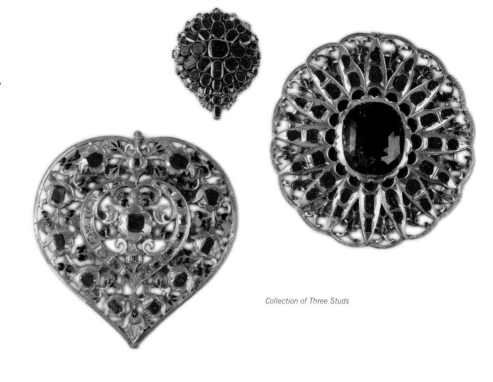

Collection of Three Studs

Single Button

Pair of Buttons

Pair of Buttons

Collection of Three Studs
17th century
Russia
Gold, precious stones, embossing, enamel, carving

Small Stud (above center)
1.7 x 1 inches (4.2 cm x 2.5 cm)
MR-3709/2

Round stud (above right)
3.2 inches (8.2 cm) diameter
MR-3709/6

Heart-shaped Stud (above left)
3.1 x 3.2 inches (7.9 cm x 8.1 cm)
MR-3709/9

Collection of Five Buttons
17th century
Russia

Pair of Buttons (middle right)
17th century
Kremlin Workshops
Moscow, Russia
Gold, polished glass, casting, enamel
1.1 x .5 inches (2.7 cm x 1.2 cm) each
MR-2449, MR-2450

Single Button (middle left)
Second half of the 17th century
Russia
Gold, agate, pearls, casting, enamel
1.7 x .9 inches (4.2 cm x 2.3 cm)
MR-2444

Pair of Buttons (bottom left)
First half of the 17th century
Kremlin Workshops
Moscow, Russia
Gold, precious stones, casting, enamel
2.2 x 1.2 inches (5.5 cm x 3 cm) each
MR-2316, MR-2317

"Birth of Christ" Icon

The artistic methods displayed in the icon suggest it to be the work of an icon painter of the late 19th century—the use of handwritten script, the lines of the blackened drawings, and the manner in which the hills are portrayed. In addition, the miniature details of the composition, the vibrancy and combinations of colors, and the introduction and execution of architectural forms follow icon-painting traditions already perfected at the end of the 17th century.

✦

"HARROWING INTO HELL" ICON WITH FRAME

This small icon was part of the iconostasis of the Archangel Cathedral where members of the Romanov dynasty were buried. The presence of the icon in the cathedral was linked to the Russian funeral rites, which determined which icons would be brought to the tombs of the deceased in the church and left there.

The subject of the icon is Christ's defeat of the powers of darkness during the three days between the Crucifixion and the Resurrection, a symbol of the victory of life over death. Beneath his feet lie the broken gates of Hell, with its shattered locks, keys, and chains. Below, shrouded figures rise from their tombs. On either side of Christ stand Adam and Eve, whom he holds with each of his hands; also featured are the biblical kings Solomon and David and prophets from the Old Testament.

Catholic artists often portrayed differing variations of the Resurrection, in which Christ is seen rising above his tomb, surrounded by astonished soldiers. Russian icon painting of the 17th century revealed for the first time elements of Western iconography; this work shows two iconographic variants united in the same composition.

"Harrowing into Hell" Icon with Frame

"Birth of Christ" Icon
17th century–19th century
Russia
Wood, gesso, tempera
12.2 x 10.3 inches (31 x 26.2 cm)
KP-51690

"Harrowing into Hell" Icon with Frame
First half of the 17th century
Moscow, Russia
Silver, precious stones, wood, gesso, tempera, gilding, embossing, carving
11.6 x 9.8 inches (29.4 cm x 25 cm)
Zh-540/1-2

"BIRTH OF CHRIST" ICON

The painter of this icon has faithfully and painstakingly represented the birth of Christ according to the Gospel. Remarkable is the number of narratives contained within the tiny composition.

In the top center is a depiction of the Nativity: the confinement of the Virgin Mary, the baby Jesus in the manger, the kneeling shepherds, and the praising angels. In the top corners are the Magi—the three wise men—following the star of Bethlehem leading to Christ. The middle portion of the icon shows a narrative sequence of the Magi offering gifts to Christ, the angel warning Joseph to flee to Egypt, Joseph and the old pastor expressing their doubts, the angel appearing to the Virgin Mary, and the flight out of Bethlehem to Egypt, with Mary and Jesus on horseback.

The lower portion of the icon presents the Magi before King Herod, the massacre of the innocents, the weeping of the women of Bethlehem, St. Elizabeth hiding in a cave with John the Baptist, Rachel weeping over her children, and Zacharias before the throne.

MEMORIAL WINE VESSEL (BRATINA)

This bratina, part of a set of memorial vessels, was filled with honey-sweetened water and placed on the tomb of the deceased during the funeral rite. The striking design consists of a pattern of adjoining rows of chased triangles. The inscription around the rim explains that it was made after the death of the Czarevna Irina, daughter of Mikhail Feodorovich, who died soon after birth.

MEMORIAL WINE VESSEL (BRATINA) FOR CZAREVICH IVAN IVANOVICH

This gilded silver bratina is decorated with an ornamental stamped and carved design on a black background. On the vessel's crown is an inscription noting that it was made for Czar Mikhail Feodorovich for the coffin of Czarevich Ivan Ivanovich, the eldest son of Czar Ivan the Terrible. The twenty-seven-year-old Ivan, heir to the throne, died in 1581 after a fight with his father at the Czar's country residence. Although the cause of the fight is still unknown, the Czar became angry with his son and hit him in the head with a staff. The Czarevich died a few days later. Ivan the Terrible managed not only to kill his own son, but he also put an end to the Rurik dynasty as well. The Czarevich was buried in the Archangel Cathedral of the Kremlin.

CEREMONIAL KUTIA DISH FOR THE TOMB OF CZAR IVAN ALEXEYEVICH

The creation of these dishes was intended for the Russian Orthodox funeral ritual. During the church funeral for the dead, a dish with *kutia*—a mixture of grain and honey—was placed on the coffin. The grain decomposing in the earth and germinating again, signified resurrection, while the honey represented the sweetness of the future blessed life.

As the inscription on the dish indicates, it was meant to be used on the coffin of Czar Ivan Alexeyevich, who is buried in the Archangel Cathedral. In the 17th century a funeral service was conducted every day in memory of the dead. There were several such dishes that were kept in the church for these services. A dish, candlestick, and goblet for church wine were placed on the coffin. This dish for Czar Ivan Alexeyevich is one of the most exemplary. A rendering of the two-headed eagle—the emblem of the Russian state—appears in the middle of the dish. Along the rim are circular indentations for the placement of the grain, on the very edge of the dish is a stripe of emeralds.

Memorial Wine Vessel (Bratina)

Memorial Wine Vessel (Bratina) for Czarevich Ivan Ivanovich

Ceremonial Kutia Dish for the Tomb of Czar Ivan Alexeyevich

Memorial Wine Vessel (Bratina)
First half of the 17th century
Kremlin Workshops
Moscow, Russia
Silver, embossing, carving, flat chasing, gilding
3.9 inches (10 cm) height, 4.3 inches (11 cm) diameter
MR-4185

Memorial Wine Vessel (Bratina) for Czarevich Ivan Ivanovich
First half of the 17th century
Russia
Silver, embossing, niello, carving, gilding
3.1 inches (8 cm) height, 4.6 inches (11.8 cm) diameter
MR-4135

Ceremonial Kutia Dish for the Tomb of Czar Ivan Alexeyevich
1696
Kremlin Workshops
Moscow, Russia
Gold, silver, precious stones, gilding, niello, forging, embossing, carving
15.2 inches (38.5 cm) diameter
MR-4227

Altar Cross
1677
Moscow, Russia
Gold, precious stones, pearls, embossing,
enamel, niello
14.8 inches (37.5 cm) height, 7.8
inches (19.7 cm) width
MR-1879

Candlestick
1699
Kremlin Workshops
Moscow, Russia
Silver, emeralds, glass, embossing,
engraving, enamel, gilding
10.4 inches (26.4 cm) height, 7.5
inches (19 cm) diameter
MR-3388/1-2

ALTAR CROSS

This gold cross embodies the traditional form of the
Russian altar cross. It has eight corners with the
Crucifixion in the center. The design of the cross
effectively combines the use of gold, precious stones,
pearls, and niello. The cross was made on the order of
Czarina Evdokia Alexeyevna, the sister of Peter I.

There were two daughters with the name of Evdokia
born to Alexei Mikhailovich and his wife, Maria
Miloslavskaya. The first Evdokia died at age nineteen, in
February of 1669. When the couple gave birth to another
daughter that same year, she was named Evdokia, after
her deceased sister. This second Evdokia had this cross
made in memory of her father, Czar Alexei Mikhailovich,
for the Archangel Cathedral.

CANDLESTICK

When royal personages died, it was customary for
members of the family to make donations to cathedrals
and monasteries. This silver candlestick decorated with
142 emeralds was one such donation. The inscription on
the interior of the candlestick's base tells how the Czarina
Marfa Apraxina placed it in Moscow's Archangel
Cathedral, the resting place of the Great Princes and
Czars of Russia until the end of the 18th century. In 1682
Czar Feodor Alexeyevich, the elder brother of Peter the
Great, died and was buried in the cathedral. His widow
presented this candlestick to the cathedral in his
memory.

Altar Cross

Candlestick

COFFIN CLOTH OF CZAREVICH DMITRY ALEXEYEVICH

In the Orthodox funeral rite, the coffin cloth was ceremonially draped over the coffin of the dead. Each church made its own coffin cloth, which always portrayed the Cross of Golgotha, a symbol of suffering, death, and the afterlife. For the burial of members of the royal household, coffin cloths were used that were of a more personal nature and recalled the memory of the deceased. These were laid on the tombs of members of the royal family on the days set aside in the Orthodox calendar for mourning: forty days after the death; a year after the death; and three years after the death.

The coffin cloth on display here is that of Dmitry Alexeyevich, the first son of Alexei Mikhailovich, who was born October 22, 1648 and died on October 6 the following year. An inscription of pearls woven into the green velvet border of the cloth states that it was placed on the coffin of the Czarevich Dmitry Alexeyevich "by order of Czar Alexei Mikhailovich, on the sixth day of October 7158 [1649]." Thirty-eight silver gilt badges have been applied to the central crimson section of the cloth, forming the eight-pointed Cross of Golgotha. The badges, made by smiths of the Silver and Gold Chambers of the Kremlin Workshops, contain carved images of Orthodox feast days and saints. During the days of mourning for the czars and their older sons, their coffin cloths were carried to the family tomb in the Archangel Cathedral.

The images on the badges of the coffin cloth represented the patron saints of the deceased, his parents, living members of the royal family, and those of the dynasty in general. The cloths usually took at least a month to make; the inscription, woven with pearls, took fifteen to twenty days. It is known that sketches for coffin cloths were made by artists—often icon painters and calligraphers—from the Kremlin Workshops; the sketch for this cloth was carried out by the artist Karp Timofeev.

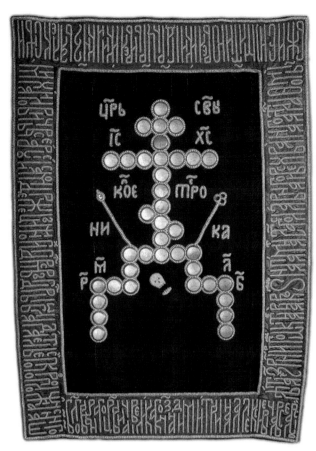

Coffin Cloth of Czarevich Dmitry Alexeyevich

Coffin Cloth of Czarevich Dmitry Alexeyevich
1649-50
Kremlin Workshops
Moscow, Russia
Cloth: First half of the 17th century, Italy
Embroidery: 1649, Russia
Velvet, damask, silver, precious stones, pearls, gold, weaving, carving, gilding, embroidery
55.1 x 38.6 inches (140 cm x 98 cm)
TK-2158

CHAPTER IV

The Royal Parades of the Czars

The Royal Parades of the Czars

by O.B. Melnikova

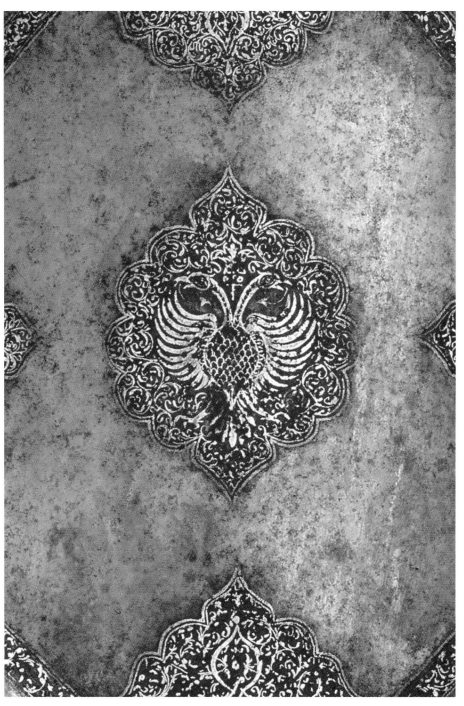

Detail of Steel Plate Armor (Zertsala)

The royal parade was the name given to the ceremonial excursions undertaken by the Russian Czars when they left their residence in the Kremlin and set off on military campaigns, pilgrimages, and hunting expeditions. Like nearly all aspects of court ceremony during the Romanov era, the royal parade was a highly orchestrated affair.

Written records from the time described the elaborate preparations made for each royal parade. The order of the procession was worked out, and lists were drawn up of the participants in the ceremony and the requisite royal equipment and attire. Horse trappings from the royal stables and weapons from the armory were distributed for use in the parade. Each item was dictated according to the purpose and significance of the excursion. The number of horses, carriages, and other vehicles was carefully calculated. Only the highest ranking boyars, *stolniki* (courtiers), and noblemen from the *Duma* were allowed to accompany the Czar, while the Czarina was escorted by wives and widows of boyars. Boyars and noblemen, armed and mounted on richly equipped horses, presented themselves at the Kremlin in their finest robes.

There were three principal kinds of royal parade in 17th-century Russia: military reviews, royal campaigns and pilgrimages (normally of a religious nature), and hunting trips (often occurring at the same time as the royal campaigns).

MILITARY REVIEWS

Military reviews were significant events, generally preceding a declaration of war or a campaign by the Czar's forces. The sovereign's regiment (The Bolshoi Gosudarev) played the most important role; it was made up of elite representatives of the Russian gentry and was directly under the sovereign's orders. Military reviews lasted for several days and were held on the Devichy Field near the Novodevichy Monastery just outside Moscow. Banners, armor, and weaponry were distributed to the regiments from the Kremlin Armory for use in the review. A "campaign" armory reserved for the Czar was set up, which contained the most exquisite sidearms, firearms, sabers, broadswords, and *konchary* (cavalry swords) with jeweled hilts and silver-gilt scabbards; there were one-of-a-kind pistols in embroidered holsters, arquebuses with barrels and stocks inlaid with gold and encrusted with ivory and mother-of-pearl, and fine armor with chased gold ornament. The Czar's ceremonial weapons were, of course, of the highest quality and usually consisted of three *saadaki* (bow and arrow sets), lances, spears, and arquebuses. These were carried in front of the sovereign by the royal weapons bearers, or *ryndy*, dressed in white or scarlet caftans. The armor bearer rode behind the sovereign with the royal helmet in his hands.

When a military review signaled the beginning of a campaign, the army paraded from the Devichy Field through Moscow, and then into the Kremlin. When the armed forces returned home from battle, they were greeted by another ceremony. If they were victorious, the event was particularly splendid. Accounts of Alexei Mikhailovich's entry into Moscow after the successful Polish campaign described the royal procession as glittering with gold and precious stones; the richly attired army carried banners as they formed two columns to line the route to the Kremlin. The bells of Moscow's many churches rang out. The boyars headed the procession, followed by twenty-four royal parade horses outfitted with jeweled harnesses, horsecloths, and saddles embroidered with gold and pearls. Next came the royal sleighs and carriages. The Czar himself entered the Kremlin on foot preceded by the *streltsy* (guards).

ROYAL CAMPAIGNS AND PILGRIMAGES

The second type of ceremonial procession was the royal campaign, which frequently included pilgrimages to monasteries. Pilgrimages were timed to coincide with religious holidays and were named after the monastery or town at which the pilgrimage was aimed. Some of the best-known were the Trinity, Mozhaisk, Nicholas, Rubtsovskoe, and Pokrovskoe pilgrimages. Particular events in the life of the state and of the royal family—consecrations, marriages, and royal births—were always marked by pilgrimages.

Every year on September 25th, the appointed feast day of St. Sergius of Radonezh, a pilgrimage was made to the Troitse-Sergiev (St. Sergius) Monastery, a political and religious center forty-three miles from Moscow. In 1675 during the reign of Alexei Mikhailovich, Adolf Lizek, a secretary at the Embassy of the Holy Roman Empire, recorded a detailed description of this very pilgrimage which was called the Trinity Pilgrimage. Lizek recorded the stunning number of participants, weapons, and vehicles employed during these occasions.

The procession of the Trinity Pilgrimage was fronted by the infantry; first came a cannon with two gunners on either side, followed by a pair of grooms leading the magnificent skewbald horse of the commander. The commander sat astride his horse flanked by bodyguards in red uniform. Behind walked the standard bearer and a band of trumpeters and drummers. Twenty companies of streltsy with arquebuses in their hands and ceremonial axes on their shoulders, brought up the rear. The procession moved slowly into the field where an army of 14,000 strong stood awaiting the arrival of the Czar. This was the advance guard which prepared the sovereign's route and pitched camps along the way. The cavalry arrived at midday, armed with arquebuses; 432 of these weapons, with gilt locks and ebony stocks and butts, had been distributed from the Royal Treasury. The Czar's two favorite mounts were led in the middle of the cavalry. Behind the cavalry came a long row of carriages containing the royal bedclothes, dresses, linen, toiletries, furniture, domestic tableware, icons, and weapons. A special carriage was put aside for gifts presented to the Czar during the journey.

The Czar's retinue was made up of many different servants, from sentries and stokers to a doctor and a watchmaker. The long line of carriages was drawn by sixty-two horses, each wearing a cloth embroidered with gold and silver. On either side of the route, 200 streltsy cleared the way. Finally, a row of carriages appeared bearing the Czar, the boyars, and all those who had been ordered to take part in the expedition. An equally opulent procession of the Czarina and her daughters then emerged from a different gate of the Kremlin. The procession moved slowly, making its first stop only just beyond the boundaries of the city, where an entire fortress had been erected with ditches, ramparts and towers. Grand marquees and tents had been set up within, where participants could rest and change their clothing. The whole journey to the Troitse-Sergiev Monastery took five days or more. After prayers, the distribution of alms, and solemn feasts in the monastery, the procession returned to Moscow to an equally magnificent greeting.

When the Czar set off on a pilgrimage with his family, the Czarina and Czarevnas were escorted by their own magnificent procession, accompanied by the necessary ceremonial elements. The procession included troops of cavalry at the head and the rear, horses led on foot, the carriages of the Czarina, Czarevnas, the wives and widows of the boyars, plus the boyars themselves and crowds of ordinary people there to witness the dazzling spectacle. The windows of all the carriages were heavily curtained, so that no one could see the Czarina, the Czarevnas, or the boyars' ladies. There was also a magnificent spectacle of rouged ladies in red dresses, white ribboned hats, and yellow boots sitting astride white charges. These were the chambermaids and seamstresses who lived with the Czarina in the Terem Palace. Twenty-five to thirty-five horses were sent from the royal stables for each procession.

The Russian Czarinas made their own pilgrimages to monasteries and churches. Many documents have been preserved describing the pilgrimages of Czarina Evdokia Lukianovna, wife of Czar Mikhail Feodorovich Romanov. As many as forty carriages and over 1,000 horses were used in her processions. The carriage drivers wore caftans of cerise velvet with pearls, and green velvet caps trimmed with sable.

HUNTING TRIPS

Processions which accompanied royal hunting trips were formed quite differently. Members of the royal hunt—huntsmen on horseback and on foot, falconers, and so on—always accompanied the Czar on his pilgrimages and even on his military reviews, so that he could hunt during halts. Royal excursions were also occasioned in which the sole aim was to hunt. When the Czars went out to hunt "unofficially," their retinue was very small.

Only those servants directly involved with the royal hunt, and a few invited guests, accompanied the Czar.

When a hunting trip was initiated for the amusement of the whole royal family or when foreign emissaries had been invited to take part, the excursion was particularly ceremonious. The procession consisted of ranks of soldiers, horses sparkling with jewels, huntsmen with hounds and hawks, grooms, hundreds of servants, and finally an enormous convoy of carts containing everything needed for the hunt and for the ceremonial feast. The whole procession moved slowly to the scene of the hunt, where an advance team had secured the necessary supplies. Game birds were enclosed in pens, and tents were erected. Samuel Collins, an English doctor in the service of Czar Alexei Mikhailovich, described the scene as the most magnificent hunt he had ever seen. The tents of the Czar, the Czarina, and their children stood in a circle, in the center of which a temporary church had been erected. Barriers and guards stood a rifle shot away from the tents, preventing onlookers from entering the scene of the hunt.

One unifying element was traditionally present in all Russian ceremonial processions. Both the parades of the Czar and Czarina, and the processions in which the Czar did not take part (such as ambassadorial meetings), always featured the "horses of the royal saddle" led by members of the Office of the Stables. These horses were of an Eastern breed and were the principle decorative element of the procession. The "Grand Horse Attire"—the valuable trappings of the horses, distributed from the stables for ceremonial processions—delighted and amazed spectators. Saddles, stirrups, and harnesses were faced with gold and silver and covered in precious stones; the horsecloths were studded with pearls. The horses also bore forehead ornaments

(*reshma*), neck tassels (*nauz*), silver knee-cops (*nakolennik*) on the legs and clanking chains stretching from bridle to saddle, which jangled as the horses moved.

The accoutrements of the royal parade continued to be a prominent feature of Russian life until the end of the 17th century, when Peter the Great replaced them with a procession based on a Western European model.

Detail of Broadsword with Dragon's Head Pommel

Mace of the Boyar Prince Boris Mikhailovich Lykov
Early 17th century
Eastern Europe
Silver, wood, forging, gilding, embossing
30.3 inches (77 cm) total length
OR-3790

Helmet (*Erikhonskaya Shapka*) of Boyar Prince Feodor Ivanovich Mstislavsky
16th century
Turkey
Steel, white metal, precious stones, turquoise, cloth, forging, embossing, carving, gold inlay
8.4 inches (21.3 cm) diameter
OR-118

MACE OF THE BOYAR PRINCE BORIS MIKHAILOVICH LYKOV

The mace is one of the oldest weapons known to man, but in the early 16th century, use of the mace as a weapon diminished, and it became more a symbol of power and might. In the 17th century, maces such as this one from the Kremlin Armory were often presented to military leaders on their promotion to a post of command in the Russian army.

This weapon belonged to the Boyar Prince Boris Mikhailovich Lykov, a prominent political figure of the early 17th century. He was a distant relative of the Romanovs on his mother's side, and a personal friend of Feodor Nikitich Romanov, the Patriarch Filaret. Prince Boris played a significant role in the election of the young Mikhail Feodorovich Romanov as Czar in 1613. The ownership of the mace was established by the monogram on the smooth plate at the end of the shaft: BKBML, which stood for "Boyar Prince (Kniaz) Boris Mikhailovich Lykov."

The body and shaft of the mace are entirely covered with turquoise and silver-gilt, the latter decorated with a flat-chased stylized ornament. The decoration bears the mark of Eastern European armorers, who in the 16th and 17th centuries were strongly influenced by accomplished Turkish masters.

HELMET (*ERIKHONSKAYA SHAPKA*) OF BOYAR PRINCE FEODOR IVANOVICH MSTISLAVSKY

Royal military headgear was afforded an important place in the Kremlin Armory's collection of Russian ceremonial armaments. In the 16th and 17th centuries, during processions—particularly royal military reviews—it was the job of the *oruzhnichy*, the head of the Kremlin Armory, to carry the royal helmet, which was a particular type of ceremonial headgear that had first appeared in Turkey at the end of the 16th century. The helmet had a pair of ear guards, a neck guard, and a sliding nasal bar to protect the face. It was known as an *erikhonskaya shapka*, from the Russian word "*erikhonitsya*", meaning "to stand out, impress by one's beauty."

The beautiful helmet on display here, of 16th-century Turkish origin, came to the Royal Armory in 1622. After Prince Feodor Ivanovich Mstislavsky died without heir, valuable articles which had belonged to the ancient and powerful line of the Mstislavskys became the property of the Sovereign. This helmet has always been highly valued and carefully guarded by the Armory. It is made from Damascus steel. Vertical flutes carved in the crown accentuate the beauty of its shape. The delicate tip is studded with red rubies and blue turquoise, and attached to a flat-chased patterned plate fashioned with more rubies and turquoise. The surface is richly damascened in gold. A sapphire in a high mount lies in the center of the delicately carved vertical nose bar. The interior is lined with soft red silk cloth.

Mace of the Boyar Prince Boris Mikhailovich Lykov

Helmet (Erikhonskaya Shapka)

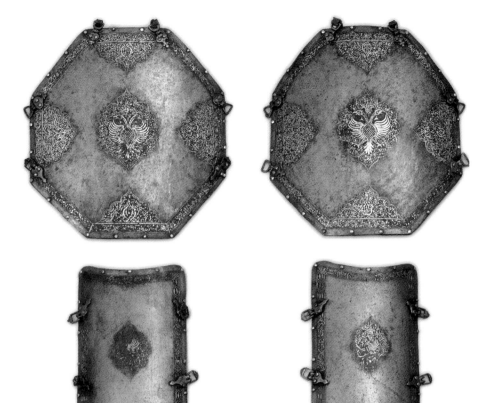

STEEL PLATE ARMOR (ZERTSALA)

The term *zertsala* first appeared in Russian documents of the 16th and 17th centuries to refer to armor composed of thick metal plates and fastened together with straps, laces, or chains. Usually the zertsala was made from between two and four pieces, but could contain as many as forty pieces. This armor was worn by itself, over a battle uniform, or in combination with other armor. The plates were typically crafted from polished steel, decorated with gold, silver, and sometimes precious stones. The patina of this armor was likened to both polished silver and to the surface of an old-fashioned mirror.

Today, the Kremlin Armory houses approximately fifty sets of simple four-piece zertsalas made in both Russia and the East. Only a few of these sets are decorated. This particular zertsala, made in the second half of the 17th century, is lavishly decorated. In the center of each plate is the Russian two-headed eagle, gilded on a silver background. Originally, plates were lined with green and red velvet.

MAIL SHIRT

Mail shirts, formed with interlocking wire rings, first appeared in Russia in the 13th century and gradually replaced the heavier chainmail, so that by the 16th or 17th centuries they had become the most widely used armor in the Russian cavalry. The flexibility of the shirt meant that it could be used with other protective covering. A thick quilted garment was normally worn beneath it. The breast and back were protected by additional lames, or plates; the upper arm was protected by an armored plate called a rerebrace, and the lower arm by a vambrace.

This mail shirt is a fine example of the traditional metal-weaving techniques of the Moscow masters. Its cut shows that it was designed for a horseman—the hem was shortened at the back so as not to hinder the wearer sitting in the saddle, and the lengthened front section protected the upper part of the cavalryman's legs. Mail shirts made in Moscow were the heaviest of all the mail shirts of 17th-century Russia.

Steel Plate Armor (Zertsala)

Mail Shirt

Steel Plate Armor (*Zertsala*)
Second half of the 17th century
Kremlin Workshops
Moscow, Russia
Iron, copper, silk, forging, inlay
10.8 inches (27.5 cm) length (octagonal plates)
8.5 inches (21.5 cm) length (rectangular plates)
OR-4180/1-4

Mail Shirt
17th century
Kremlin Armory
Moscow, Russia
Iron, forging, riveting
35.8 inches (91 cm) total length
OP-4714

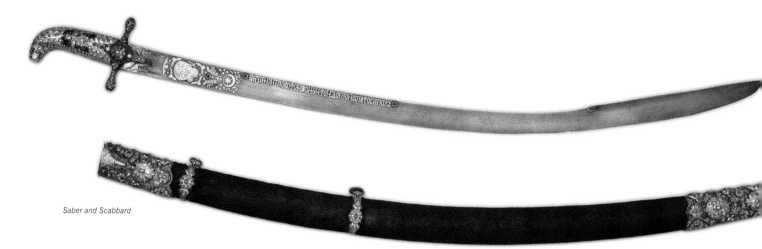

Saber and Scabbard

Saber and Scabbard of Czar Ivan Alexeyevich
Second half of the 17th century
Turkey
Gold, burnished steel, wood, leather, precious stones, glass, forging, gold inlay, carving, enamel
41.7 inches (106 cm) total length, 36.6 inches (93 cm) length of blade, 36.6 inches (96 cm) length of scabbard
OR-4567/1-2

SABER AND SCABBARD OF CZAR IVAN ALEXEYEVICH

The saber—as a curved-bladed hacking weapon—was well known in Russia even before the Mongol invasion. By the end of the 15th century, it had completely ousted the straight European sword and became the weapon of choice of the Russian gentry cavalry. In the Kremlin Armory there is a wide assortment of Russian, Turkish, Iranian, Hungarian, and Polish swords. The blades of these swords were usually made out of gold or gilded silver and decorated with enamel and precious stones. The sabers were worn on the czar's belt or fastened to the saddle of the lead horse during military campaigns, parades, and hunting expeditions.

The blade of this saber is made from Damascus steel; it is rounded with a double-edged tip, slightly widened at the blade's arc. The gray color of the tip attests to the quality of the steel. This saber was created by an unknown Muslim master who lived during the Ottoman Empire. On the upper front side of the blade inlaid in gold is a depiction of the "Everlasting Light of the Virgin Mary." On either side of the image are impressions of cherubs and angels holding a crown in their hands. Under the image of the Virgin Mary, the master placed renderings of two candles, and above the angels the sun and the moon. Along the head of the blade in Greek is the gold inlaid inscription: "Immaculate Virgin Mary Help Your Slave." On the backside of the sword in gold inlay is a representation of St. George on a horse with a snake. The scabbard has been given an equally well-crafted treatment, with thin layers of gold, a colored enamel design, and settings of precious diamonds.

The design and iconography of the saber is evidence that the saber was not made in Russia; the "Everlasting Light of the Virgin Mary" is of Western origin. The construction and decoration of the handle and the scabbard are executed in a purely Eastern manner characteristic of Turkish masters.

This saber and scabbard belonged to Ivan Alexeyevich and was first mentioned in the Kremlin Armory records in 1727. The weak, deformed brother of—and co-ruler with—Peter the Great, Ivan Alexeyevich was never involved in military affairs. The saber was probably given to him by an ambassador from the East, though no documentation exists as to its provenance.

Detail of Saber

BROADSWORD AND SCABBARD

This broadsword is typical of the bladed sidearms carried in Eastern Europe and Russia during the 16th and 17th centuries; weapons such as this one originated in the Near and Middle East and differed from Western European broadswords in the wider double-edged blade and the saber-like shape of the hilt. The decoration of the scabbard also sets it apart, as distinguished by its two methods of chased ornamentation and the use of turquoise and precious stones. In Russia, broadswords of this type were owned by the richest and noblest members of the military class, and were used primarily as parade weapons. These unique weapons first entered the country as military trophies, as gifts from ambassadors, or as trade imports; they often became models for Russian weapon makers.

This sword is first recorded in the inventory of the Armory of 1686-87 among royal broadswords under the Number 1, which indicates the high value accorded it by the compilers. It was believed to have been produced in the Armory Workshop of the Moscow Kremlin in the middle of the 17th century.

The blade is straight and double-edged. In the upper part, near the hilt, is a hallmark of two sickle-like semicircles. In the 16th century these sickle hallmarks were used by Italian armorers from Genoa. The hilt is of silver-gilt. The ends of the quillons (the handle's cross guard) and the pommel (the handle's knob) are in the shape of dragons' heads. Similar decorations were already popular in Eastern countries (Central Asia, Turkey, and Persia) in the 14th and 15th centuries. In these countries the dragon was considered a symbol of war. The scabbard is covered in silver-gilt with chased floral ornament, and decorated with turquoise and rubies, set in high mounts.

Broadsword and Scabbard
First half of the 17th century
Russia
Steel, wood, silver, turquoise, cloth, precious stones, forging, gilding, flat chasing
39.8 inches (101 cm) total length, 34.6 inches (88 cm) length of blade, 39 inches (99 cm) length of scabbard
OR-4445/1-2

Broadsword and Scabbard

Pair of Flintlock Pistols
17th century
Kremlin Armory
Moscow, Russia
Iron, wood, silver, copper, forging, flat
chasing, engraving, carving on wood,
gilding
Upper pistol: 16.6 inches (42.1 cm)
length of carbine, 24.1 inches (61.2 cm)
total length; 15 mm caliber
Lower Pistol: 16.6 inches (42.1 cm)
length of carbine, 24.3 inches (61.6 cm)
total length; 15 mm caliber
OP-2952/1-2, OP-2953/1-2

**Quiver and Bow Case (*Saadak*) of Czar
Alexei Mikhailovich**
1666
Master Dmitry Astafev
Kremlin Armory
Moscow, Russia
Leather, silver, cloth, embroidery, gilding,
enamel, filigree
30.3 inches (77 cm) length of quiver,
16.9 inches (43 cm) length of bow case
OR-4471/1-2

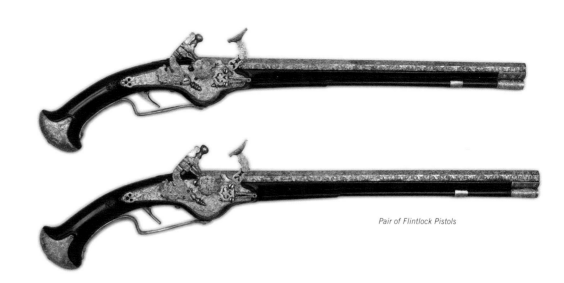

Pair of Flintlock Pistols

PAIR OF FLINTLOCK PISTOLS

In the second half of the 16th century, a pair of pistols in
special holsters was a necessary weapon for the Russian
horseman, as well as a part of the ceremonial costume of
the Czar. The Kremlin Armory possesses a multitude of
pistols made either by the Kremlin Workshops or abroad.
Less frequently, these pistols were brought as gifts to the
Czar from merchants and ambassadors. Masters from
Holland were highly praised in the 17th century as being
among the best weapon makers. Their pistols were
known for both their decorative and practical excellence,
and so it is not by accident that Russian masters during
this time copied the designs of these masters. All the
metal parts of this pair of pistols are decorated with
engraved ornamentation, forming a design of leaves and
plant shoots on an embossed background. The flintlocks
are carved to look like dolphins, and the handles of the
guns are made of hard wood, delicately carved. It is quite
possible that these were made for Alexei Mikhailovich.

+

QUIVER AND BOW CASE (SAADAK) OF CZAR ALEXEI

The saadak was the most important Russian ceremonial
armament. This saadak belonged to Czar Alexei
Mikhailovich and was made from red Persian leather;
this special kind of goat hide was used in the East and in
Russia for the production of battle equipage. Along the
outer edge of the cases, stylized foliage has been
embroidered in silver thread. The Russian emblem of the
two-headed eagle under three crowns is portrayed in the
center. In the upper corner of both cases is a silver plate
decorated with enamel and precious stones. An enameled
lion on its hind legs stands in the right corner of the
kolchan (arrow case). The strap of the saadak is made
from silk with silver enamel. The leather work was
completed in 1666 by Master Dmitry Astafev, and the
silverwork was done by the silversmiths of the Kremlin
Workshops. Historical documents explain that this
saadak was presented to Czar Alexei Mikhailovich at an
Easter celebration.

Quiver and Bow Case (Saadak) of Czar Alexei Mikhailovich

Double-Barreled Arquebus with Flintlock

Double-Barreled Arquebus with Flintlock
Second half of the 17th century
Kremlin Armory
Moscow, Russia
Iron, wood, mother-of-pearl, forging,
carving on metal, engraving, gilding
60 inches (152 cm) total length
OR-4995/1-2

Sword (*Konchar*) and Scabbard
17th century
Russia
Steel, wood, silver, ivory, velvet,
turquoise, forging, gilding, niello, carving
46.9 inches (119 cm) total length, 39.4
inches (100 cm) length of blade, 46.5
inches (118 cm) length of scabbard
OR-4545/1-2

DOUBLE-BARRELED ARQUEBUS WITH FLINTLOCK

This double-barreled arquebus is a unique example of a hunting firearm from the 17th century. The barrels are positioned one above the other, and it was possible to change the positions of the barrels by rotating a pivot on the butt-end of the gun. Each barrel has a cut decoration on the breech and muzzle. A heraldic two-headed eagle is portrayed on a flat-chased foliate ground. The flintlock, typical of the second half of the 17th century, is also of interest. Only part of the lock—the cock and the mainspring—is attached to the neck of the butt, while each barrel has a separate frizzle, powder pan, and steel spring.

✦

SWORD (KONCHAR) AND SCABBARD

According to scholars, the word *konchar* comes from the Turkish *kandzar*, meaning sword or dagger. The word, however, is also consonant with the Slavic word *konets*, or *konez*, in its meaning of "sharp." For example, in Russian, *konchatiy* is the adjective for a sharp knife, and in Czech, a *koneiz* is a foil (a sidearm with a long narrow blade). The Hungarian word for this weapon—*egyestorok*, a "cutting edge"—is also extremely close in meaning.

There are two types of konchars: the fighting konchar, with a long blade and, as a rule, a saber hilt; and the parade konchar, which has a small blade and is decorated with precious metals and stones. The distinctive feature of the weapon was that it was not carried on the swordbelt, but attached to the saddle.

This konchar is smaller than other known examples. It may have been made for one of the czareviches. The form of the hilt is also different. Its grip is extended, ending in a pommel in the form of a dragon's head. The cross-guard with its dragon-head quillons is reminiscent of a saber hilt. The scabbard is wooden, covered in cerise velvet. The chape, mouth-locket, and suspension rings are of silver, decorated with delicate stylized niello and turquoise.

Sword (Konchar) and Scabbard

95

Saddle
Mid-17th century
Istanbul, Turkey
Silver, emeralds, pearls, wood, velvet,
altabas, gold thread, leather, weaving,
embroidery
12.2 inches (31 cm) height of pommel,
6.3 inches (16 cm) height of cantle,
16.1 inches (41 cm) overall length of
saddle
K-230

Detail of Saddle

SADDLE

This saddle from the Treasury of Czar Alexei Mikhailovich is remarkable for its beautiful shape and delicate decoration. It has a low, round cantle rising to a narrow pommel at the front, flanked by oval wings. This shape is seen in the work of the finest saddle makers of Istanbul in the middle of the 17th century. Documents show that such saddles were brought to the Russian Czar from Istanbul by ambassadors of the Turkish Sultan and by Greek traders. Royal saddles had mounts of gold or silver and were richly decorated with precious stones.

This saddle is covered with velvet in the Czar's color, red. Leaves, tulips, and carnations are embroidered on the seat in fine silver thread. Intertwining leaves and pomegranate flowers are embroidered on the side flaps in gold thread. The mount of the saddle seems, from a distance, to be of gold, but is, in fact, covered with Turkish altabas—silk cloth interwoven with silver. The carnations and tulips on the border are made from pearl and the calyces of the flowers are made of large pierced emeralds sewn onto the cloth.

Saddle

Pair of Knee-cops for a Horse

Pair of Knee-cops for a Horse
Second half of the 17th century
Workshops of the Kremlin Stables
Moscow, Russia
Silver, gilding, embossing, flat chasing
4.1 inches (10.5 cm) height of each
K-129, K-130

Pair of Stirrups
17th century
Turkey
Silver, iron, semi-precious stones, gilding,
forging, embossing
6.5 inches (16.5 cm) height of each
K-407/1-2

ΛIR OF KNEE-COPS FOR A HORSE

16th- and 17th-century Russian ceremonial
ocessions, royal horses wore silver knee-pieces, or
knee-cops," on their legs (shown above). These were
de hoops made in halves and attached by hinges and
ns. The interior of the knee-pieces was cushioned with
d silk or velvet to protect the horse's legs. Many knee-
ps were produced in the Workshops of the Kremlin
ables and in the Kremlin's Silver and Gold Chambers.
his pair is made of pure silver, with a flat-chased
ndulating foliate ornament. The purpose of the holes
ong the edges was for the attachment of the interior
lvet or cloth lining.

PAIR OF STIRRUPS

These massive stirrups (shown below) with expensive
trimming from the royal stables were produced by
Turkish masters of the Ottoman Empire in the 17th
century. An extended, wide rectangular base served as a
sturdy mount for the rider. The sides of the trapezoid
rise over the base, and the upper parts connect to the
cross-piece in the center. An oval ring in the center of
each cross-piece was designed for the supporting belts
which were connected to the saddle.

This pair of stirrups is made of iron and covered in
gilding. The center of each base contains a decorative
rosette, while the outer sides are covered in gilded silver
and stamped with a flower pattern onto which semi-
precious stones have been fastened.

Pair of Stirrups

Horse Cloth (Caparison)

HORSE CLOTH (CAPARISON)

The purpose and form of *caparisons*, or horse cloths, varied: some covered the breast and hind end of the horse, some were placed beneath the saddle, and others covered the saddle. Parade caparisons were generally made in the Kremlin Stables Workshops from imported cloth, embroidered with pearls and decorated with precious stones.

This caparison, according to documents of the time, came to the Stables Treasury in the mid-17th century from Turkey as a gift to Czar Alexei Mikhailovich. The caparison is made of dark red velvet, and decorated with silver-gilt studs, set with rubies on a ground of stylized pomegranates and toothed leaves, and embroidered with pearls.

✦

PAIR OF PISTOL HOLSTERS

Holsters were a virtual requirement for the attire of every horseman and, of course, for the 17th-century ceremonial regalia for the Czar's horse. The holsters featured here are two of the best specimens in the Czars' collections, in terms of their craftsmanship and design. The pistol holster was traditionally attached to the pommel of the saddle and designed by the Czar's harness makers. These leather holsters are blanketed with smooth green velvet. The velvet lapels and the flaps covering the cartridges are embroidered with gold and silver thread and studded with pearls. Rubies and emeralds are set in raised mounts. In the middle of each flap is a two-headed eagle under a crown, embroidered in pearls, which show that the holsters were the property of the Moscow sovereigns.

Horse Cloth (*Caparison*)
17th century
Turkey
Velvet, silk moiré, Bukhara silk, satin, fringe, rubies, pearls, silver-gilt, weaving, casting, embossing, embroidery
68.5 x 61 inches (174 cm x 155 cm)
TK-2620

Pair of Pistol Holsters
17th century
Workshops of the Kremlin Stables
Moscow, Russia
Gold, silver, rubies, pearls, emeralds, leather, velvet, gold thread, weaving, braid, embroidery, casting
20.9 inches (53 cm) length of each holster
OR-4901, OR-4902

Pair of Pistol Holsters

RIDLE (OGOLOV)

he decorative bridle was an essential and unique
omponent of royal horse trappings for ceremonial
rocessions. The leather straps of the *ogolov* were
ttached to the horse's head and further strengthened by
n iron bit and reins made of silk. For royal parades, two
ypes of bridles were used: Russian-made bridles from
ne Workshops of the Kremlin Stables, and imported
nes— usually from Turkey. Turkish horse trappings
vere highly valued in Russia before the time of Peter the
ireat, and were widely used by the czars and nobility.
urkish bridles are recognizable by the extreme richness
f the trimmings, and by the abundance of precious
ones.

he straps for this bridle were made from soft red
Moroccan leather, which is entirely covered with silver-
lt plates studded with rubies and turquoise. Flowers
nd trefoils are chased on the plates, many of which
ontain roundels of nephrite, inlaid with additional
ubies and turquoise.

everal different types of bridles were used, each with a
istinct name and function. This is an ogolov with an
sheik—an additional strap which tied around the
orse's neck. Its use was purely decorative. The fine
entral pendant, which was attached to the forehead of
ne horse, is also unusual. A nephrite mount holds a six-
ointed star encrusted with gold and precious stones.

Bridle (Ogolov)

BREAST ORNAMENT (PAPERST) FOR A HORSE

The *ogolov* and the *paperst*—the head and breast
trappings of the horse—were always made in a matching
style. The silver-gilt plates which cover the straps of the
paperst are similar to those on the ogolov. The paperst
consists of three straps which were attached to the saddle
by hooks. The smiths who produced the ogolov-and-
paperst ensemble paid careful attention to the decoration
of the forehead pendant of the former and the central
plate of the latter. This paperst of Turkish origin has
rubies and turquoise set in nephrite mounts covering
most of the surface of the figured silver plate.

Bridle (*Ogolov*)
17th century
Turkey
Gold, silver, rubies, turquoise, nephrite,
leather, copper, gilding, embossing, inlay
work, forging
43.3 inches (110 cm), 19.7 inches (50
cm) length of straps
K-235

Breast Ornament (*Paperst*) for a Horse
17th century
Turkey
Gold, silver, rubies, turquoise, nephrite,
leather braid, gilding, embossing, inlay
work, weaving
25.2 inches (64 cm), 29.1 inches (74
cm), 21.3 inches (54 cm) length of straps
K-414

Breast Ornament (Paperst) for a Horse

Head Band (*Reshma*) for a Horse
First half of the 17th century
Turkey
Gold, silver, rubies, emeralds, nephrite, gilding, embossing, black enamel, inlay work
4.5 inches (11.5 cm) height, 8.9 inches (22.5 cm) diameter
K-1087

Neck Tassel (*Nauz*) for a Horse
17th century
Workshops of the Kremlin Stables
Moscow, Russia
Silver, gold thread, silk, gilding, carving, embroidery
29.9 inches (76 cm) total length, 23.6 inches (60 cm) length of tassels
K-685

Head Band (Reshma) for a Horse

Neck Tassel (Nauz) for a Horse

HEAD BAND (RESHMA) FOR A HORSE

The *reshma* is a jeweled silver or gold plate which was placed on the Czar's horse (on the bridge of the nose) during ceremonial processions. It was attached to the bridle by silver chains.

The surface of this silver reshma is covered in a delicate foliate ornament on a blackened ground; this was a technique favored by Turkish metalworkers of the 16th and 17th centuries. The gifts of ambassadors, tradesmen, and representatives of the Orthodox Church would often include elements of a horse's harness—*reshmy*, breast ornaments, bridles, and saddles—and weapons in silver cases decorated in a method similar to the reshma. The mountings of bright nephrite, encrusted with rubies and emeralds framed by gold petals, lent a particular brilliance to the reshma.

✦

NECK TASSEL (NAUZ) FOR A HORSE

The horse's tassel, which hung beneath the horse's neck, was one of the most ancient equestrian decorations. It initially served as an amulet, but later came to signify the power and rank of the rider. Such tassels can be traced to the Ottoman Empire in the early 15th century. In the 16th and 17th centuries, the tassel became an essential element of ceremonial processions.

This shiny tassel has a length of about two feet and is a shimmering braid of silk and silver threads. It is attached to a spherical dome with a thin engraved gilded rim with a ring in the center. A berry-colored band is looped through the ring and tied around the horse's neck. The smooth surface of the dome is decorated with six stamped spherical shapes with a gilded flower design.

Bridle Chain

Bridle Chain
17th century
Workshops of the Kremlin Stables
Moscow, Russia
Silver, base metal, embossing
112.6 inches (286 cm) total length
K-107/15

BRIDLE CHAIN

his massive silver chain is nearly ten feet in length. The ſteen broad, curved links are decorated with nagnificent flat-chased ornament of undulating stems, owers, and leaves.

1 the 16th and 17th centuries, chains such as this one were special feature of royal parade horse trappings. They were ttached to the horse's neck to act as a leading rein, and ere held by an attendant who walked beside the parade orse or rode on another horse. Bridle chains were part of le "Grand Attire" used on the most solemn occasions.

Silver bridle chains were greatly admired by spectators during ceremonial processions, particularly by foreign observers, many of whom referred to the chains in their accounts of Russia. Adam Olearius, a member of the Holstein Embassy to Moscow, wrote in 1634: "Instead of reins, the horses wore enormous silver chains. The links of the chain were more than two inches in width, but the silver was no thicker than the blunt edge of a knife, so that it was almost possible to pass your hand through the great rings; these chains made a mighty noise when the horses moved."

Detail of Bridle Chain

CHAPTER V

Ambassadorial Ceremony

Ambassadorial Ceremony

by I.A. Bobrovnitskaya

Detail of *Czar Alexei Mikhailovich Receives the Ambassador of the Holy Roman Empire, 1662* Engraving from *The Collection of Drawings from the Travels of A. Meerberg, 1661-1662* (St. Petersburg, 1827)

he highly ritualized court ceremonies for foreign ambassadors were first cultivated in Russia towards the end of the 15th century under Ivan the Great and finally crystallized in the 17th century—not coincidentally, it should be pointed out—during the Romanov reign.

The ceremonial meetings, receptions, and negotiations for foreign emissaries, in concert with the sending abroad of Russian emissaries, played a vital role in building the foundation for the young Russian state in the early 1500s. Links with European and Eastern countries had been largely destroyed in the years of domination by the Mongol Tartars, also known as the Golden Horde. It fell upon Russia to re-establish these connections completely. At the same time, foreign states were making overtures towards the Russian state, hoping to find in Moscow a friend and ally.

Living permanently at his assigned post, the resident emissary—whom we would call today an ambassador or diplomat—was not officially a participant in the diplomatic practice until the second half of the 16th century. However, still throughout the 17th century, this new breed of diplomatic representative was forced to share the stage with the "occasional diplomacy" of prior history, so named because of the ad hoc foreign embassies that were hastily established in response to critical international events. In Russia, ambassadors, emissaries and heralds served a variety of purposes. They were

assigned to conduct peacetime negotiations, to settle questions of trade privileges, to conclude union agreements, and to establish borders, often at the accession of a new monarch, after the birth of a royal heir, or upon military victories over neighboring states.

Hundreds of ambassadors from all over the globe could be found in the streets of Moscow during the Middle Ages; they made a rich and solemn spectacle, a rainbow parade of national costumes and customs.

Many foreign visitors wrote about diplomatic etiquette at the Moscow court. In addition, Russian records (called the "Ambassadorial Books") exist in which the arrival of a foreign mission or embassy in Russia was carefully recorded. These ancient documents survive to this day and allow us to recreate Russian ambassadorial customs in minute detail.

FOREIGN AMBASSADORS IN RUSSIA

In advance of their imminent arrival in Russia, foreign ambassadors were obliged to inform the *voivode* (provincial governor) of the appropriate Russian border town. The voivode would then send his representative to meet the group at the border. At this point, the foreigner declared where the embassy came from, the rank of the emissary, and the size of his retinue. The information was then immediately relayed to the capital by heralds. The voivode would keep the emissaries with him until further orders were received. Finally, permission for ntry would arrive from Moscow and the missaries' lengthy journey began. Their inerary from the border to the capital was arefully worked out. Special policemen were ssigned for the "protection" of the mbassadors and were also charged with the istenance of the embassy throughout the ourney. This might be far from an easy task: ome embassies numbered up to 1,000 people.

he procession made its final stop just outside Moscow. Here the emissaries were met by two r three courtiers sent on behalf of the Czar. ach of the courtiers offered a ceremonial reeting and made formal conversation as to he status of the envoy's health, the quality of he journey, the mood of the czar or czarina, nd so on. The embassy was also informed of he day of its entry into the capital. The date of ntry depended on the weather and time of ear, but, as a rule, the arrival was arranged for he morning.

Designated representatives—up to 200 men— net the emissaries in Moscow. At an agreed pon site, the foreign ambassadorial procession eaded by the "chief ambassador" and the Russian "welcoming party" moved slowly owards one another. The retinue lined up eside the ambassadors and the principal Russian participants, and everyone was nstructed to dismount from their horses and arriages.

The ambassadors were required to doff their hats and listen to a ceremonial royal greeting conveyed by the senior member of the welcoming party. After an exchange of greetings and speeches, the participants remounted their horses, and the procession moved solemnly to he guest quarters reserved for the ambassadors and their entourage.

While in the capital, the foreign guests were supported with funds from the Royal Treasury;

abundant provisions were delivered daily to the ambassadorial residence from the royal kitchens. Notes from foreign ambassadors recorded the immense largesse of the czars. One ambassador wrote that "the food provided for the embassy would have been enough for 300 men, let alone 30." Anther recorded that during his sixteen-week-long stay his embassy of 33 men consumed "48 bulls, 336 rams, 1,680 chickens, 112 geese, 224 ducks, 11,200 eggs, 10 deer, and 336 pounds of butter."

The meeting with the Czar was the high point and the denouement of the ambassadorial ceremony. The pomp and wealth that accompanied the proceedings took on deep symbolic meaning, as if the event represented the very well-being and prosperity of the state itself. Ambassadors were informed in advance of the date of the meeting, the rules of court etiquette, and how they were expected to conduct themselves en route to the Kremlin.

The royal meeting was both an honor for the ambassador and an expression of respect for the monarch; it was also a highly theatrical public event which took place before a large crowd of people. Upon entering the Kremlin, and before reaching the steps of the czar's palace, the ambassadors were required to dismount from their horses. This was a strict rule of the audience—and it was also customary in secular Russian life of the 16th and 17th century, as it was considered disrespectful to the host to arrive at his house on horseback.

Ambassadorial gifts were considered *de rigueur* during the ceremonial procession and were exposed to public view. The opulence and splendor of the gifts were intended to reflect the glory of the Czar. One surviving account described how a Western ambassador who had been robbed on his journey had nothing to present to the Czar apart from a chiming clock

Detail of *Czar Alexei Mikhailovich Receives the Ambassador of the Holy Roman Empire, 1662* Engraving from *The Collection of Drawings from the Travels of A. Meerberg, 1661-1662* (St. Petersburg, 1827)

which had been miraculously spared. During the public procession it was clear to all that the clock alone was insufficient, after which a number of valuable articles were lent from the Treasury and presented by the ambassador to the Czar in his own name.

The foreign diplomats were led into the enormous parade hall of the Granovitaya (Faceted) Palace, where the "royal place"— consisting of a dais with a throne—stood. The Czar sat in his royal place in his brilliant finery. At his right hand, by the window, was a stand on a base. Near the Czar, on either side of the stand, were *the ryndy*, four bodyguards, members of noble families, dressed in ermine robes, tall hats, and boots, each holding an axe made from gold and silver. The Czar wore a precious crown and held a scepter and orb. The scepter remained in the Czar's hands throughout the ceremony, but the massive jeweled orb was difficult to hold for extended periods of time, and so the Czar would often rest the orb on the stand next to his throne.

On a bench beside the throne was a hand basin on a silver-gilt dish covered with a towel. The Czar rinsed his hands after he had proffered them to be kissed by the ambassador and members of the ambassador's staff, for in the words of one foreign writer, "the Russian sovereign, when offering his hand to an ambassador of the Roman faith, considered that he had been touched by a profane and unclean man." In the 17th century this custom, which aroused great interest in foreign diplomats, became little more than a curiosity.

The boyars, representatives of the Russian aristocracy since the Middle Ages, were essential participants in the ambassadorial audience. Wearing long robes, they sat silently on benches along the walls of the chamber, only occasionally standing up and taking off their tall fur hats at the mention of the Czar's name.

Detail of *Czar Alexei Mikhailovich Receives the Ambassador of the Holy Roman Empire, 1662* Engraving from *The Collection of Drawings from the Travels of A. Meerberg, 1661-1662* (St. Petersburg, 1827)

These figures, reminiscent of stage extras, underlined the theatricality of the spectacle. The words and gestures of the participants had but one aim: to underline the prestige of the sovereign and his domain.

THE ROYAL HAND & THE AMBASSADORIAL FEAST

The exchange of gifts was an essential element of the ceremonial rite. Eastern emissaries brought rich garments, carpets and other textiles, and precious stones. Most significant of the gifts sent by Western monarchs were gold and silver utensils. Western European diplomats often presented the Russian sovereign with goblets. These might be extremely unusual: sometimes in the shape of exotic fruits, of real or fantastical beasts and birds; sometimes they were made in the form of ships with tiny figures of sailors, or allegorical figures or quaint fairytale characters. There were amusing goblets, double and triple goblets, goblets with moving parts driven by a concealed mechanism. Silver and gold, rock crystal, mother-of-pearl and coconut shells, elephant tusks and even ostrich eggs were used in these works. Gifts presented to the Czar were carefully recorded and put into the Treasury for safekeeping. Foreign diplomats also received gifts of corresponding value in return; these usually consisted of furs, most often sable.

After the exchange of gifts, the Czar ordered the ambassadors to approach the "royal hand." The kissing of the royal hand was the next stage in the ceremonial rite of the royal audience, although Muslim ambassadors were not permitted to kiss the hand; instead, the Czar placed his palm on their heads.

The ceremonial feast, which the sovereign hosted for foreign diplomats, was as essential an element of the ceremony as the feasts given in honor of guests in private life. At the same time, the ambassador considered an invitation to the royal table a great honor.

In contrast to other aspects of ceremonial etiquette at the Moscow court, foreign tradition had little influence on the ceremonial feast. On the whole, the feast reflected the influence of traditional Russian folk customs. The notion of "ambassadorial honor" at court was closely related to the "honor of the guest" in ordinary life. The feast generally took place in the Hall of Facets, which in any event was the most striking of the royal rooms, but was even more finely decorated on these occasions.

The ambassadors were led into the Hall of Facets, where the Czar and his courtiers were already sitting at their places. The sovereign sat at a separate table raised one step above the rest. No one, apart from the czareviches, was allowed to sit at this table, a fact which underlined the special position of the Czar and his heirs. The closer the placement to the Czar, the more honorable; in addition, it was more auspicious to sit beside the royal table than opposite it, and more auspicious still to sit on the Czar's right than on his left. The ambassadors did not sit down at the same time, but separately, in the company of those whose official status was equal to their own. In accordance with their placement at the tables, the guests were offered "presentations of wine and food" by the sovereign. The receiving of dishes from the hands of the Czar was considered the highest favor and represented a solemn act; the name of the dish was announced and those who were to partake were obliged to stand up. Most venerated of all were the "remains"—goblets from which the Czar had taken a sip and dishes from which he had tasted—since these were considered a direct tie to the sovereign. Before the ambassadorial feast, the Czar distributed bread as a symbol of hospitality. This custom originated in Russian daily life, as the host of a private gathering in Moscow

would do the same. Unlike the bread, the ritual salt was not distributed to everyone. As one ambassador wrote: "to receive a saltcellar from the sovereign is a high honor indeed, since salt expresses not only favor but love." The ambassadorial feast continued for five or six hours; throughout this time nobody was allowed to leave the table. The prolonged length of the dinner was also a result of the many toasts made in honor of the sovereign, members of his family, and distinguished guests. The guests on whom the Czar conferred attention were required to stand as a sign of gratitude, after which everyone else stood up too, bowing gracefully and then taking their seats again. During the feast, guests stood over and over again. "We stood so often," wrote one ambassador, "that from hour to hour the movement increased my appetite."

After the first royal meeting and the feast (some of which lasted for more than a week) came the final farewells. This ceremony was also conducted by the Czar himself, who conveyed his compliments and at times a petition to each diplomat's monarch. He then offered the ambassadors a cup of mead or wine. The drinking of the beverage signaled the official end of the ambassador's sojourn at the court of the sovereign. This custom also originated in everyday life and, like many of the national traditions, was gradually formalized into a feature of court protocol. These royal rituals and ceremonies remained in place until the end of the 18th century, although they were significantly revised by the reforms of Peter the Great.

Detail of *Czar Alexei Mikhailovich Receives the Ambassador of the Holy Roman Empire, 1662* Engraving from *The Collection of Drawings from the Travels of A. Meerberg, 1661-1662* (St. Petersburg, 1827)

Riding Caftan (*Tyerlik*)
Mid-17th century
Kremlin Workshops
Moscow, Russia
Shag velvet: mid-17th century, Gdansk
Damask: mid-17th century, Italy
Velvet, gold and silk thread, embroidery,
weaving, galloon, damask
48.4 inches (123 cm) length
TK-2616

Caftan
Second half of the 17th century
Russia
Velvet: Italy
Velvet, taffeta, silk thread, weaving
60.2 inches (153 cm) length
TK-2242

RIDING CAFTAN

The riding caftan, or *tyerlik*, was the rarest kind of ancient Russian court uniform; it was stored in the State Treasury and lent only for official ceremonies. In the 17th century this style of caftan was worn chiefly by those in service at court: the *ryndy*, who stood by the throne and accompanied the Czar on ceremonial processions; the noble *zhiltsy*, who met foreign emissaries and stood at official receptions bearing halberds and partisans (ceremonial staff-weapons); and the *voznichie*, who were part of the royal entourage. Normally, the purpose of the dress would dictate the manner in which the tyerlik was decorated. Only four examples have survived to this day, one of which is on display in the exhibition.

The tyerlik consists of two main sections: a detachable tight-fitting bodice and a lower piece of material in the form of a wide skirt. The collar is small and raised, and the sleeves are in two parts: the upper arm is wide and gathered in at the elbow; while the sleeve is narrow, with a small reversed cuff at the wrist. The fastening on the front of the bodice is concealed behind a broad figured flap, fastened with hooks on the left side and on the shoulder. A wide strip of uncut long-napped velvet, golden in color, runs along the hem of the skirt. The external lining of the lapels, the cuffs, and the collar is finely decorated with interwoven thread in two colors. The bodice of the tyerlik features a two-headed eagle with three crowns embroidered in shallow relief with gold and silk thread. On the breast of the eagle is a shield with the emblem of Moscow. The garment possesses a degree of theatricality, and on more than one occasion, Nicholas II, the last Russian Czar, chose a tyerlik as his costume when attending masked balls at court.

CAFTAN

Caftans are first mentioned in Russian documents of the 15th century. Thereafter, and particularly in the 17th century, the name "caftan" referred to any loose-fitting, ankle-length, secular garment, with many buttons, long sleeves, and a lining. It could be worn as either an undergarment or an outer garment, in summer or winter. The garment on display in the exhibition was for indoor use, of a type worn by members of the aristocracy on ceremonial occasions. It is made from smooth cerise velvet, with a braid-edging and long tapered sleeves. It is fastened from top to bottom by forty-seven pear-shaped buttons covered with cerise silk and attached by dark purple thread. The caftan was a particularly elegant and sedate garment, with its flowing, loose form and extreme length, stretching almost to the floor, which encouraged a smooth and dignified gait, as was considered appropriate in the Middle Ages. The full costume was completed with the aid of a high fur hat and staff.

Riding Caftan (Tyerlik)

Caftan

Ambassadorial Axe
Early 17th century
Attributed to Turkey
Damask steel, silver, wood, gold, embossing, gold inlay, gilding, forging, flat chasing
11 inches (28 cm) length of blade,
50 inches (127 cm) total length of axe
OR-2235

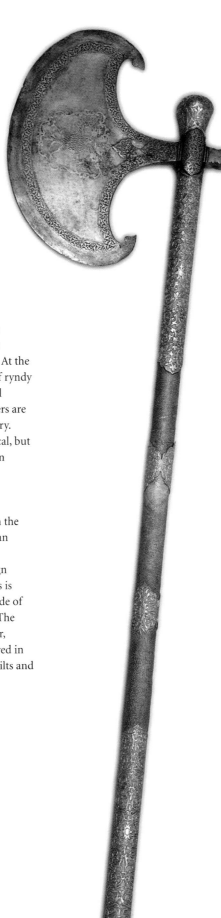

AMBASSADORIAL AXE

Beginning in the mid-16th century, the *ryndy* (the weapon bearers and bodyguards of the Czar) were known to have carried axes in defense of the Czar. At the turn of the century, the honor guard, composed of ryndy armed with axes, was a staple of the ambassadorial ceremony. Axes of both Turkish and Russian makers are mentioned in documents from the Kremlin Armory. Their purpose and basic construction were identical, but the form and character of their heraldic decoration varied.

The axe on display here is most likely the work of Turkish craftsmen. It is made of Damascus steel in the traditional half-moon shape. It differs from Russian specimens in its slightly smaller size and greater curvature of the blade. A damascened foliate design decorates the edge of the blade, and its royal status is underlined by the etched representation on its blade of the Russian two-headed eagle with three crowns. The axe-handle is wooden, round, and covered in silver, ending in a spherical pommel. The silver is engraved in the manner of leather used in the production of hilts and scabbards for side weapons.

Ambassadorial Axe

109

Lidded Goblet
1637
Nuremberg, Germany
Silver, base metal, embossing, casting,
engraving, gilding
33.5 inches (85 cm) height
MZ-1081/1-2

"Warrior on Horseback" Pitcher
Second half of the 17th century
Nuremberg, Germany
Silver, embossing, casting, poinçon
19 inches (48.3 cm) height
MZ-286

Handwashing Pitcher
1685-1700
Master Johann Lorenz Biller
Augsburg, Germany
Silver, base metal, embossing, engraving,
casting, gilding
20.3 inches (51.5 cm) height
MZ-1621

LIDDED GOBLET

Western European goblets were used in Russian life for a variety of purposes: as dresser ornaments, as awards for successful military campaigns and faithful service, and as gifts presented on solemn occasions and ceremonies—such as the coronation of the Czar, weddings, namedays, and christenings. On his accession to the throne in 1646, Czar Alexei Mikhailovich received nearly 200 standing cups, the majority of which were of German origin.

This tall, elegant, bell-shaped goblet was made in Nuremberg, the most important center of gold- and silversmithing in Germany in the 16th and 17th centuries. Its most striking features are the large convex ball shapes which give it a massive appearance and reflect the nuanced qualities of the surface. This style of molding reminded Russians of apples and were referred to in Russian documents as *yablochniy*, or "apple-like."

"WARRIOR ON HORSEBACK" PITCHER

The Czars' sideboards, which decorated the halls for ceremonial receptions, were filled with fantastic silver sculptures: lions on their hind legs with regalia, storks, deer, invented creatures, characters from fairy tales, and mythological heroes. Table decorations in the Baroque era were often pitchers for handwashing, mechanical toys, or fountains. They entertained the guests and displayed the riches of their owners.

In the 17th century, the horse-and-rider motif occupied a special place among this genre. The prototype for these decorations was a rendering of King Gustav II of Sweden on a horse, done by the goldsmith David Shwestermuller. In the Kremlin Armory today there are seven silver riders on horseback, two of which are pitchers for handwashing. The pitcher was a part of the ceremonial handwashing, a Russian tradition which metaphorically expressed the Czar's good intentions.

HANDWASHING PITCHER

Vessels of the type on display here were traditionally used to decorate the dressers of the Granovitaya (Faceted) Palace until the end of the 19th century. In form, the pitcher is reminiscent of classical vessels, with its long neck, arched handle, and circular base. The body and lid of the vessel show a gilded ornament of densely interwoven acanthus leaves and pendants of fruit, a design characteristic of European art of the turn of the 18th century. The stamped roundels on the long neck and the delicately pearled beading on the lid contribute greatly to the overall decorative effect. This pitcher is a fine example of the mature Augsburg baroque style.

Lidded Goblet

"Warrior on Horseback" Pitcher

Handwashing Pitcher

Soup Tureen (Rassolnik)

Soup Tureen (*Rassolnik*)
1610-1625
Master Hans Jacob I Bauer
Augsburg, Germany
Silver, casting, embossing, engraving,
gilding
12.2 inches (31 cm) height
MZ-550

Incense Burner
First quarter of the 17th century
Germany
Silver, base metal, wood, embossing,
casting, engraving, gilding
20.9 inches (53 cm) height, stand size
15.7 x 15.7 inches (40 cm x 40 cm)
MZ-246/1-2

INCENSE BURNER

This remarkable object (below) in the form of a silver-gilt mountain on a four-sided base was both a practical vessel for burning incense and a superbly lavish table decoration. It was a gift from the Danish King Christian IV to Czar Mikhail Feodorovich. It is in the shape of a steep mountain crowned by a castle with watchtowers; paths and stairways run down the mountain's sides. The castle is a model of the famous fortress of Kronborg at Helsingör (Elsinore), the seat of the Danish kings (and the setting for Shakespeare's Hamlet).

OUP TUREEN (RASSOLNIK)

. *rassolnik* tureen, in the form of a dish or a bowl on et, from the beginning of the 17th century was a opular kind of ware. Rassolniks were made from arious materials, but most were made out of silver. In ie 1620s it was fashionable for goldsmiths to make sets f rassolniks representing, allegorically, the four seasons, ie four elements, the five senses, or the twelve zodiac gns. Mixing and matching dozens of such pieces of lentical theme, their owners creatively contrived whole ompositions for the halls of the royal palace. At first, mall rassolniks were used for wine vessels, but later iowcased fruit and oysters.

1any luxurious types of vases were among the mbassadorial gifts from the King of Sweden. This tureen ith the figure of Minerva is from the Kremlin Armory nd is one of fourteen pieces given to Czar Alexei Iikhailovich. It was originally one of the eighteen vases resented by King Karl XI of Sweden in 1684.

Incense Burner

111

Silver Platter with "Diana and Nymphs" Scene (right)
1650-1660
Master Jacob II Plank
Augsburg, Germany
Silver, punching, embossing, poinçon, gilding
20.1 x 23.6 inches (51 cm x 60 cm)
MZ-367

Silver Platter with "Triumph of Peace" Scene (below)
1645-1650
Master Jacob II Plank
Augsburg, Germany
Silver, embossing, mauve paint, gilding
29.7 x 34.6 inches (75.5 cm x 88 cm)
MZ-1222

SILVER PLATTER WITH "DIANA AND NYMPHS" SCENE

In the 17th century, handwashing platters such as this one were often turned into "silver canvases" upon which talented artisans engraved or inlaid scenes both real and mythological. This baroque platter was employed in the ambassadorial handwashing service. The German master, Jacob II Plank, embossed the composition of Diana and Actaeon on the dish. This rendering of the myth features Diana, the ancient goddess of hunting and wildlife, bathing with the nymphs in the forest at the moment the young hunter Actaeon encountered her. The angry goddess subsequently turned the youth into a deer, who was then torn apart by his own hunting dogs.

SILVER PLATTER WITH "TRIUMPH OF PEACE" SCENE

Augsburg was one of most fertile sources of fine metalwork in 17th-century Europe and the Augsburg masters created numerous decorative objects in the royal collection. This platter, also by the Jacob II Plank, contains an ornately chased composition depicting the allegorized "Triumph of Peace" set in a wide scrollwork border. The female figures on the bottom of the bowl represent Peace, Glory, Plenty, and History. The putti astride an eagle, dragon, lion, and sea creature in cartouches on the side of the vessel symbolize the four elements: air, fire, earth, and water. The design is remarkable for its baroque features: brilliantly worked planes and perspectives in high relief, which create a rich play of light and dark.

Silver Platter with "Diana and Nymphs" Scene

Silver Platter with "Triumph of Peace" Scene

SNOW LEOPARD WINE VESSEL

This silver snow leopard with a heraldic shield in its paws, sits atop a massive square base. The detachable head of the leopard is attached by a heavy chain to rings in the mouths of two small embossed lion heads applied to each shoulder. The heraldic shield bears a mask in the form of a female face and is flat-chased in the style of Renaissance masters. The base is decorated with chased depictions of grass and engraved pendants of fruit. The surface of the vessel is covered in tiny cross hatches in imitation of the animal's coat. The image of the snow leopard was prevalent in English decorative art, but this example and its mate, also in the Kremlin Armory collection, are unique in English silverwork at the turn of the 17th century. These vessels, originally from the English Royal Treasury, are among the most valuable acquisitions made for the Russian Royal Treasury; they were purchased by state officials in 1629.

Snow Leopard Wine Vessel
1600-1601
London, England
Silver, embossing, casting, gilding, mauve paint
38.9 inches (98 cm) height; 64.6 pounds (29.32 kg) weight
MZ-693

Snow Leopard Wine Vessel

Detail of Snow Leopard Wine Vessel

Detail of Snow Leopard Wine Vessel

Pitcher
1612-13
London, England
Silver, embossing, casting, gilding
13 inches (33 cm) height
MZ-607

Tablecloth
1621
Karl Tissen
Denmark
Silk, canvas, weaving
13.6 x 7.2 feet (408 cm x 218 cm)
TK-2184

PITCHER

This pitcher for ale was presented to Czar Mikhail Feodorovich by the English customs agent Fabian Wilianov. It has the traditional form for English pitchers; the bulbous body, the high neck, and lid are decorated with embossing in flat relief, characteristic of the late Renaissance with fanciful representations of a shell, grapevines, and sea monsters. Flower flourishes are freely dispersed between them. The body is completed with a cast winged head, and the handle is engraved with a foliage ornament.

The job of the merchant was exceptional in the late 16th century and early 17th century. Trading privileges were the province of mercantile agents who regularly visited the ruler to kiss the royal hand. This gift was made during one such visit in 1613, perhaps to celebrate his coronation that year. This splendid English-made vessel was placed in the halls of the royal palace and in the private rooms of the Czar's family in Moscow.

✦

TABLECLOTH

In 17th-century Russia, tablecloths were important decorative adornments for the royal chambers. This wonderful blue-and-white silk tablecloth with woven illustrations was a gift from King Christian IV of Denmark to Czar Mikhail Feodorovich; it was brought to Moscow in 1622 by the Russian ambassador, Prince Alexei Mikhailovich Lvov. The delicate design on the central panel of the tablecloth represents a fully set table, consisting of large dishes with wildfowl, sturgeon, and turtles; smaller dishes with lobsters, herring, various fruit, berries, and vegetables; and twelve empty plates set between knives and two-tined forks.

Woven into the border are scenes of a royal hunt with hounds and gamebirds; a sea battle between various European sailing ships; views of a medieval town, with a

Pitcher

cathedral, town hall, and numerous tall houses. The border at the ends of the tablecloth includes heraldic badges with the coat of arms of Christian IV and the emblem of Denmark and its constituent lands and regions. The inscription "Anno [Year] 1621" and the initials of the maker—"KT"—are woven beneath the emblem of Denmark.

The tablecloth is executed in double-sided embroidery, such that the design on the front of the cloth is visible in negative on the reverse side. The entire composition of the tablecloth and in particular the careful selection of scenes around the border indicate the specific nature of the tablecloth: clearly it was an official diplomatic gift. It is also a unique example of European weaving, highly valued at the time of its making and carefully preserved ever since.

Tablecloth

Drinking Ladle (Kovsh)

Drinking Ladle (Kovsh) (left)
First quarter of the 17th century
Kremlin Workshops
Moscow, Russia
Silver, precious stones, embossing,
niello, carving, gilding
5 inches (12.8 cm) height, 13.2 inches
(33.6 cm) length
K-4142

Drinking Ladle (Kovsh) (below)
First quarter of the 17th century
Moscow, Russia
Silver, embossing, carving, gilding
11.4 inches (29 cm) length with
handle, 8.5 inches (21.5 cm) height
with handle
MR-4156

TWO DRINKING LADLES

The ladle, or *kovsh*, is one of the most archetypal decorative vessels from ancient times. As archaeological digs show, ladles appeared in Russia in the 10th and 11th centuries. Later, this typically wooden form was reproduced in metal. Silver and gold ladles were mentioned in the spiritual books of the Moscow princes, starting from the 14th century. These ladles were passed down from generation to generation. During feasts, Russians drank their favorite drink, *myod*, from ladles. Myods were boiled following ancient recipes and were usually made from berries and fruit. They differed not only in flavor, but also in color. Red myod was drunk from red ladles and white myod from silver ladles.

These two ladles belonged to Czar Mikhail Feodorovich, and follow the strict form accorded them. On the ladle above, precious stones, encased in high embossed settings have been set onto the smooth polished metal.

The spout and handle of the ladle are decorated with a delicate black enamel design; an inscription runs along the rim with the title of Czar Mikhail Feodorovich.

By contrast, the silver gilded drinking ladle shown below is slightly plainer. It is decorated around the rim with a wide ornamental stripe with an inscription noting its owner, Czar Mikhail Feodorovich. It is very similar in design to the Czar's other ladle, however, this kovsh is stouter and possesses a slightly longer handle. Ladles such as these were used during ceremonial receptions in the Granovitaya (Faceted) Hall, the ceremonial hall of the royal palace

Drinking Ladle (Kovsh)

Drinking Cup

Drinking Cup (above)
First half of the 17th century
Kremlin Workshops
Moscow, Russia
Gold, precious stones, embossing,
carving, niello, cornelian, flat chasing
1.3 inches (3.4 cm) height, 2.4 inches
(6.1 cm) diameter, 3.2 inches (8.2 cm)
width with handle
DK-21

Drinking Cup (below)
17th century
Russia
Silver, casting, embossing, flat chasing,
gilding
2 inches (5 cm) height, 4.8 inches (12.2
cm) width with handle
MR-5167

TWO DRINKING CUPS

In the records of the Czar's storerooms in the 17th century, there were many expensive gold and silver vessels. There were also vessels made out of semi-precious stones such as crystal, agate, cornelian, and jasper. Sometimes wares were created from more exotic materials such as coral, mother-of-pearl, ostrich eggs, and coconut shells. Some of these objects were given to the Czars as presents, while others were purchased abroad for the Russian court.

The drinking cup featured above was formed from transparent red cornelian. Its gold frame has been decorated with precious stones, emeralds, and rubies. The title of Czar Mikhail Feodorovich runs along the cup's rim, and a decorative handle with a black enamel design adorns it.

Simple drinking cups were used mainly for imbibing hot liquids. Since they were generally made out of inexpensive metal, many people were able to own these cups, which were popular in the 17th century in Russian homes of merchants and lower gentry. Cups commissioned for the czar's table were created with added flare and fantasy.

The gilded-silver cup shown at left was kept in the Kremlin's storeroom, and is less opulent than the one above. The sides are decorated with foliate embossing depicting animals and birds: an eagle with spread wings, an eagle with a crown, a lion, a pelican, a unicorn, and other creatures. A swan adorns the bottom of the cup, while on the rim is an inscription stating the benefits of drinking wine, but also the misfortunes of abusing it.

Drinking Cup

PRIVATE PLATE BELONGING TO THE PATRIARCH JOSEPH

During ceremonial dinners in the Czar's palace, food was served on silver plates. The uncharacteristically minimal decoration on this large plate features a stamp with a plain inscription, although every letter of the inscription is beautifully and expressively drawn. It is believed to be the handiwork of a particular master (whose identity is not known) in the Kremlin Workshops in the 17th century who specialized in etching. He inscribed the titles of the Czars on more than 200 silver plates and 20 ladles, executing the design directly on the object; later these drawings were "finished" by another master by means of engraving or inlaying. The inscription on this plate states that it was the personal property of the Patriarch Joseph.

CUP OF CZAR MIKHAIL FEODOROVICH

This cup with a broad base supported by three miniature lions is typical of the tall wide-mouthed cups utilized in everyday life in old Russia. Words of prayer—asking God to protect Czar Mikhail Feodorovich and to grant victories to his czardom—are written on the rim of the cup and on three large medallions on the cup's body. It is believed that this cup was crafted during one of the most complicated times of Czar Mikhail's reign, when the young ruler fought off Polish and Swedish invaders who challenged his sovereignty after the death of Boris Godunov.

Cup of Czar Mikhail Feodorovich

Cup of Czar Mikhail Feodorovich
First half of the 17th century
Kremlin Workshops
Moscow, Russia
Silver, embossing, carving, gilding
7 inches (17.8 cm) height, 5 inches
(12.7 cm) diameter
MR-4169

Private Plate Belonging to the Patriarch Joseph
Mid-17th century
Kremlin Workshops
Moscow, Russia
Silver, gilding, embossing, carving
9.6 inches (24.3 cm) diameter
MR-4165

Private Plate Belonging to the Patriarch Joseph

Bowl (*Stavets*) of Czar Peter Alexeyevich
Last quarter of 17th century
Moscow, Russia
Silver, embossing, niello, carving, gilding
5.7 inches (14.6 cm) diameter
MR-4028/1-2

Pitcher of Czarevich Ivan Alexeyevich
1676
Kremlin Workshops
Moscow, Russia
Silver, embossing, filigree, enamel,
casting, carving, gilding
12.6 inches (32.1 cm) height, 6.8
inches (17.2 cm) width with handle
MR-3420

Wine Vessel (*Bratina*)
1642
Master Feodor Evstigneev
Kremlin Workshops
Moscow, Russia
Gold, embossing, carving
7 inches (17.7 cm) height, 1.7 inches
(4.4 cm) diameter of crown
MR-4133/1-2

Bowl (Stavets) of Czar Peter Alexeyevich

Pitcher of Czarevich Ivan Alexeyevich

Wine Vessel (Bratina)

BOWL (*STAVETS*) OF *CZAR PETER ALEXEYEVICH*

Among the Russian vessels that were used during
ceremonial dinners in the Czar's palace, a few of these
lidded bowls, or *stavets*, still remain. The use and
meaning of these low, cylindrical bowls have not been
fully explained. It is known that wooden bowls were
frequently found in Russian monasteries and that silver
ones were used at court. Some historians have speculated
that these bowls were used for dessert.

The motif of this stavets employs the two headed eagle—
the crest of the Russian state. An inscription along the
rim of the vessel states the title of Peter the Great and the
date that he was appointed Czar. Hence, the bowl was
made after 1682, when ten-year-old Peter was crowned
along with his older brother Ivan.

PITCHER OF *CZAREVICH IVAN ALEXEYEVICH*

Washbasin sets, consisting of a pitcher and a bowl, were
used to rinse the hands while at the table. They were
already known at court in Moscow in the 16th century.
The sets which are kept in the Kremlin Museums are
mostly of foreign origin; often they were presented to the
state as ambassadorial gifts. Among the work of Moscow
silversmiths are two pitchers which were commissioned
for the young Czareviches Ivan and Peter by their older
brother Feodor Alexeyevich soon after his accession to
the throne. The two bowls which were part of the sets
have not survived. Documents from the time show that
the Czar Feodor even dictated their decorative character,
stipulating that "the sides of the bowls should be

decorated with silver badges with enamel designs, and
the basins should be engraved with grasses." The shape of
the pitcher is traditional and, as was common at that
time, the handle is similar to German vessels of this type.
It is quite likely that in creating these sets, craftsmen
utilized imported, readymade components.

WINE VESSEL (*BRATINA*)

This *bratina* has a pointed lid; the smooth joining of the
lid to the body of the vessel recalls the cupola of a
Russian church. Ordinarily, these drinking cups carried
an inscription of its owner or an appropriate Russian
proverb. The inscribed sentiment on this bratina reads:
"True love is like a vessel of gold: it can never be broken,
and if it should ever bend, then reason will mend it." In
the works of the masters of the Kremlin Workshops, the
carved message always served a dual purpose, equally
decorative and moral.

WINE VESSEL (BRATINA)

Gold and silver *bratinas*, or wine vessels, were widely employed in the Czars' and boyars' daily lives; bratinas are quintessential Russian vessels. The form of the bratina derived from clay and wooden wares. *Kvas*, a drink made from bread and wine, was passed around the table from hand to hand in these vessels. Their simple form was decorated in a multitude of ways. The smooth surface was usually covered in a foliage design and decorated with engraved compositions with circular and triangular stamps. The alternation of smooth ungilded and engraved gilded scales created an interesting play of light and gave the vessel a reptilian elegance. This bratina belonged to members of the Moscow gentry, the brothers Feodor and Parfeny Venevitov.

Wine Vessel (Bratina)

POURING VESSEL (ENDOVA)

Vessels similar in form to the bratina were used in Russia over many centuries. This pouring vessel, known as an *endova*, differs from a bratina in that it has a spout. The collection of old Russian tableware in the Armory is unique in both size and value; this, however, is the only endova in the collection. It would traditionally be filled with mead, beer, or wine, and was used to replenish smaller vessels. The decoration of the endova is based on the alternation of smooth, polished swirled bands with flat-chased foliate bands. Around the top of the spherical, bulbous vessel runs a smooth band with an

inscription which describes how the endova was made for the Boyar Vasily Ivanovich Streshnev, a relative of the Czarina Evdokia Lukianovna—the second wife of Mikhail Feodorovich. In the mid-17th century, Streshnev was the head of the Kremlin's Silver and Gold Halls, where jewelers used precious metals to create wonderful objects for the royal court.

Wine Vessel (*Bratina*)
1643
Master Peter Evstigneev
Kremlin Workshops
Moscow, Russia
Silver, embossing, carving, gilding
7 inches (17.8 cm) height, 5 inches
(12.7 cm) diameter
MR-4196

Pouring Vessel (*Endova*)
1644
Kremlin Workshops
Moscow, Russia
Silver, embossing, carving, poinçon, gilding
6.7 inches (17 cm) height, 9.8 inches
(25 cm) diameter of crown
MR-4189

Pouring Vessel (Endova)

Towel
17th century
Russia
Calico, silk thread, gold thread, weaving, embroidery
7 x 2 feet (210 cm x 60 cm)
TK-544

TOWEL

In royal times, the towel was one of those decorative articles where design outweighed practicality. This towel, made of calico, is ornamented with embroidery in different colored silk and gold thread. The bright colors of the fantastic foliate designs and the richness of the trimming make this example particularly fanciful. Such towels were used during the ambassadorial presentation of gifts and at banquets and other formal receptions.

Towels were brought to the royal court from Turkey and the Crimea; Russian versions were also made in the Workshops of the Kremlin. There was a special worksho known as the Czarina's Chamber, where the Czarina herself took an active part in the production of items of royal dress and other small articles, including parade towels.

Towel

Bowl

Bowl (left)
Late 17th century
Solvychegodsk, Russia
Silver, embossing, filigree, enamel,
gilding
7.2 inches (18.3 cm) diameter
MR-1233

Bowl (middle)
Late 17th century
Solvychegodsk, Russia
Silver, embossing, filigree, enamel,
gilding
6.2 inches (15.7 cm) diameter
MR-1206

Bowl (bottom)
Late 17th century
Solvychegodsk, Russia
Silver, embossing, filigree, enamel,
gilding
7.2 inches (18.3 cm) diameter
MR-1232

THREE SOLVYCHEGODSK BOWLS

[E]legant silver bowls with painted enamel were extremely [p]opular thanks to the craftsmen of Solvychegodsk. The [p]articular feature of enamel-work done in Solvychegodsk [w]as the combination of multi-colored painted designs on [a] smooth white background. The enamel took on bright [c]olors, with yellow and brown tones. Foliate ornament [d]ominated the decorative composition. This type of [d]ecoration was an important part of the jeweler's art [fr]om early times. Until the 17th century, foliate [o]rnaments on enamel were treated symmetrically and [c]onventionally; at the end of the century, however, new [fe]atures appeared. Many of the enamel flowers are easily [r]ecognizable—tulips, poppies, irises, and cornflowers. It [i]s not just the naturalistic form, but also the scale of the [fl]owers that makes them so lifelike. The flowers, with [th]eir long, smoothly curved details seem to braid the [s]urface of the vessel. This colorful, vibrant aesthetic [m]arked an important point in Russian art of the 17th [c]entury and signaled a return to realism and a revitalized [in]terest in the natural world.

[T]he painted enamel of these three Solvychegodsk bowls [fe]atures depictions of flowers as well as animals. The [r]epresentation of wild animals and birds, both real and [fa]ntastic, was possibly borrowed from enamel-work on [o]ther pieces of representational art—book miniatures, [fo]r example. One of the potential sources for this type of [w]ork was a 17th-century album of miniatures with [d]rawings of animals. In 1692 three books about animals [w]ith detailed illustrations and descriptions were [p]roduced by masters of the Kremlin Workshops.

Bowl

Bowl

CHAPTER VI

Court Life
in the 18th & 19th Centuries

Court Life
in the 18th & 19th Centuries

by M.V. Martynova and T.N. Muntian

*Czar Nicholas II and Czarina Alexandra
Feodorovna in Masquerade Costumes*
1903
Photograph

COURT LIFE IN THE 18TH CENTURY

The 18th century ushered in a new series of dramatic acts in the history of the Russian state and the ruling Romanov dynasty, bringing significant changes in the ceremonial rites of the royal court.

The rituals of Russian life had been built up over many centuries. The reigns of Czar Alexei Mikhailovich and his son Feodor Alexeyevich in the second half of the 17th century introduced numerous reforms, yet it was not until the time of Peter the Great (who ruled from 1682 to 1725) that changes crucial to the development of the Russian state took hold. This was a time of ambitious and fundamental renewal, which in some cases even toppled centuries-old foundations. Peter's irrepressible energy and zeal for reform led to the remarkable rebirth of a new society and a new secular culture.

The symbol of Peter's reforms was the new capital, St. Petersburg, founded on an uninhabited piece of land—recently captured from the Swedes—at the mouth of the Neva River. A 19th-century historian wrote: "St. Petersburg was the embodiment of all that Peter loved and the rejection of all that he hated: his love of the sea and the fleet, his need for open spaces, his regard for the outward expression of culture, his hatred of antiquity, and his fear of the mute, hostile old capital."

By the end of Peter's reign, St. Petersburg was a fair-sized town, spread out on both shores of the Neva. Unlike in Moscow, buildings in St. Petersburg were made exclusively of stone. Under Peter's descendants, the new capital, known as the "Palmyra of the North," evolved into a city of elegant architectural ensembles with magnificent palaces enclosing opulent interiors and surrounded by stately parks and gardens.

CHANGES IN APPEARANCE, DRESS, AND WEAPONRY

After the court nobility moved to St. Petersburg, life at court soon followed the European model, and in general the 18th century marked a step towards European modernity in the Russian people. Some of these reforms might seem trivial or superficial by today's standards, but these changes, however slight, demonstrated the supremacy of the Czar and the obedience of his subjects.

In 1698 Czar Peter issued a special decree forcing men to shave off their beards. For centuries, beards had been the pride of Russian men, and a sign of strength and virility. Those who failed to comply were heavily fined. Next, Peter prohibited his subjects, apart from peasants and clergy, from wearing the traditional form of Russian dress. His decree, or *ukaz* (in Russian), of 1700 ordered that men "in Moscow and in other towns wear foreign dress in the Hungarian manner." This meant loose-fitting garments of a type already seen in ancient Russia. The new fashion was, in the words of the Czar, intended to make Russian citizens look like Europeans."

The new forms of clothing were soon assimilated at court. Particular attention was paid to parade costumes used during festivals and ceremonies. The wardrobes of the Russian high society—men and women alike—came to include hundreds, sometimes thousands, of articles of clothing. Additionally, the creation of new hairstyles transformed the appearance of Russian women. Before Peter's reign, women were rarely without traditional head covering. European dress demanded a variety of coiffures. At the beginning of the 18th century, there were only three hairdressers in Moscow who knew how to style hair in the European manner.

In the same manner as changes to clothing and appearance occurred, so too with traditional weapons. The light, elegant European sword replaced the Eastern-influenced heavy sword and knife. The size of the weapon, the type of the blade, and the decorative formation of the handle were subverted to the demands of fashion, just as clothing was. During the 18th century, swords that were used to defend honor and life were prized most for their aesthetic qualities. Accordingly, jewelers oversaw the manufacture of swords and turned to engravers and artists for their decorative compositions. The techniques and materials used in adorning these swords were similar to those employed in the decoration of snuffboxes, cases, watches, and other personal accessories. Such weapons in Russia were produced in the Court's Diamond Workshop. This workshop operated from around 1750 until 1797 and was located on Vasilevsky Island in St. Petersburg. In addition to housing the lavish jewelry of Czarinas Elizabeth Petrovna and Catherine the Great, the Diamond Workshop also stored a large collection of weapons—over 70 pieces— including magnificent swords and knives of both Russian and foreign craftsmanship.

SOCIAL "GATHERINGS" & IMPERIAL PARTIES

When Peter the Great visited France, he was particularly impressed with the informal gatherings of French noblemen. In 1718, the year after his return, he established "gatherings"—ceremonial public meetings of courtiers. In ancient Russia, nobles led enclosed lives, played host only to those close to them (usually relatives) during festival times. Guests were received according to a longstanding ritual whereby the host's wife greeted guests at the door, kissed them, and raised a glass of wine to them, after which the women and men dined separately in different parts of the house.

Until the end of the 17th century, the Czarina and the Czarevnas were shielded from public view. They rarely took part in court life and observed court ceremonies only through secret windows. Now, however, they began to appear openly at court. Peter ordered that gatherings of nobles should include their wives and daughters and that courtiers take turns hosting gatherings in their own homes. Domestic life also witnessed the influence of European fashion. In the homes of nobles and courtiers, walls were hung with carpets, and rooms were appointed with elegant lamps and mirrors with intricately carved frames. Sets of furniture were commissioned for parade halls, dining rooms, offices, and bedrooms. The Czar himself made special rules for the host of these events: the host was to dedicate several rooms of the house to his guests. The biggest of these was for dancing; the second for playing chess, a game which Peter loved; the third for conversation and smoking; and the fourth for ladies to play at forfeits and other parlor games.

Previously, meetings of nobles had been constrained by the etiquette of the Middle Ages. Now, men and women were challenged by the new art of social interaction and the order of formal court celebrations. Gatherings soon turned into balls with strictly defined rituals for the reception of guests. A ball

became an integral element of all official ceremonies—coronations, weddings, and diplomatic receptions. Parties at court were rounded off by ceremonial banquets, also notable for their great opulence. The rituals surrounding these banquets were cloaked in the aura of fantasy. Banquet tables would usually have in their center an elegant cascading fountain surrounded by candles. Parade banquets would often involve more than a thousand courtiers. The meal would be accompanied by instrumental and vocal music, while dishes from all over Europe were served by both Russian and foreign waiters.

The jeweler Jeremiah Poze, who made Catherine the Great's magnificent imperial crown, left delightful descriptions of court life. He described one particular party held in the stupendous Hall of Mirrors: "A multitude of bodies wandered around in masks and rich costumes; they gathered in groups or danced quadrilles. All the rooms were lavishly illuminated: at any one time, no fewer than one thousand candles burned, and the whole effect was as magnificent and opulent as could be."

Like all other ceremonies and festivities at court, masked balls were carefully ritualized. Peter the Great issued decrees setting forth the exact sequence of events at a party. Participants in the masquerade were informed in advance of their costumes, and were then given a number which instructed them of their specific roles in the masked spectacle. Under Czarina Elizabeth Petrovna, masked balls were held on Tuesdays, and attendance was compulsory; those who failed to turn up were fined 50 rubles.

The programs for masked balls varied enormously. In planning them, the monarch often exhibited exceptional inventiveness and humor. In 1744, for example, Czarina

Elizabeth Petrovna hosted a number of court masked balls where the men were required to appear unmasked wearing enormous skirts and sporting ladies' hairstyles, while the ladies were dressed in men's court outfits.

The magnificent masked ball held by Catherine the Great (who ruled from 1762 to 1796) in Moscow soon after her coronation was especially noteworthy. It was entitled "The Festival of Minerva" since the Czarina liked to identify herself with the ancient Roman goddess of wisdom and the arts. According to the invitations, the ball was to represent "the infamy of the vices and the glory of good works." The masquerade, which lasted for three days, took place on the streets of Moscow. A vast costumed procession was composed of groups which represented, in symbolic and theatrical form, the seven human vices. This human parade was completed by a train of chariots bearing figures dressed as ancient gods, with Minerva at their head. They were surrounded by muses, poets, musicians, philosophers, and allegorical figures representing science and the arts. More than 4,000 people and 200 ox-drawn chariots took part in the procession. This exhibition, which required an enormous amount of stage machinery, was directed by F. G. Volkov, the founder of the first professional theater in Russia.

Masked balls and special celebrations were also convened to commemorate military events, such as victorious battles and the launching of ships. In 1774, numerous festivals in honor of Russia's victory over Turkey were held. Catherine the Great rode around Moscow in a golden carriage, pulled by wildly decorated horses led by ceremonial court escorts. With the arrival of the Czarina in the capital, a ceremonial church service in the Assumption Cathedral was attended by court members dripping with gold and diamonds. Following

Masquerade Ball in the Court of Czarina Elizabeth Petrovna
Mid-18th century
Lithograph

this service was a ceremony in the Granovitaya (Faceted) Palace to decorate the heroes of the war. The principal festival took place on the vast green Khodynskoe Field, just outside Moscow, where temporary structures had been erected under the direction of the renowned Russian architect, V. I. Bazhenov. Spectators watched from a platform in the form of a ship with masts and sails. The festival included theatrical spectacles and a masked ball, which ended with brilliant fireworks portraying the Battle of Chesme, in which Russia defeated the Turkish fleet in 1770. From the time of Peter the Great, "fire games", as fireworks were originally known, were a favorite diversion at the Russian court at coronation ceremonies, carnivals, masked balls, and peace declarations, among others.

A ROYAL PASTIME: THE HUNT

The acceptance of Western European culture,

the changing nature of court life, and the transfer of the capital to St. Petersburg gradually altered one of the oldest forms of amusement favored by the Czars—the hunt.

Peter the Great, the great enlightener of Russia, was not a great fan of the sport: "This is not my entertainment. Even without wild animals, I still have something to fight with: outside society with my enemies and inside society with my uneducated and coarse people." All of the future Russian leaders of the 18th century, including the Czarinas, were passionate hunters. Peter II was particularly fond of hunting. His successor, Czarina Anna Ivanovna, also loved to hunt and had many weapons. According to historical accounts, she was a great shot. Her contemporaries recalled that the Czarina placed loaded rifles at the windows of various rooms in the palace so she could practice her favorite pastime when the whim struck her. The newspaper *The St. Petersburg Times* in 1740 announced to its readers that from July 10 to August 26, the Czarina killed 9 deer, 16 wild goats, 4 boars, 1 wolf, 374 rabbits, 68 wild ducks, and 16 sea birds.

During the reigns of Elizabeth Petrovna and Catherine the Great, the ceremonial hunt was a noisy, happy, gallant holiday. The Czarinas especially liked what was called "Circus Hunting" in which people on foot and on horseback participated in the hunt, accompanied by musicians and servants. The goal of such a hunt was to herd the prey until it was exhausted, after which it was killed with a precise blow of a hunting dagger. Catherine the Great was said to have been an expert rider. In her youth she was able to ride equally well in both a woman's saddle and a man's saddle.

The Russian court of the 18th century attempted to outdo the French court in both

wealth and magnificence. Outrageous sums of money were spent on ladies' costumes and other luxurious items—snuff boxes, watches, jewels, precious weapons and the like. The jeweler Jeremiah Poze wrote: "The ladies' dress was particularly lavish, as were their gold accoutrements. They would wear an extraordinary number of diamonds; even in private life, ladies never went out without wearing precious jewelry." The foremost exponent of this extravagance was Czarina Elizabeth Petrovna. During the fire of 1753 in Moscow, 4,000 of her dresses were burned; yet after her death, her wardrobe was found to still contain more than 15,000 dresses.

During the 18th century, court etiquette took on a decidedly European flavor and defined not only the conduct of courtiers but also their appearance. A series of decrees illustrates how strictly court dress was regulated. Czarina Anna Ivanovna, for example, with an extravagance typical of the century, forbade people from appearing at court in the same dress on more than one occasion. According to the Czarina Elizabeth Petrovna's decree of 1743, court ladies were not permitted to attend balls in dresses of the same color as that of the sovereign. Pronouncements from the beginning of the reign of Catherine the Great ordered that all subjects should appear at court in "Russian" costume; later, ladies were forbidden to wear anything other than "Greek" costume.

Vast sums would often be spent in complying with these royal orders. When Peter III was to marry Catherine the Great, Czarina Elizabeth ordered that courtiers be given a donation a year in advance, to enable them to have new dresses made.

The constant issuance of decrees, rules, and orders concerning all aspects of court life established a new system of court etiquette in

e 18th century. This etiquette achieved its
nal form towards the end of that century
nd, to a large extent, continued to define
ourt life in the 19th century.

LIFE AT COURT IN THE 19TH CENTURY

erhaps because of the previous century's
ramatic social transformation, the Russian
ourt of the 19th century was one of the
randest in Europe, and St. Petersburg arose as
ne of Europe's most elegant capital cities.
ourt ceremonies of the time, combining
Eastern luxury" with the "refined taste of the
Vest," fittingly upheld the prestige of the
ussian monarchs.

he magnificence of St. Petersburg impressed
oreign diplomats and travelers alike. The
Marquis de Custin, for example, could not
ame a single ceremonial reception in all of
urope which could compare with "the
elebration held by Emperor Nicholas I on his
aughter's wedding day in the Winter Palace:
ow rich its jeweled dress, how varied and
pulent the uniforms, what magnificence and
armony in the whole ensemble." The
efinement and lavishness of the ladies' dresses
1ade a particularly strong impression.

he uniforms of the cavalry were particularly
criking: the Guards in white and silver, the
Iussars in red and gold with their fur-lined
apes slung over their shoulders, and the
Jhlans with bright stripes and lapels. They
ooked romantic, elegant, and regal. Parade
niforms worn by courtiers and senior official
vere remarkable for the profusion of gold
mbroidery: the more senior the rank, the
1ore extravagant the decoration.

he dresses of court ladies were also richly
mbroidered. At the coronation of Nicholas I
n 1825, the cut, color, decoration, and
naterial of the dresses worn by court ladies

were strictly defined. Such dresses were
consequently known as "Russian"—or,
unofficially, as "Frenchified sarafans"—since
they contained some elements of the national
female costume. The color of loose-fitting
court dresses, and their decoration—either
silver or gold embroidery—would depend on
the particular calling of the ladies, and to
which court they belonged, whether it was the
royal court or the court of a Grand Duchess.
Court ladies wore elaborate head coverings,
with white veils glistening with precious
stones, pearls, and brilliant-cut diamonds,
while the young maids of honor would wear
red or blue velvet hair bands during most
ceremonial feast days, particularly during
"Parades of the Highest-born," which usually
took place after the royal family returned to St.
Petersburg from one of their country
residences.

HIGH SOCIETY

The New Year saw the return of the royal
family to the capital, and heralded the opening
of the winter season in high society, which
included Italian and Russian operas, theatrical
performances, concerts, receptions, parties,
and balls. The St. Nicholas Ball was the first
event in a series of similar celebrations, and
was considered a ceremony more important
even than the "Parade of the Highest-born." It
took place in the St. Nicholas Hall of the
Winter Palace—described as "a temple of
magnificence," more suitable for such
ceremonies than any other palace in Europe.

More than 3,000 guests were invited to the St.
Nicholas Ball (in 1890 the figure reached
4,000), representing the cream of high society.
The guests gathered in a sea of gold and
diamonds; ministers, senators, members of the
State Council, heads of the St. Petersburg city
council, leaders of the provinces, and senior
representatives of the gentry abounded. On

Detail of *Entrance of Czar Nicholas II and Czarina Alexandra Feodorovna at the Opening of the Season of Court Balls, May 16, 1896*
1903
Lithograph

this evening, the whole of St. Petersburg beau monde were presented to their Highnesses, and as per the social hierarchy, different sections of Russian society were invited separately to subsequent events.

Typically, the Czar and Czarina entered the Concert Hall from the Malachite Hall, where the Chief Steward of the Royal Household, the Steward of the Royal Household, and pageboys awaited them. At exactly half past nine, two black footmen in fantastic Mauritian costumes threw open the doors and their Highnesses entered the St. Nicholas Hall to the strains of the polka from Glinka's opera *A Life for the Czar.*

Other less grand balls were also held in the smaller Anichkov Palace on the banks of the Fontanka River. From 1816 on, this was the residence of heirs to the throne after their marriage; Anichkov Palace was particularly fancied by Nicholas I. Balls were held here later in the year, when the guests danced all week in the white drawing room. It was also a favorite place of Alexander III (ruler from 1881 to 1894), who lived there for more than a quarter of a century while he was heir to the throne. In addition to building up a magnificent collection of works of art, he was known to host amateur theatrical events, concerts, and festive parties.

Court life under Alexander III brought a plethora of changes. For example, Alexander required that the court staff be exclusively Russian. Also during his rule, a national orchestra and choir were formed; the musicians played at balls in new red parade caftans of a Russian cut and performed from a stage covered in red broadcloth. The Czar himself had a bushy beard and wore his trousers tucked into his boots. In the words of the artist V. Surikov, Alexander was "a true representative of the people."

During the reigns of Alexander III and Nicholas II (the last Romanov Czar), the traditional Nikolaevsky Ball became an even grander event. During the ball, held on January 19, 1883, dinner for the 2,800 invited guests was served in the Crest, Grigorievsky, Alexandrovsky and White Halls of the Winter Palace. During these festivities, the Czarinas truly reigned supreme.

At the St. Nicholas Ball of January 23, 1885, many of the halls of the Winter Palace were lit with electricity for the first time. Czar Alexander III attended the ball in the red parade uniform of the Royal Cavalry Regiment, with the star and ribbon of the Order of St. Andrew the First Called. The Czarina Maria Feodorovna wore a diamond tiara and necklace, and a dress of silver gauze decorated with garlands of white roses and ivy leaves, on which brilliant-cut diamonds sparkled brightly.

The St. Nicholas Balls during Nicholas II's rule were graced by the Czarina Alexandra Feodorovna. She was tall, with a magnificent bearing. The Czarina was extremely fond of large pearls and, according to one account, wore a beautiful necklace which hung down to her knees.

Court receptions and other festivities were unusually lively during the reigns of the last two Romanovs, but they were not held as frequently as in previous times. This was due in part to the endless sequence of balls held in many other high-society homes in St. Petersburg and in part because both Alexander III and Nicholas II valued the privacy and intimacy of family life. The illness of Nicholas' heir, Alexei Nikolaevich, and the difficult disposition of the Czarina Alexandra Feodorovna meant that the life of the royal family became ever more solitary and confined. Nicholas II, like his father before

...im, was quite indifferent to matters of court ...fe and cared little for ceremonies, etiquette, ...r grand speeches. Czarina Alexandra ...eodorovna fulfilled her numerous ceremonial ...nd dynastic duties, but was said to have ...resided over these affairs with an icy ...etachment.

LIFE IN MOSCOW

...nd what, then, of the ancient Russian capital, ...Moscow? Here, too, the city had its own ...nique style. Muscovites were not used to the ...efined opulence of St. Petersburg, and ...estivals in Moscow were famous for the ...rand, limitless hospitality of true Russians. ...When celebrations were held honoring the ...rrival of the newest heir to the throne, ...Muscovites tried to outdo the splendor of St. ...Petersburg. When Moscow hosted a ball in ...onor of the marriage of the Duke of ...dinburgh and the Grand Duchess Maria ...Alexandrovna, the daughter of Alexander II, ...wo fountains illuminated by multicolored ...lames were set up at the entrance to the ...Grand Hall of the Noble Assembly. One of the ...ountains, situated opposite the royal box, was ...n the form of an enormous goblet. The royal ...ox, a luxurious marquee of purple velvet with ...a lining of white satin, was decorated with ...lowers and beautiful Sèvres porcelain vases. ...orty servants lined the stairway, and the ...allroom was filled with enormous wreaths of ...resh hyacinths.

...n the 19th century the prevalent attitudes ...owards the nation's past were gradually ...econsidered both inside and outside Russia. ...Other countries began to appreciate the ...nique history and people of Russia; interest ...n the art and cultural life of Russia grew. ...These tendencies were encouraged by Nicholas ...(who ruled from 1825 to 1855) in his state ...policy and found expression in the three tenets ...which defined the official ideology of the state:

"orthodoxy, autocracy, and nationality."

Costume balls were one opportunity for the aristocracy to wear the clothes of their ancestors, and the finest of such balls were held in the ancient capital, Moscow. The nobility in St. Petersburg, following Moscow's lead, also wanted to display their love and respect of old Russia. On January 25, 1883—the year of the coronation of Alexander III—a special ball was held in St. Petersburg, in the palace of the Grand Duke Vladimir Alexandrovich. Over 250 guests were invited to the ball: ministers, courtiers, officers of the guards, and professors from the Imperial Academy of Arts. In addition to the host, three other brothers of the Czar were present at the ball: the Grand Dukes Alexei, Pavel, and Sergei Alexandrovich.

The guests arrived at around ten o'clock in the evening and were promptly greeted by servants dressed in picturesque costumes from various eras of Russian history: Varangians, Scythians, Novgorod, and Moscow streltsy. The halls of the palace were filled with boyars and boyarinas, falconers, musicians, singers, and *ryndy* (traditional weapon bearers). Maria Feodorovna's costume was inspired by original works of art depicting Russian empresses from the 17th century. Her relatives met her with salt and bread, enacting the traditional ritual. The revelry and opulence lasted well into the night.

The early 20th century witnessed the terrible and tragic events in Russian Imperial history, events which inevitably put an end to the Russian Imperial Empire. In a brief span of years, the world of luxurious palaces and balls—so magical and yet so far removed from the rest of Russia—disappeared into the past.

Detail of *Entrance of Czar Nicholas II and Czarina Alexandra Feodorovna at the Opening of the Season of Court Balls, May 16, 1896*
1903
Lithograph

Portrait of Emperor Peter I
19th century
Unknown Artist
Russia
Oil on canvas
63 x 45.7 inches (160 cm x 116 cm)
Zh-1947

Portrait of Empress Catherine I
Early 18th century
Unknown Artist
Attributed to Russia
Oil on canvas
53.5 x 37.4 inches (136 cm x 95 cm)
Zh-1975

Portrait of Emperor Peter I

PORTRAIT OF EMPEROR PETER I

The first European artist to depict Peter the Great was the English portrait painter G. Neller. In 1698 King William III of England ordered a life-size portrait of the Russian Czar while Peter was in Great Britain. Today, that portrait is in the collection of Queen Elizabeth II and located at Kensington Palace in London. After his first European portrait, Peter the Great was painted by numerous other European artists as well as by many Russian masters.

The portrait shown here was painted by an unknown artist and is based on the portrait done by a Frenchman named Jean-Marc Natte in 1717 in Paris. At the time, Peter the Great was visiting Paris with the intentions of ending the Northern War and arranging the marriage of his daughter Elizabeth I (8 years old at the time) to the French prince Ludwig XV (7 years old at the time). Not long before this, Natte had done a portrait of Catherine, Peter the Great's wife. Catherine was so excited with the French master's work that she urged Peter to have his portrait painted as well. During the 18th and 19th centuries, this portrait of Peter was used time and again by various artists as the model for their depictions of the Czar. This version belongs to a number of portraits of Peter the Great posed in armor against the background of the battlefield.

PORTRAIT OF EMPRESS CATHERINE I

This portrait of Catherine I presents an unusual representation of the Empress. Except for the scepter and orb, the portrait does not exude any other attributes of high power. It is possible that this portrait was rendered before Catherine I became the Empress, and perhaps was commissioned to coincide with the announcement of her coronation on November 15, 1724.

This idealized portrait of Catherine was made by an unknown artist believed to be of Russian origin. The aristocratic beauty and heightened nobleness given to Catherine by the artist does not reflect her contemporaries' views of her. The deep love that Peter I felt toward Catherine raised her from her lowly position—she was the daughter of a Lithuanian peasant—to one of power, making her the first Empress of Russia. Before converting to the Orthodox faith, she was known as Marfa Skavronskaya. She first met Peter when she was captured by the Russian army, and was remembered as having a kind heart and the ability to influence and soften her husband's sharp character.

Portrait of Empress Catherine I

PORTRAIT OF EMPEROR PETER II

This portrait of Peter II was executed in the style of 17th and 18th-century royal European portraiture; it is based on the work of Johann Paul Ludden from Braunschweig who traveled to St. Petersburg in 1728 and painted several portraits of the Emperor by order of the Imperial court. This rendering has a decidedly theatrical character. Peter II is situated in the center of the canvas, on a dark background which contrasts with his light silhouette.

Peter II's short reign was unremarkable. His grandfather, Peter the Great, spent little time raising and educating his heir, because he did not believe that Peter II would ever rule. Having lost both of his parents early, and after the death of Catherine I, Peter II ascended the throne at the age of twelve and became a puppet in the hands of his appointed guardians, A. D. Menshikov and Prince Dolgoruky, who were favorites of Peter the Great. Peter's only official state business was his engagement on November 30, 1729, to the eighteen-year-old beauty Catherine Alexeyevna Dolgorukova. He died on January 7, 1730.

SWORD AND SCABBARD OF EMPEROR PETER II

Beginning in the 18th century, a small European sword with a light blade and elegant handle emerged as an

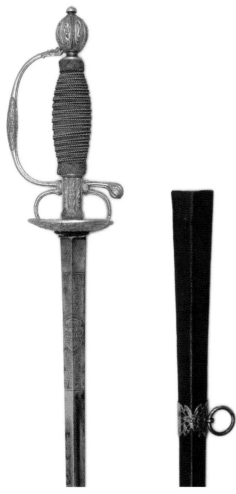

Sword and Scabbard of Emperor Peter II

Portrait of Emperor Peter II

important element of Russian court attire. This sword has a straight triple-edged blade with concave sections. The upper part of the blade is decorated on both sides with gold ornamental engraving, creating a wavy, stem-like motif. The handle of the sword is wooden and bears a stylized monogram(in Latin) with the initials "P S" and the Roman numeral "II," an abbreviation for Peter II, the grandson of Peter the Great. The sword became part of the Kremlin Armory collection on February 16, 1766, bequeathed by Empress Catherine II.

Portrait of Emperor Peter II
19th century
Unknown Artist
Russia
Oil on canvas
63.8 x 46.1 inches (162 cm x 117 cm)
Zh-1948

Sword and Scabbard of Emperor Peter II
1720s
France
Steel, silver, wood, leather, forging, engraving, carving, gilding
37 inches (94 cm) total length, 30.7 inches (78 cm) length of blade, 31.5 inches (80 cm) length of scabbard
OR-4031/1-2

Caftan, Camisole, Hat and Gloves of Emperor Peter II
1727-1730
France
Caftan and Camisole: Heavy cloth, silk, silver and gold thread, embroidery, weaving
39 inches (99 cm) length of caftan, 35 inches (89 cm) length of camisole
Hat: Felt, galloon, thick linen, weaving, braiding
3.9 inches (10 cm) height of crown, 23.6 inches (60 cm) circumference
Gloves: Kid leather
8.7 inches (22 cm) length
TK-1879, TK-1880, TK-2755, TK-244/1-2

Caftan and Camisole of Emperor Peter II
1727-1730
France
Caftan: Velvet, brocade, silk, gold thread, weaving, embroidery, braiding
45.1 inches (114.5 cm) length
Camisole: Brocade, silk, gold lace, embroidery, weaving
41.3 inches (105 cm) length
TK-2909, TK-2910

CAFTAN, CAMISOLE, HAT AND GLOVES OF EMPEROR PETER II

By oral accounts, Catherine II, on November 23, 1766, was presented the wardrobe of Emperor Peter II, which after his death had been kept in the storeroom of the Kremlin Palace. The extravagances of dress in the first half of the 18th century were extreme. The Kremlin Museums today house 24 ceremonial caftans, 21 camisoles, 10 pairs of pants, 25 pairs of stockings, 9 hats, and 22 pairs of gloves in addition to numerous hunting uniforms, house coats, outerwear, and undergarments belonging to Peter II.

This particular caftan and camisole were made of dark-green heavy cloth and lined with light-green taffeta. The hem, cuff, and decorative flaps on the pockets are embroidered with gold thread in a design of a flower garland. The costume also contains a pair of pants made of the same dark-green heavy cloth with silver braid and bronze buckles. The set is completed with a black felt hat sewn with gold galloon on the edge and also a pair of white kid leather gloves with cuffs.

Caftan, Camisole, Hat and Gloves of Emperor Peter II

Caftan and Camisole of Emperor Peter II

CAFTAN AND CAMISOLE OF EMPEROR PETER II

Emperor Peter II, the grandson of Peter the Great, came to the throne in 1727 at the age of twelve. He ruled until his death from smallpox in 1730. This costume consists of a caftan of coarse-cut velvet, and a camisole of patterned brocade. Typical 18th-century dress would also include a pair of breeches and a shirt trimmed with lace, as well as stockings, shoes, hat, and other accessories. The caftan was worn open, but drawn in at the waist, and the buttons and buttonholes that ran from the neck to the ornamented hem were purely decorative. Three slits in the side-seams and at the back enabled the wearer to ride a horse and to carry a sword beneath the caftan. Neither caftan nor camisole had collars, owing to the fashion of wearing full-bottomed wigs. This camisole was made from the same cloth as the caftan. Parade versions of these costumes were made of patterned brocade or velvet, and also from plain cloth with a trimming of galloon or gold thread.

The reign of Elizabeth, the daughter of Peter the Great, was considered the very happiest of times in Russia during the 18th century. When the thirty-two-year-old Empress took the throne, she did not have a mind for political life, but smartly surrounded herself with people to fulfill the needs of her country. The court of Elizabeth was one of the most splendid in Europe. She created a festive air and celebrated the baroque style in literature, music and architecture. Italian, French, and Russian theatrical performances were frequently presented. Incredibly fashionable, she had more than 15,000 dresses, 1,000 pairs of shoes, and two trunks of silk stockings in her wardrobe.

Portrait of Empress Catherine II
19th century
Unknown Artist (after Alexander Roslin)
Russia
Oil on canvas
102.8 x 73 inches (261 cm x 185.5 cm)
Zh-1978

Portrait of Empress Elizabeth Petrovna
18th century
Unknown Artist
Russia
Oil on canvas
63 x 45.7 inches (160 cm x 116 cm)
Zh-1954

trait of Empress Catherine II

ORTRAIT OF EMPRESS CATHERINE II

this dramatic full-length portrait, Catherine II is picted in the so-called Slavic dress, covered with amonds and wearing a cloak fastened with a diamond oach. Around her neck is the Order of St. Andrew the rst Called on a ribbon, and a star of St. George resented to her in 1769). She has a crown on her head, d in her right hand she holds a scepter mounted with a amond eagle. Next to her on a velvet pillow is an orb d a large crown, created for her coronation in 1762. er right hand gestures towards a granite bust of Peter I hind her, which represents both the political direction Catherine's reign and the continuation of Peter I's eas.

is portrait is one of the many copies of the ceremonial rtrait of the Empress made in France by the Swedish tist Alexander Roslin in 1777–1778. Roslin, by all counts, did not like Catherine II, and in his own words lled her physiognomy "vulgar and crude."

ORTRAIT OF EMPRESS ELIZABETH PETROVNA

is portrait of Elizabeth Petrovna was produced from e original by Luis Caravacca, who was specially invited Russia by Peter the Great in 1757 to produce a remonial portrait of Elizabeth Petrovna. The tendency Russian royalty towards French art was in line with e tastes of other European monarchs in the mid-18th ntury. This type of portrait satisfied the Russian need r refined style in painting and was consistent with the mosphere of Elizabeth's court, which was refined in ntrast to the more vulgar tendencies of the Petrine era.

Portrait of Empress Elizabeth Petrovna

135

Dagger and Sheath
18th century
Western Europe
Handle: 18th century, India
Jewelry work: 18th century, attributed to Iran
Steel, wood, leather, jade, inlay work, precious stones, forging, enamel, imprinting
26.8 inches (68 cm) total length, 21.6 inches (55 cm) length of blade, 22.4 inches (57 cm) length of sheath
OR-365/1-2

DAGGER AND SHEATH

The structure and decor of this dagger is very unusual. It is composed of individual pieces originating from different countries and was assembled at roughly the same time. The handle has been made in the shape of a pistol, and was carved from greenish nephrite by an Indian artisan. The entire surface area is covered in inlaid foliage ornament. The stems and branches are made from gold wire, and the leaves act as settings for dark green emeralds. The flowers are made from rubies and carved light gray nephrite. Along the ridge of the handle is a narrow gold groove in which smooth red rubies have been set. The jewelry work is similar to that of masters working in Iran in the 18th century, though it is wholly plausible that it was crafted in a European workshop. The steel flexible single-edged blade is made by European masters. The wooden sheath, covered in leather with a stylized foliage imprint, was also done by European masters. The hook and tip are decorated with settings of rubies and emeralds. The dagger was made for either Empress Elizabeth Petrovna or Empress Catherine the Great.

Detail of Dagger Handle and Hilt

Dagger and Sheath

HUNTING DAGGER AND SHEATH

This dagger and sheath (at right) were made after 1741 for either Elizabeth Petrovna or Catherine the Great. The single-edged blade of dagger has a double-edged tip, and the cast handle is engraved with gold- and silver-stylized foliage with a setting of garnets. The wooden sheath is covered in black leather; the tip and hook of the sheath are gilded silver with similar decorations as the dagger's handle.

+

HUNTING DAGGER WITH KNIFE AND FORK

The hunting dagger here is accompanied by a small knife and fork set used in the celebratory feast after a successful hunt. The subtle decoration of this set suggests that it could be handled by either a man or a woman. The handles of each utensil are made from a very rare material for knives: fragile white porcelain; each handle is decorated with a gallant scene consistent with the spirit of the hunt. The double-edged blade is straight, the upper part decorated with gold stylized ornamentation. The dagger itself was made in Saxony, which was praised for its porcelain and weaponry.

This hunting dagger came from the Oranienbaum Chamber, which was located in a small city on the shore of the Finnish Bay of the Baltic Sea not far from St. Petersburg. This was one of the places where Empress Elizabeth Petrovna liked to hunt in the first half of the 18th century; there was a small palace and surrounding grounds there, which in 1747 was given to Peter Feodorovich (the future Emperor Peter III) and his wife Catherine Alexeyevna (the future Empress Catherine the Great). In the palace was a hall with an arsenal—called the Oranienbaum Chamber—and a unique collection of hunting and battle weapons. Many of these weapons came from the collections of Peter Feodorovich's relatives, who spent much time in the palace, along with the Empress Elizabeth Petrovna herself.

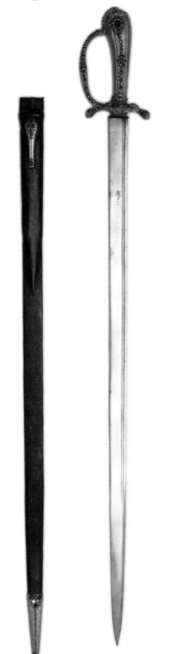

Hunting Dagger and Sheath

Hunting Dagger and Sheath
18th century
Western Europe
Steel, wood, silver, leather, forging, carving, gilding, precious stones
33.5 inches (85 cm) total length, 27.6 inches (70 cm) length of blade, 28.7 inches (73 cm) length of sheath
OR-4449/1-2

Hunting Dagger with Knife and Fork
Mid-18th century
Saxony, Germany
Steel, silver, porcelain, forging, gold inlay, carving
24 inches (61 cm) total length of dagger, 8.3 inches (21 cm) length of knife, 7.5 inches (19 cm) length of fork
OR-3919/1-3

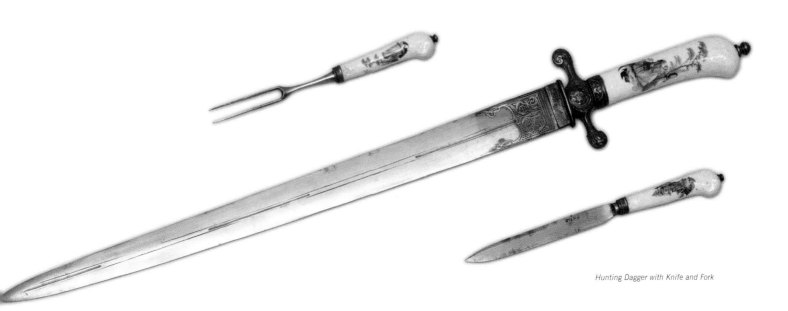

Hunting Dagger with Knife and Fork

Court Sword
Mid-18th century
Steel, gold, silver, diamonds, forging, casting, carving, gold, silver, diamonds
35 inches (89 cm) total length, 28.9 inches (73.5 cm) length of blade
OR-4458/1-2

COURT SWORD

The court sword was a lighter version of the officer's sword. The fashion for these swords appeared in Europe in the 17th century, but their popularity reached a high point in the 18th century. In both their creation and use, functionality was secondary to ornament.

The impeccably crafted court sword shown here was made of gold and decorated with a floral design consisting of undulating stems and high silver settings for diamonds. The sword's six-edged blade is pure steel. The upper section of the sword has traces of engraving, which may have originally been covered with gold. Also inscribed on the blade is the name "Antonio Pichinio," a famous Italian swordmaker active in the early 17th century. It is unlikely, however, that the sword is his handiwork, and the inscription is perhaps more symbolic than factual. The name of the sword's true maker has been lost. This sword would have been part of a well-to-do man's attire, and it may have been one of the many foreign and Russian swords obtained by Czarina Elizabeth Petrovna in the 1740s.

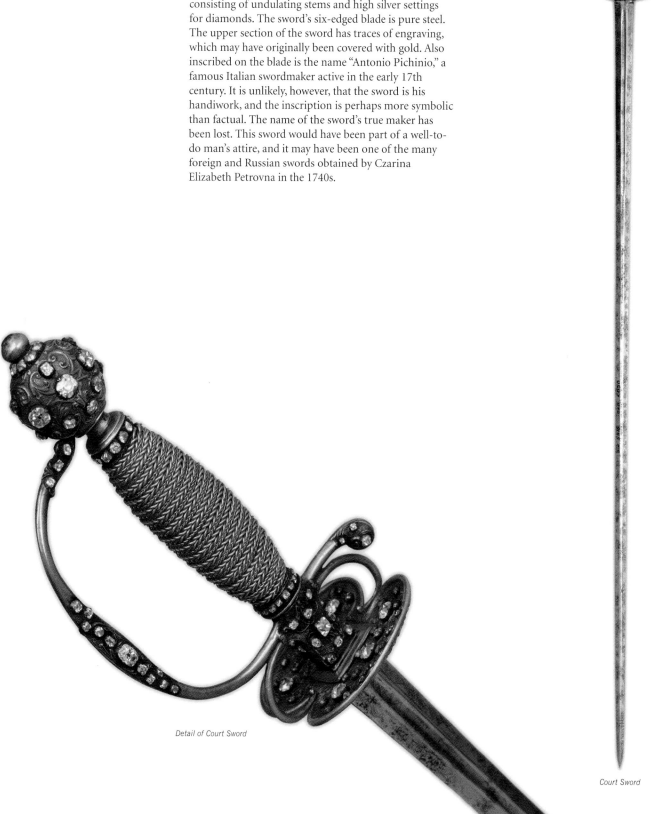

Detail of Court Sword

Court Sword

Hunting Knife and Sheath with Small Knife and Fork
1750s
Attributed to Germany
Steel, silver, jasper, wood, leather, forging
19.7 inches (50 cm) total length of hunting knife, 15.4 inches (39 cm) length of scabbard (excluding handle), 6.7 inches (17 cm) length of small knife, 6.3 inches (16 cm) length of fork
OR-385/1-4

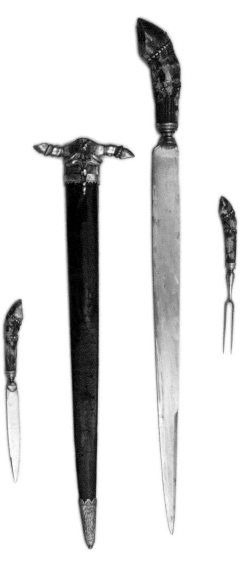

Hunting Knife and Sheath with Small Knife and Fork

HUNTING KNIFE AND SHEATH WITH SMALL KNIFE AND FORK

During the second half of the 18th century, royal hunting trips were more like theatrical events, and sidearms became one of the main decorative props—style prized over the performance of the weapon. An indispensable ceremonial hunting weapon, for both men and women, was the knife. The hunting knife was smaller than the dagger in size.

This hunting garniture consists of a large knife, a sheath, and a small knife and fork. All their handles are made out of jasper in the form of deer's hooves. The blades of the large and small knives, as well as the fork, are made of steel. The mouth and tip of the sheath are gilded-silver, decorated with engraving. The mouth of the sheath is quite original; on top of the mouth is soldered a cross with ends shaped like miniature deer's hooves. The construction of these items is similar to that of hunting weapons made in the 16th–18th centuries in the region of Saxony (North Germany).

Detail of Hunting Knife and Sheath

139

Saber and Scabbard of the Grand Duke Alexander Pavlovich
Late 18th century
St. Petersburg, Russia
Maker of blade: Master Hadji Sanfar
16th century
Turkey
Damask steel, wood, silver, snakeskin, gold inlay, leather, cornelian, forging, gold inlay, gilding, casting, carving on the blade
40 inches (101 cm) length of saber, 33.1 inches (84 cm) length of blade
OR-4458/1-2

SABER AND SCABBARD OF THE GRAND DUKE ALEXANDER PAVLOVICH

This saber is a unique example of the Russian weaponry and decorative art of the second half of the 18th century. It was presented by Catherine the Great as a gift to her favorite grandson, Grand Duke Alexander Pavlovich, the future Emperor Alexander I.

The following Arab inscriptions are damascened in gold on the blade: "The Year of Sultan Suleiman 957 [1540-1541]"; "There is no God but Allah"; "God the Almighty"; and "Allah Saves the Supplicant." The word "Prosperity" is repeated three times along the blunt edge of the saber. On the sharp edge, using the same damascening technique, the following inscription appears in Greek: "God Save and Protect Me In My Humble Struggle; Take This Weapon and Shield and Succor Hercules."

The decoration of the saber hilt and scabbard is executed in the classical style. The handle of the hilt shows two male figures bound in chains inside a frame of military trophies. Rising above them is a female figure carved from cornelian. The cross-guard features interwoven serpents— symbols of justice. In the center of the cross-guard, on one side is a portrayal of the Greek goddess of victory, Nike, with a wreath in her hand, and on the other a figure of a lamenting woman. The most remarkable feature of the sword's decoration is the use of engraved gems, possibly taken from the famous collection of Catherine the Great, which was kept in the Hermitage. The front of the handle of the hilt contains two carved gems: one portraying the Roman Emperor Augustus, and the other, on the reverse, portraying Alexander the Great; these symbolized the future role of Grand Duke Alexander Pavlovich as Emperor of Russia. Catherine the Great viewed Alexander as her successor, rather than her son, the future Emperor Paul I.

The scabbard is faced with green snakeskin and is reminiscent of the scabbards of ancient Roman swords. The silver mouth, hoops, and chape are decorated with depictions of military accoutrements. A silver-gilt band of laurels runs along both edges of the scabbard.

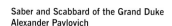

Detail of Saber

Saber and Scabbard of the Grand Duke Alexander Pavlovich

HUNTING DAGGER

he hunting dagger, a short-bladed knife, appeared in ussia only after the royal hunting expeditions were formed under the rule of Peter I. The one seen below n the left) belonged to the collection of Empress Anna anovna, though it is unlikely that she ever used it. Its raight single-edged blade is forged from steel. The per part is decorated with free ornamental engraving imitation of Damascus steel. In the center, in Latin, is e circular inscription, "Pamplona," the name of the city d then-capital of the Spanish Province—and quite ssibly the place of the dagger's maker. The handle is ade of deer antlers.

HUNTING DAGGER

This dagger (on the right), from the St. Petersburg Imperial collection, was made after 1741 for either Elizabeth Petrovna or Catherine the Great. The single-edged blade of the dagger has a double-edged tip and a faintly visible, asymmetrical central border. The upper part of the blade is decorated with an ornamental foliate pattern on a wavy background, while the surface of the background is gilded. The dagger's handle is made of steel. The handle has a smooth polished surface, decorated with diamonds, steel balls, buttons, and a carved stylized foliate design.

Hunting Dagger (left)
18th century
Western Europe
Blade: Attributed to Spain
Steel, copper, deer horn, forging, engraving, carving
31.9 inches (81 cm) total length, 25.9 inches (66 cm) length of blade
OR-3960

Hunting Dagger (right)
18th century
Western Europe
Steel, forging, engraving, gilding, carving
28.3 inches (72 cm) total length, 24 inches (61 cm) length of blade
OR-3956

Hunting Dagger

Hunting Dagger

Carbine with Flintlock (left and middle)
1780s
Master Gavril Permianov
St. Petersburg, Russia
Iron, wood, silver, horn, forging, carving,
burnishing, engraving, gold inlay
38.2 inches (97 cm) length of carbine,
14.4 mm caliber
OR-2171/1-2

Light Flintlock Rifle (right)
1780
Master Gavril Permianov
St. Petersburg, Russia
Iron, silver, horn, forging, engraving,
burnishing, gold inlay, gilding, carving
41.4 inches (105.2 cm) length of rifle,
6 mm caliber
OR-2152/1-2

GROUP OF FIVE WEAPONS MADE IN ST. PETERSBURG

This group of five weapons was used by the Russian
court for different aspects of the hunt during the 18th
century. The carbine with flintlock (directly below) as
well as the large-gauge, longer-barrelled shotgun with
flintlock (third from right) were used for hunting big
game and sport. Because of its size, the light flintlock
rifle (fourth from right) was probably made for a woman
or child. It is possible that this was the gun of Alexander
Pavlovich, the grandson of Catherine II and future
Emperor Alexander I. These three weapons were made in
St. Petersburg by Master Gavril Permianov.

The pair of weapons on the far right consist of a rifle an
musket. The rifle differs from the flintlock rifle in that it
has a longer barrel and a smaller caliber. This type of rif
had greater accuracy and distance. The musket, a rifle
with a barrel that ends in a wide mouth, was best suited
for hunting birds. These two rifles were the product of a
different St. Petersburg gunmaker, Master Johann Adolp
Grekke, but they were equally well-crafted and beautiful

Detail of Carbine with Flintlock

Carbine with Flintlock

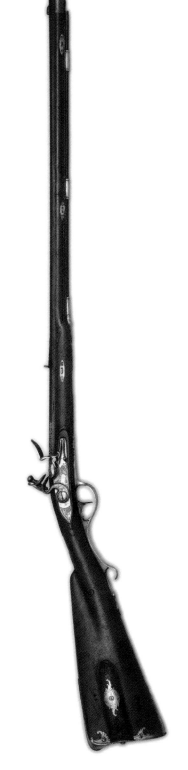

Light Flintlock Rifle

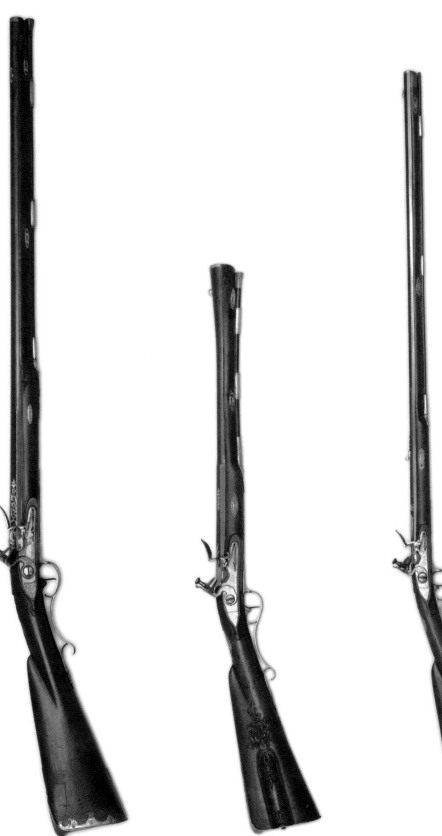

Shotgun with Striking Flintlock (left)
1780
Master Gavril Permianov
St. Petersburg, Russia
Iron, steel, silver, wood, horn, engraved inlay, burnishing
47.1 inches (119.6 cm) length of shotgun, 18 mm caliber
OR-50007/1-2

Musket (middle)
1770s–1790s
Master Johann Adolph Grekke
St. Petersburg, Russia
Iron, steel, silver, forging, bone, engraving, gold inlay, gilding, wood carving
35.4 inches (90 cm) length of rifle, 19.8 inches (50.3 cm) length of barrel, 57 mm x 33 mm caliber
OR-4895/1-2

Rifle (right)
1783
Master Johann Adolph Grekke
St. Petersburg, Russia
Iron, steel, wood, silver, horn, forging, engraving, burnishing, gilding
42 inches (106.7 cm) length of rifle, 5 mm caliber
OR-2175

Shotgun with Striking Flintlock   *Musket*   *Rifle*

Long-barreled Hunting Rifle with Flintlock
Mid-18th century
Tula, Russia
Iron, steel, wood, forging, engraving, embossing, carving, gilding
56.7 inches (144 cm) total length, 15 mm caliber
OR-1120

Pair of Pistols
Mid-18th century
Tula, Russia
Iron, wood, forging, engraving, drop-forging, gilding, flat chasing
Top Pistol: 17.3 inches (43.9 cm) total length, 11.3 inches (28.8 cm) length of barrel; 15 mm caliber
Bottom Pistol: 17.3 inches (43.9 cm) total length, 11.3 inches (28.7 cm) length of barrel; 15 mm caliber
OR-2996/1-2

LONG-BARRELED HUNTING RIFLE WITH FLINTLOCK & PAIR OF PISTOLS

During the reign of Empress Elizabeth Petrovna, guns made in the city of Tula were considered the most prestigious weapons of their kind by the Russian aristocracy. Guns from Tula, which were influenced by the trends of decorative gun-making in France, were valued for their excellent workmanship and fine appointments.

The exquisite rifle and pair of pistols seen here hail from Tula and were designed as a hunting set. The main part of the barrel of the rifle is made out of one piece. The locks of the rifle and the pair of pistols are covered with high relief engraving of stylized plant ornamentation on a gold embossed background, while the stock of the rifle and the handles of the pistols are made from walnut wood.

The provenance of this set is interesting. All three items were fabricated before 1745 and given to the Russian Foreign Ministry that same year as gifts to be presented to the proposed Embassy of Iran, but the embassy was never realized, and in 1747 the guns entered into Empress Elizabeth's Cabinet in 1747. In 1757 Empress Elizabeth gave the guns to Count Ivan Ivanovich Shuvalov to use while hunting with the Empress, though they remained in her private arsenal.

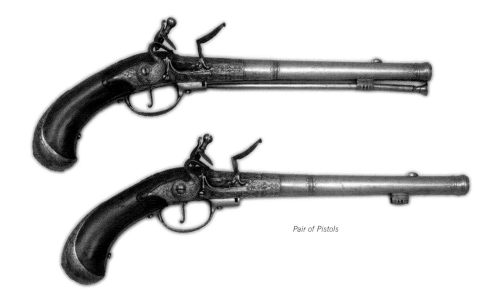

Pair of Pistols

Long-barreled Hunting Rifle with Flintlock

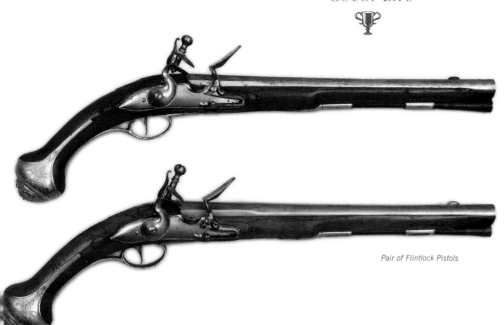

Pair of Flintlock Pistols

AIR OF FLINTLOCK PISTOLS

he pair of flintlock pistols above came from the
eapons collection of Czarina Anna Ivanovna. Though
uite simple in composition, they are extravagant in
ecoration. The pistols were made by Johann Christoph
Iling, a Swede, who was employed in Moscow for four
ears as the Czarina's head court-craftsman. Although
ese pistols were considered officer's weapons, they were
so used for hunting, a favorite pastime of the Czarina's.

hese pistols, along with various weapons belonging to
eter I and Peter II, were part of the original collection
hich, from the 1730s onward, was called the Imperial
Veapons Hall. From 1733 to 1735, Anna Ivanovna's
ollection of weapons was moved to St. Petersburg and
laced in a small house belonging to the Czarevich Alexei
etrovich.

UNTING RIFLE WITH FLINTLOCK

his elegant hunting rifle with a burnished Spanish-style
arrel, is imprinted with the mark of the famous Madrid
aster Diego Venture. In the 1740s and 50s the barrel
ork of the Spanish gun makers was extremely sought-
ter in Russia. The flintlock of this rifle is done in the
rench style. On the flintlock-side, in high-relief carving

with a gilded background, is the inscription "St.
Petersburg: Peter Lebedev." The short forearm and butt-
stock is decorated in relief carvings with a stylized
ornamental design. On the other side of the flintlock, in
the same technique, is a rendering of a wild boar hunt.

This weapon belonged to the personal collection of
Empress Elizabeth Petrovna, who was a passionate
hunter. The gun's maker, Peter Lebedev, who was still an
apprentice in the 1740s, eventually became the head of
the royal court's weapons workshop and served in this
role until the 1760s.

✛

PAIR OF FLINTLOCK PISTOLS

These superb pistols featured below were made in Tula in
the mid-18th century, the "golden era" of Russian
decorative gunsmithing. The Tula craftsmen often found
inspiration in the richly decorated hunting weapons of
France and Germany, imbuing their works with
extraordinary qualities, which included the liberal use of
gilding on the barrels, magnificent relief carvings of
foliate design, military accoutrements, wild beasts, birds,
shells, and scrolls. The monogram of Czarina Elizabeth
Petrovna is visible on the barrels of the pistols; on the
breech is the inscription "Tula 1750."

Hunting Rifle with Flintlock

Pair of Flintlock Pistols (above left)
First half of the 18th century
Johann Christoph Illing
St. Petersburg, Russia
Iron, wood, copper, horn, forging, casting,
engraving, gilding, carving
Top Pistol: 20.9 inches (53.1 cm) total
length, 13.1 inches (33.4 cm) length of
barrel; 14 mm caliber
Bottom Pistol: 20.6 inches (52.3 cm)
total length, 13.1 inches (33.4 cm)
length of barrel; 14 mm caliber
OR-3033/1-2, OR-3034/1-2

Hunting Rifle with Flintlock (above right)
Mid-18th century
Master Peter Lebedev
St. Petersburg, Russia
Iron, steel, wood, forging, engraving,
burnishing, embossing, gilding, carving
58.3 inches (148 cm) total length
43.3 inches (110 cm) length of barrel
OR-2373/1-2

Pair of Flintlock Pistols (left)
1750s
Tula, Russia
Iron, steel, wood, silver, forging, gilding,
carving
18.1 inches (46 cm) total length of each
OR-2772, OR-2773

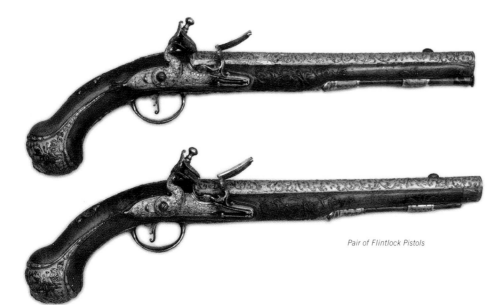

Pair of Flintlock Pistols

Garden Carriage of Empress Anna Ivanovna
1739
Moscow, Russia
Velvet: 20th century, Moscow
Carriage: oak, heavy cloth, copper
Painting: oil, gilt along the brackets
10.2 feet (3.1 meters) length, 4.6 feet
(1.4 meters) width, 4.9 feet (1.5 meters)
height
K-3

GARDEN CARRIAGE OF EMPRESS ANNA IVANOVNA

This extremely rare two-seated carriage with a driver's seat was designed and used for casual trips around the palace gardens. This is evident from its light and compact construction; in addition, the wheels are set close together but with wide wheel-frames, so as not to dig too deeply into the garden paths.

In both shape and décor, the carriage exhibits elements of the baroque style. It is decorated with gilt brackets and relief carving in the form of shells and foliate scrolls. The panels of the body bear renderings of the Russian crest and a female figure on a green background, which, judging from the iconography, represents the Empress Anna Ivanovna. The interior of the carriage was originally lined with green broadcloth, and later replaced in the 20th century with velvet.

Garden Carriage of Empress Anna Ivanovna

SNUFF BOX

Europeans were introduced to tobacco at the end of the 15th century after Christopher Columbus discovered the New World. Boxes made from horn, bone, or wood were used to store the tobacco, but by the end of the 17th century, precious metals and stones were also employed in creating them. The peak of the fashion for snuff boxes was reached in the 18th century during the Age of Rococo. They were often given as gifts and sometimes had portraits or historical scenes painted onto the lids.

The most prestigious snuff boxes were made of gold and, in the middle of the 18th century, of colored gold from France; this soft metal allowed for intricate relief embossing. The lid was created by French masters and is decorated with a portrait of Empress Elizabeth Petrovna in a crown with the medal of St. Andrew the First Called. The body of the box is decorated with allegories of war, sea voyage, art, and science.

REMOVABLE HANDLE FOR A CANE

Removable handles for canes in the 18th century were sometimes made to match snuff boxes in similar materials and motifs. The everyday objects of aristocratic families in both Europe and Russia were often extremely luxurious and frequently arrived from distant, exotic countries such as India, China, Africa, and the New World. It was fashionable, in some Russian quarters, to retain a young Arab boy as a house servant. This handle is decorated with an Arab lad emerging from the mouth of an enormous gold fish.

Snuff Box

Snuff Box
1757–1758
Paris, France
Gold, silver, diamonds, casting, embossing
3.4 x 2 x 1.7 inches (8.7 cm x 5 cm x 4.2 cm)
MZ-1904

Removable Handle for a Cane
Mid-18th century
Paris, France
Agate, gold, precious stones, iron, carving, casting, embossing
4.6 inches (11.7 cm) width, 4.4 inches (11.2 cm) height
DK-841

Removable Handle for a Cane

Desk Set
Mid-18th century
France
Gold, silver, precious and semi-precious stones, mother-of-pearl, steel, mirror, embossing, casting, carving, flat chasing, stone carving
Box: 3.1 inches (7.8 cm) length, 2.4 inches (6.0 cm) width, 1.9 inches (4.8 cm) height
MZ-4128

Dagger and Sheath
18th century
India
Steel, gold, jade, wood, precious stones, forging, carving, inlay work
15 inches (38 cm) total length, 10.2 inches (26 cm) length of blade
OR-3888/1-3

Telescope
First quarter of the 18th century
Western Europe
Heliotrope, gold, silver, precious stones, glass, carving, embossing, casting
4.2 inches (10.6 cm) length, 1.1–.75 inches (2.8 cm–1.9 cm) diameter
DK-1429

Desk Set

Dagger and Sheath

DESK SET

Portable desk sets in the form of small boxes came into use in Russia in the 18th century. They contained an array of writing instruments, including ink, brushes, blotters, scissors, and a needle for sewing sheets of paper together. Each of these objects—and the case itself—was the creation of a master craftsman. Dark semi-precious stones were the most popular decorative materials for the sets and served as a contrast to the gold ornamental designs, which depicted subjects like ocean waves and sea shells. Exotic scenes from far-off countries and folkloric costumes were also common motifs in Europe and Russia in the mid-18th century.

DAGGER AND SHEATH

Fancy imported articles were highly prized as works of art, expensive toys, and collectibles, brought to Russia as gifts from ambassadors and merchants, or as souvenirs from world travelers. The interiors of the Czar's Palace were filled with exotica from India, Turkey, Iran, China,

Japan, and Indonesia, including hundreds of knives and swords housed in the Kremlin Armory. The most precious of these was a large group of traditional Indian swords and knives made in the 17th and 18th centuries, to which this dagger belonged.

The dagger has a double-edged blade forged from Damascus steel, which gives it a light gray patina. The handle, mouth, and tip of the sheath are carved from light green nephrite. The unknown Indian master covered the handle with stylized ornamentation inlaid with gold and red rubies. The body of the sheath is made of wood and covered with gold leaves using the stylized technique known as basma which created a stunning interwoven foliate motif.

TELESCOPE

Heliotrope, the material used for this telescope, was very fashionable during the Age of Rococo. Set onto the heliotrope is a stylized floral motif with gold rosettes and precious stones. When theater-going emerged as a national pastime, these tiny telescopes became de rigueur. They were ordered from the best jewelers and were often given as gifts.

Telescope

Medallion with the Hair of Empress Elizabeth Petrovna

MEDALLION WITH THE HAIR OF EMPRESS ELIZABETH PETROVNA

This small two-sided glass medallion is enclosed with a gold frame. Inside, on a birch disk is a lock of light brown hair belonging to Elizabeth Petrovna, daughter of Peter the Great. In the upper part of the medallion in French is the inscription "Empress Elizabeth." In addition to this medallion, five others were created with the hair of Peter I, his grandfather Czar Mikhail Feodorovich, his father Czar Alexei Mikhailovich, his daughter Anna Petrovna, and his grandson Czar Peter II.

POCKET WATCH ON A WATCH FOB

From the moment of its appearance in the 16th century, the pocket watch served not only as a time piece but also as an item of great decorative value. In the 18th century, watches became a luxury item. They were round and made of expensive metals and semi-precious stones. Since the 1740s, heliotrope, which contrasted with the gold ornament and was in the spirit of the Rococo, was a favorite material. In the 18th century, watches were most often worn on fobs—chains of flat links with a wide hook. This special chain was worn on a man's robe or woman's dress together with other precious charms.

Medallion with the Hair of Empress Elizabeth Petrovna
Late 18th century-early 19th century
Russia
Gold, glass, hair, birch bark, engraving
1.9 x 1.7 inches (4.9 cm x 4.4 cm)
F-1820

Pocket Watch on a Watch Fob
First half of the 18th century
England
Heliotrope, gold, silver, diamonds, metal, glass, carving, embossing, engraving
Watch: 1.9 x 1.9 inches (4.8 cm x 4.8 cm)
Watch fob: 5.1 inches (13 cm) length
MZ-4121/1-2

Pocket Watch on a Watch Fob

Portrait of Emperor Paul I

PORTRAIT OF EMPEROR PAUL I

This portrait of Emperor Paul I is a reproduction of a painting by V. L. Borovikovsky, done in 1800 for the conference hall of the St. Petersburg Academy of Art. The original painting was meant to commemorate Paul I as the master of the Order of St. John of Jerusalem (also known as the Knights of Malta) in 1798.

This idealized painting is essentially a coronation portrait, and includes all the official symbols of power. Paul I is depicted in all his glory and might. A crown of diamonds on his head, he wears a dalmatic—the ancient clothing of the Byzantine emperors—and is posed near the throne. The traditional set of ceremonial objects accompany him: an orb on a velvet pillow and a scepter in his right hand.

Paul's troubled childhood and his estrangement from his mother, Catherine II (the Great), made him irritable and suspicious of the people around him. (He is often referred to as "the Russian Hamlet.") Catherine II wished to keep Paul off the throne in favor of her grandson, Alexander, Paul's oldest son. Paul, independently of his mother's wishes, continued to work on his political campaign and on restructuring Catherine the Great's rights of succession. Upon Catherine's death, he declared himself emperor.

Portrait of Emperor Paul I
1844
Unknown Artist
Russia
Oil on canvas
122.4 x 79.1 inches (311 cm x 201 cm)
N-1971

THRONE AND FOOTSTOOL OF EMPEROR PAUL I

Russian thrones stood on a high stepped dais beneath a canopy and were often the only piece of furniture in an enormous state room. Particular attention was paid to the construction and decoration of thrones, and often they were designed by the most important architects of the time. Six identical thrones were commissioned by Paul I based upon the throne made in England for the Empress Anna Ivanovna. Unlike the original, which is silver, these six thrones were made of gilded wood by the court furnisher Christian Meier. Documents show that they were commissioned in 1797.

Two of the six thrones have survived to this day. One is kept in St. Petersburg at the Hermitage, and the other, on display here, is in the Moscow Armory. The velvet back of this throne is decorated with an opulent gold-embroidered rendering of the Russian state crest with a Maltese cross, which became part of the state insignia by order of Paul I in 1799.

Throne and Footstool of Emperor Paul I

Throne and Footstool of Emperor Paul I
1790s
Russia
Birch, velvet, gold embroidery
71.7 inches (182 cm) height, 33.9 inches (86 cm) width
R-36

Horse Cloth (*Caparison*)
Late 18th century
St. Petersburg Tapestry Manufactory
St. Petersburg, Russia
Wool thread, silk, canvas, embroidery, weaving
6. 3 feet x 4.9 feet (193 cm x 150 cm)
TK-1473

Officer's Dress Uniform, Camisole, Pants, Hat, Boots and Gloves of Emperor Paul I
1796-1797
Russia
Dress Uniform: cloth, velvet, gold, silver, linen, weaving, embroidery, enamel, wool; 43.3 inches (110 cm) length
Camisole: cloth, canvas, copper, weaving, gilding; 29.1 inches (74 cm) length
Pants: buckskin, ribbon, bone, weaving; 43.3 inches (110 cm) length
Hat: felt, leather, linen, feathers, lace, gold thread, weaving, braiding; 22.4 inches (57 cm) circumference
Boots: leather, steel; 22.4 inches (57 cm)
Gloves: buckskin; 11.8 inches (30 cm) length
TK-3018, TK-3019, TK-1939, TK-1552, TK-1907/1-2, TK-212/1-2

Horse Cloth (Caparison)

Officer's Dress Uniform of Emperor Paul I

HORSE CLOTH (*CAPARISON*)

The monogram of Emperor Paul I and the Russian national crest with a white Maltese cross at the center are embroidered onto this horse cloth. This representation of the crest, introduced by personal order of Paul I on August 10, 1799, was official for less than two years. In April of 1801, Paul's successor, Alexander I, resurrected the former state crest without the Maltese cross.

The formal nature of the horse cloth suggests that it was used for court parades, and it could be that this very cloth was featured in the ceremonial meeting between the nephew of Paul I and Prince Eugene of Württemberg, who came to Russia at the beginning of 1800.

Production at the St. Petersburg Tapestry Manufactory, where this horse cloth was made, was at its height in the second half of the 18th century. At that time, more than 150 craftsmen and craftswomen worked there. They had an astounding command of the intricacies of tapestry weaving, as well as of embroidery techniques that imitated weaving. The decoration around the border of the horse cloth, for instance, imitates the border design of a tapestry carpet and are embroidered in silk thread, using cross, satin, and Gobelin stitching.

OFFICER'S DRESS UNIFORM, CAMISOLE, PANTS, HAT, BOOTS AND GLOVES OF EMPEROR PAUL I

The coronation of Paul I took place on April 5, 1797. Paul was the first of the Russian monarchs to appear in full military uniform. He wore a dress uniform from the Preobrazhensky regiment, the first of two regiments of the Russian military guard. His dress coat is made from green cloth with a green wool lining. This style of officer's coat was worn by all the members of this regiment from November 1797 until late 1798. On the left side of the chest are pinned two silver, gold and enamel stars—the orders of St. Andrew the First Called and St. Vladimir. A camisole was generally worn under the dress coat and was made from white material and buttoned with eleven gilded bronze buttons. Two similar buttons were used to attach the pants to the vest with long leather straps. The only indication of the uniform's officer status was the white plume of feathers on the hat. The black felt hat is decorated with gold galloon on the edge, and the buttonholes are made with braided gold lace and the cockade is in the form of a many-pointed star made out of gold foil. The high narrow heels of the boots are made from black lacquered leather. White gloves with cuffs, sewn from kid leather, traditionally completed the officer's uniform.

PORTRAIT OF EMPEROR ALEXANDER I

This portrait of Alexander I, in an officer's uniform wearing the ribbon and star of St. Andrew the First Called, is similar to two particular ceremonial portraits of the Emperor, both of which were made to commemorate the victory over Napoleon's armies at the Battle of Waterloo. After the capitulation of Paris on March 18, 1814, and the removal of Napoleon from the throne on June 22, 1815, foreign troops entered Paris for a second time and liberated Europe. Having reached his ultimate objective, Alexander I, the leader of the coalition of the anti-Napoleonic forces, was represented in this ceremonial portrait in a highly romantic manner.

The portrait on display here is very similar to the two original versions painted in 1815. The first portrait was carried out in Paris by Napoleon's court painter, while the second one was ordered from the English painter Thomas Lawrence by King George IV of England, to honor all twenty-four leaders of the anti-Napoleonic coalition for the Waterloo Hall in England's Windsor Palace.

SNUFF BOX

Mounted on the lid of this gold snuff box is an oval cameo of white and pink agate with portraits of Emperor Alexander I and his wife Elizabeth Alexeyevna. Beneath the cameo is the inscription "Girometti." Around the cameo in black enamel on a camphor ground are written: "November 19, 1825" and "May 4, 1826." These are the respective dates of the deaths of Alexander I and Elizabeth Alexeyevna.

The snuff box was made by Johann Wilhelm Keibel, a court goldsmith. In 1826 Keibel made a small Imperial crown for the wife of Nicholas I and a number of order decorations and medals. Keibel's workshop continued in existence until 1910. The cameo is the work of the famed Italian stone engraver and medal-maker Giuseppe Girometti.

Portrait of Emperor Alexander I

Snuff Box

Portrait of Emperor Alexander I
19th century
Unknown Artist
Russia
Oil on canvas
39.4 x 27.6 inches (100 cm x 70 cm)
Zh-1951

Snuff Box
1826
Box: Master Johann Wilhelm Keibel
Cameo: Giuseppe Girometti
St. Petersburg, Russia
Gold, enamel, agate, carving, flat chasing
1.2 x 3.5 x 2.4 inches (3 cm x 9 cm x 6 cm)
MR-642

Dessert Plate Depicting "The Kidnapping of Ganymede" (right)
From the "Olympic Service"
1804-1807
J. Jorge
Sèvres Porcelain Manufactory
France
Porcelain, paint, covering, gilding
9.3 inches (23.5 cm) diameter
F-202

Dessert Plate Depicting "Clio, the Muse of History" (bottom left)
From the "Olympic Service"
1804-1807
J. Jorge
Sèvres Porcelain Manufactory
France
Porcelain, paint, covering, gilding
9.3 inches (23.5 cm) diameter
F-206

Dessert Plate Depicting "Hercules Killing the Amazon Queen Hippolyte" (bottom right)
From the "Olympic Service"
1804-1807
J. Jorge
Sèvres Porcelain Manufactory
France
Porcelain, paint, covering, gilding
9.3 inches (23.5 cm) diameter
F-200

"The Kidnapping of Ganymede"

"Clio, the Muse of History"

"Hercules Killing the Amazon Queen Hippolyte"

ECTED ITEMS FROM THE "OLYMPIC SERVICE"

e Olympic Service was one of the most beautiful
vice sets created by France's legendary Sèvres
rcelain Manufactory. This service, totaling 166 pieces
1 including tea service for 16 people and 31 vases for
le decorations, was completed in the beginning of the
h century. It was created by the order of Napoleon I
the period from 1804 to 1807 and was to be used at
wedding of his brother Jerome to a German princess.

is group—each one extravagantly decorated and
ished—of three plates, a server, sugar bowl, and vase
s part of the dessert service, the most interesting parts
which are the 69 dessert plates, three of which are on
play here. The decorations for these plates were taken
m ancient Greek mythology, hence the name of the
vice. The myths depicted are of a moralistic nature
d relate thematically to family bliss and love. Such
dding gifts were traditionally passed down from
eration to generation, but this particular service had
ifferent fate. Napoleon gave the set—as both a gift
d a token of friendship—to Alexander I, to honor a
aty between Russia and France. Alexander I was said
have been weary of the gift. For the first 25 years, the
vice was located at the Winter Palace in St.
ersburg, but in 1832, by order of Nicholas I, the
vice was moved to Moscow.

Dessert Server

Dessert Server (left)
From the "Olympic Service"
1804-1807
J. Jorge
Sèvres Porcelain Manufactory
France
Porcelain, paint, covering, gilding,
sculpted patterning
7.2 inches (18.3 cm) height
F-181

Sugar Bowl with Lid (botom left) **and
Vase for Ice Cream Depicting "the Four
Elements"** (bottom right)
From the "Olympic Service"
1804-1807
J. Jorge
Sèvres Porcelain Manufactory
France
Porcelain, paint, covering, gilding,
sculpted patterning
Sugar Bowl: 9.4 inches (24 cm) height,
8.9 inches (22.5 cm) diameter
Vase: 11.8 inches (30 cm) height, 8.5
inches (21.5 cm) diameter
F-218/1-2 , F-92/1-3

Sugar Bowl with Lid

Vase for Ice Cream

Portrait of Emperor Nicholas I
19th century
Workshop of Franz Kruger
Russia
Oil on canvas
39.4 x 27.6 inches (100 cm x 70 cm)
Zh-2000

Plate (below foreground)
1843-61
The Kornilov Brothers Factory
St. Petersburg, Russia
Porcelain, glaze, gilding, overglazing
11 inches (28 cm) diameter
F-434

Plate (below background)
1893
Imperial Porcelain Factory
St. Petersburg, Russia
Porcelain, glaze, gilding, painting
8.7 inches (22 cm) diameter
F-731

Portrait of Emperor Nicholas I

PORTRAIT OF EMPEROR NICHOLAS I

In this painting, Nicholas I, standing against a cloudy s. is presented in a uniform of the cavalry regiment with Order of St. Andrew the First Called, the Order of St. Vladimir, and the English Order of the Garter. In the tradition of the Russian court, the highest state award of Imperial Russia was the title of Head of the Cavalry. Th title was granted to Nicholas I in 1796, soon after his birth. In the background of the portraits is a soldier an horse of the Russian army and a group of Cossacks in hats.

This portrait of Nicholas I is attributed to the worksho of the famed artist Franz Kruger, the court painter of th Prussian King Frederick William III. Kruger was knowr as a master of ceremonial portraits and mass scenes. In 1832, the artist was summoned by Nicholas I from Berl to St. Petersburg, where he quickly gained favor with th Czar and his family, who valued Kruger's smooth, preci technique. The artist made numerous portraits of Nicholas I.

In 1844 Nicholas I visited London, and to commemora his trip, Queen Victoria commissioned a portrait of herself for the Russian ruler, who, in turn, chose Kruger to create his portrait. The original painting, on which this version is based, can be seen in England, at Windsc Palace.

SELECTED ITEMS FROM THE KREMLIN SERVICE

The Kremlin Service was commissioned by Emperor Nicholas I for the Great Kremlin Palace, and productio was commenced by the Imperial Porcelain Factory in 1839. Intended for use at the most important state banquets, the service was extraordinary for the numbe of pieces it contained (nearly 1,000 articles total). At th behest of the Emperor, it was designed by F. G. Solntse a gifted decorative artist, archaeologist, researcher, and expert in Russian art.

The Kremlin Service represents the first attempt to app the Russian Historical style to porcelain. Well-versed ir the Armory's collection, Solntsev took as the basis for h design some of the finest examples of the decorative ar of the 17th century. The model for the decoration of th dinner service, for example, was a pitcher from the washbasin set of Czarina Natalia Kirillovna, which was made of gold and decorated with colored enamel and precious stones. As a result, the pieces in the dinner service were richly gilded, painted in bright colors, and decorated in a way that imitates the chasing of the gold and the sparkle of the stones and enamel in the origina The three plates, cup and saucer, vase, and stand seen here illustrate the success of the artist in lending to porcelain the beauty of gold.

The Kremlin Service was in use from the moment it wa fired, and as pieces wore down or broke, it became necessary to replace them. For much of the second half of the 19th century, replacements and additions to the service were undertaken by the private firm of The Kornilov Brothers, whose works were lauded for the hi

Plates from the Kremlin Service

Plate and Cup with Saucer from the Kremlin Service

Plate and Cup with Saucer from the Kremlin Service (left)
Designed by F.G. Solntsev
Imperial Porcelain Factory
St. Petersburg, Russia
Plate: First half of the 19th century
Porcelain, glaze, gilding, painting
9.4 inches (24 cm) diameter
Cup and saucer: 1892
Porcelain, glaze, gilding, painting
Cup: 2.4 inches (6 cm) height, 3.5
inches (9 cm) diameter
Saucer: 5.3 inches (13.5 cm) diameter
F-856, F-879, F-838

Vase from the Kremlin Service (bottom left)
Designed by F. G. Solntsev
1901
Imperial Porcelain Factory
St. Petersburg, Russia
Porcelain, glaze, gilding, painting
7.1 inches (18 cm) height, 9.3 inches
(23.5 cm) diameter
F-916

Sweetmeat Stand from the Kremlin Service (below)
1839
Designed by F. G. Solntsev
St. Petersburg, Russia
Imperial Porcelain Factory
Porcelain, bronze, glaze, painting,
gliding, stamping, casting
19.7 inches (50 cm) height
F-996

Sweetmeat Stand from the Kremlin Service

Vase from the Kremlin Service

ﬁality of their materials and the skillful elegance of their
ﬁish.

̖ creating the service in this Russian Historical style,
ﬁlntsev did not confine himself to the use of
ﬁtiquarian ornamentation. Solntsev used traditional
ﬁapes of metalware alongside more typical shapes for
ﬁrcelain. The small vase (near right) in this exhibition is
ﬁsed on a 17th-century *rassolnik* vase , which was a
ﬁallow cup on top of a long, graceful stem. The vase's
ﬁinted decoration of palm branches and roses matches
ﬁat of the table and dessert services.

Flask
1891
Firm of Garrard
London, England
Silver, casting, base metal, engraving,
embossing, overglazing
30.5 inches (77.5 cm) height
MZ-720

Two-handled Cup with Lid
1902
Firm of Garrard
London, England
Silver, casting, gilding, embossing
15.2 inches (38.5 cm) height
MZ-3984/1-2

FLASK

The silver body of this large flask is decorated with a band of ovoli in relief around its stout lower half; two bacchanalian masks are embossed on each side and are connected to the large cap of the flask by chains. Engraved on the front of the body is the two-headed eagle of the Russian Empire, with the inscription: "To Emperor Alexander III and Empress Maria Feodorovna, on the occasion of their silver wedding." On the back is another inscription listing the names of members of the Danish and English royal families.

It was traditional in European silverwork of the turn of the 20th century to reflect forms from previous epochs. This flask is a copy of an early 18th-century vessel, based on the leather water canteens used by pilgrims in the Middle Ages.

Flask

Two-handled Cup with Lid

TWO-HANDLED CUP WITH LID

The smooth body of this cup is decorated with applied scroll cartouches, flower festoons, vines, and small masks of lions and satyrs. The royal insignia of Great Britain is engraved on one side beneath a crown, and the two-headed eagle crest of the Russian Empire on the other. Engraved on the lower part of the body is the inscription "To His Imperial Highness, The Czarevich, Hereditary Grand Duke Alexei Nikolaievich, on the occasion of his christening, August 1904. From his affectionate great-uncle and godfather, King Edward VII."

The cover of the cup is crowned with a stylized pineapple finial, and is decorated with tiny masks, flowers, and bunches of grapes; around the base of the cover are cartouches containing an eagle, salamander, serpent, and fish symbolizing the four elements—air, earth, fire, and water.

The cup has its roots in English silverwork of the 18th century, with its characteristic bell shape, tall cover with finial, and the combination of engraving and cast decoration in relief on a smooth polished ground.

Miniature Portrait of Nicholas II
Late 19th-early 20th century
Unknown Artist
Russia
Silver, enamel
4.7 x 3.7 inches (12 x 9.3 cm)
MR-9066

Miniature Portrait of Nicholas II

MINIATURE PORTRAIT OF NICHOLAS II

This miniature enamel portrait of Emperor Nicholas II represents him in an officer's uniform festooned with the ribbon and star of St. Andrew the First Called, the cross of St. Vladimir, various medals commemorating the coronation of his father, Alexander III, and two foreign orders—the Order of Daneborg (with the Danish state crest) and the Greek Order of the Savior. At the bottom of the gold tromp l'oeil frame is Nicholas's monogram, and positioned at the top is a rendering of the Russian Imperial crown. This miniature was originally located in the Grand Kremlin Palace, but is today located in the Kremlin Armory.

Fabergé Box

(Facing Page)
Fabergé Box
1903
Firm of Carl Fabergé
St. Petersburg, Russia
Silver, engraving, embossing, carving, gilding
11 x 6.6 x 10.6 inches (28 cm x 16.8 cm x 27 cm)
MP-5649

FABERGÉ BOX

This box (seen at left, and in detail below) was a gift to Nicholas II from the Ulansky Guards; it is inscribed with the mark of the firm Fabergé. The box was made to commemorate the hundred-year anniversary of the Ulansky Guards. The original members of this regiment were great princes; in 1849 Alexander II was named their leader. This tradition was adhered to by Alexander III and Nicholas II. The rectangular shape of this box is similar to a Renaissance trunk, finely and expertly ornamentated.

Detail of Fabergé Box

(Facing Page)
**Masquerade Costume of Emperor
Nicholas II**
Caftan and Belt: 1903, St. Petersburg,
Russia
Cufflinks and buttons: Second half of the
17th century, Turkey
Precious stones, gold thread, enamel,
carving, embroidery, brocade
55.9 inches (142 cm) length of caftan
TK-2921, TK-2922, TK-2923

**Hat from the Masquerade Costume of
Emperor Nicholas II**
1903
St. Petersburg, Russia
Brocade, silk, leather, gold, precious
stones, canvas, pearls, embroidery, fur,
weaving, casting, enamel, engraving,
embossing
7 inches (17.7 cm) height
TK-2924

Hat from the Masquerade Costume of Emperor Nicholas II

ASQUERADE COSTUME AND HAT OF EMPEROR NICHOLAS II

n February 11, 1903 a spectacle was staged in the
perial Theater of the Hermitage, built for Catherine II.
l those invited, apart from foreign diplomats, were
essed in costumes from the time of Czar Alexei
ikhailovich. Two days later, a costume ball was held in
e Concert Hall of the Winter Palace for the Dowager
mpress Maria Feodorovna and Grand Duke Mikhail,
ho had not been able to attend the earlier occasion.

cholas II was dressed in a costume copying the "Parade
ess" of Czar Alexei Mikhailovich; the dress of Empress
exandra Feodorovna was a copy of the dress of Czarina
aria Ilinichna (born Miloslavskaya, the first wife of
exei Mikhailovich).

is believed that the designer of the costumes of the
perial couple for this "last court ball in the history of
e empire" was the Steward of the Royal Household and
rector of the Hermitage, I. A. Vsevolzhsky. The
stumes for this ball, including those of the Imperial
uple, were made in the Office of the Imperial Theaters
St. Petersburg. Velvet and satin, in the style of Italian
xtiles of the 17th century, were specially commissioned
om the factory of A. and V. Sapozhnikov in Moscow.
ecorations from ancient royal attire were brought from
e Armory. Nicholas II personally chose the decorations
r his costume, including pearl bracelets which had
elonged to Czar Feodor Ivanovich (who ruled from
84-1598).

n April 2, 1903, the Armory was presented with the
rts of the Emperor's costume that had been decorated
th authentic adornments from royal clothing of the
th and 17th centuries. These were an outer open-
ecked caftan with a figured turned-down collar and
ng sleeves with turned-back cuffs, decorated with gold
ce, gold adornments, and buttons with enamel and
recious stones; an inner caftan with a stand-up collar
d long narrow sleeves, decorated with jeweled studs
d buttons, pearl bracelets, and a belt with figured gold
ds; and a hat with a band of sable lined with gold
ds.

Masquerade Costume of Emperor Nicholas II

CHAPTER VII

Decoration Holidays:
Orders of Knights and Their Feast Days

Decoration Holidays:
Orders of Knights and Their Feast Days

by V.M. Nikitina

Detail of *Herald of the Order of the Great Martyr St. Catherine*
1797
Illustration

Imperial Russia in the 18th century gave birth to a new aspect of ceremonial life that did not exist in previous centuries: the creation of royal Orders of Knights and their accompanying feast days. The orders themselves were special marks of excellence conferred by the state, and were considered to be the highest awards of distinction. Feast days were traditionally celebrated after the induction ceremony.

In 1698 Peter the Great founded the first and highest order of the Russian Empire, that of St. Andrew the First Called. The draft statute of the order, drawn up in 1720 with Peter's participation, included specifications for the dress of the order and for the celebration of its feast days. The Czar adopted the idea of special feast days from Western Europe where, to this day, feast days of some of the oldest and most illustrious orders are celebrated annually.

DAMES & KNIGHTS

The newly established tradition demanded that Knights of the Order of St. Andrew the First Called gather twice a year: during the winter on St. Andrew's Day and during the summer on St. Peter's Day, whereupon they formed a procession and headed to the Church of St. Andrew. The knights wore solemn parade dress with the ordained cloak (called an *epancha*) of the order. Once inside the church, the knights took part in an earnest service of prayer, after which they held a bountiful feast paid for from the funds of the

order. The knights of the order also wore their parade uniforms when participating in important state ceremonies such as the wedding and christenings of members of the Imperial family.

In 1714, Peter the Great founded the highest female order, the Order of St. Catherine, which was rarely awarded throughout the 18th century. After the death of her husband, Catherine I made the first presentation, honoring seven courtiers as "Dames of the Order." Only during the reign of Catherine the Great was the award distributed more generously. Perhaps because the order was given rarely, official instructions concerning the dress for Dames of the Order have been so well-preserved. Initially, recipients, wearing parade court dresses, convened at court on St. Catherine's Day for the celebration of the feast day; by the 1750s, however, they appeared at the court of Elizabeth Petrovna in opulent dresses specially designed for the solemn ceremony. Order dresses were made of silver brocade with gold thread and velvet decorations in the shape of falbalas and broad ribbons, trimmed with gold braid. The Dames also wore delicate velvet hats topped with a semicircle of precious stones and an exuberant red ostrich feather at the side.

Knights of the Order of St. Alexander Nevsky celebrated their yearly feast day on the date of the order's founding: August 30. This was the anniversary of the arrival in St. Petersburg's

*Dame of the Order of the Great Martyr St.
Catherine*
1797
Illustration

lexandrovsky Monastery of the relics of the
anonized prince Alexander Nevsky, which
ad previously been housed in the
ozhdestvensky Monastery in Vladimir. On
ugust 30, 1725, Catherine I awarded herself
e insignia of the Order of St. Alexander
evsky, and also conferred the order on a
roup of foreign sovereigns.

THE ORDERS OF ST. GEORGE & ST. ANNE

On her accession to the Russian throne in
1762, Empress Catherine the Great established
two new orders. The more prestigious of the
two, instituted in 1769, was the Order of St.
George, which was awarded for noble deeds;
the second was the Order of St. Vladimir,

instituted in 1782. The Order of St. George was celebrated each year in St. Petersburg on November 26 with a magnificent ceremony. At precisely eleven o'clock, Russian nobles of both sexes, dignitaries, and foreign ministers arrived at court. They assembled in the state rooms where they were joined at twelve o'clock by the Empress, who emerged from her private apartments in the dress of the order, accompanied by the heir to the throne. The entire procession made its way to the court church for a ceremonial service. The insignia of the order lay on a gold dish on a table in the main aisle. At the end of the liturgy, the awards ceremony took place, during which a special prayer was said and holy water was ritually poured over the insignia. A one-hundred-and-one-gun salute from the cannon of the St. Peter and St. Paul Fortress and the Admiralty was sounded, and the Empress took the order's cross, star, and ribbon from the dish and put them on.

After the Empress had received congratulations from the clergy, dignitaries, diplomats, and military men, a dinner for eighteen people was served in the palace dining room. That evening, a glorious ball was held, attended by court ladies in parade dresses, knights in colorful robes, and soldiers in scarves and uniforms covered with gold and medals of enamel and precious stones. Later that evening, a magnificent banquet was organized for seventy-six people, which Catherine herself hosted. The fortress and all the houses in the town were brightly illuminated for the occasion.

Catherine the Great held great respect for this order: she often took part in sittings of the Duma of the Knights of St. George, which met in the Chesme Palace, and on the order's feast days she received the knights at court. On one famous occasion, on the eve of one such feast day, the Empress felt unwell. When someone

suggested to her that she cancel the knights' reception, Catherine supposedly replied, "I would rather be carried to the reception on a bed than allow myself to incur the displeasure of these people who have dedicated their lives to receive their honor."

On the day of his coronation, April 5, 1797, Paul I, son of Catherine the Great, included in the Statute of Russian Orders the Order of St. Anne. This order had originally been founded in 1735 by his grandfather, Count Karl Friedrich of Holstein-Gottorp, in memory of Anna Petrovna, daughter of Peter the Great, but it was Paul who established the order by royal appointment. This meant the creation and hiring of special posts: a chancellor, a master and deputy master of ceremonies, a treasurer, a secretary, and heralds of the Order were all needed to administer and maintain the Order.

CEREMONIAL DRESS

Members of the Orders of St. Andrew the First Called, St. Catherine, St. Alexander Nevsky, and St. Anne were also granted the right to wear special ceremonial order apparel, woven from silk, brocade, and velvet and embroidered in gold and silver with the insignia of the order.

The costume of a Knight of the Order of St. Andrew the First Called at the end of the 18th century consisted of a long green velvet cloak lined with white silk, hung with silver tassels and cords and bearing a large embroidered star on the left side. Under this the knight wore a tabard of white brocade with gold galloon fringe and a cross embroidered on the breast. The costume of the order was completed with a black velvet hat decorated with a red feather and the saltire of St. Andrew on a narrow blue ribbon. Dress for Dames of the Order of St. Catherine was also legally

of St. Andrew the First Called; November 24 for St. Catherine; August 30 for St. Alexander Nevsky; November 26 for St. George; September 22 for St. Vladimir; February 3 for St. Anne; November 17 for the Order of the White Eagle; and April 25 for St. Stanislav.

In addition, one general feast day was designated for all knights: November 8, the day of the Archangel Michael. This day saw a wonderful procession of knights in formal dress, headed by the Emperor and Empress themselves. Under Paul I, precedence was given to Knights of the Order of St. Anne; they were followed by Knights of the Order of St. Alexander Nevsky, behind whom came Knights of the Order of St. Andrew the First Called; each class of each order was led by its official. Next came the head of the Order of St. Catherine and Dames of the Grand and Minor Crosses, accompanied by their officials. On the day of receptions and banquets in the palace, the Knights of the Order of St. Andrew sat on the right of the Emperor; next to them came the Knights of the Orders of St. Alexander Nevsky and St. Anne. Dames of the Order of St. Catherine sat to the left of the Empress.

As Russia and the Romanovs entered the modern era, the knights and officials wore their order dress more and more infrequently, and by the 19th century, the pomp and ceremony of the order uniform dissipated. The order ceremonies, however, continued— preserved by royal statute.

Detail of *Chief Master of Ceremonies for All Orders of Russia*
1797
Illustration

xed by royal decree, although half a century ﬁter a new design for the dress appeared, 10deled on an ancient Russian style with a *rafan* (cloak) and a *kokoshnik* (headdress). aul I specified that the clothing for the Order f St. George consist of an orange velvet tabard :immed with a gold and silver thread border, /ith black velvet crosses on the back and ront.

Knights were required to appear at court in the espective dress of their order on solemn feast lays, on the dates of the foundation of each rder. These were November 30 for the Order

Cross, Star and Chain of The Order of Saint Andrew the First Called
1850-1860s
Firm of Keibel
St. Petersburg, Russia
Cross: gold, stamping, engraving, enamel
Star: silver, gilding, forging, enamel
Chain: gold, stamping, engraving, enamel
(17 links total)
3.5 x 2.5 inches (8.9 cm x 6.4 cm)
dimensions of cross, 3.6 inches (9.2 cm)
length of star, 42.3 inches (107.5 cm)
length of chain
OM-2419, OM-2420, OM-2421

CROSS, STAR AND CHAIN OF THE ORDER OF SAINT ANDREW THE FIRST CALLED

The Order of St. Andrew the First Called was named in honor of the apostle who, from the time of the Kiev princes, had been the patron saint of the Russian lands. The highest Russian order of St. Andrew was awarded very rarely. It was conferred principally on members of the royal family, heads of foreign states, and "exceptional servants" of the state. The heir to the Russian throne was awarded the order at his christening.

The order had only one class. Its symbol was a saltire, or X-shaped cross, with the letters "SAPR" (St. Andrew Patron of Russia) on the ends of the arms, and an enamel image of the crucified saint. The cross is attached to the breast of a black two-headed eagle wearing three crowns, and was worn on a broad blue sash stretching from the right shoulder to the waist.

The star is made of silver with eight points interspersed with rays. In the center of the star is a two-headed eagle holding a blue cross of St. Andrew in its beak and claws and surrounded by the motto of the order: "For Faith and Faithfulness." The example seen here carries the hallmarks of Master Alexander Kordes and of the most famous St. Petersburg firm of medalists, Keibel. This firm produced the insignia of all the orders throughout the 19th century for the Chapter of Orders and the Cabinet of His Imperial Highness.

Cross, Star and Chain of The Order of Saint Andrew the First Called

CLOAK AND HAT OF THE MASTER OF CEREMONIES OF THE ORDER OF SAINT ANDREW THE FIRST CALLED

In 1720, the Russian state instituted official new appointments for the Order of St. Andrew the First Called; one such post was the Master of Ceremonies, whose role was to officiate at ceremonies and to ensure that the Imperial throne, the knights' seats, and the orders, insignia, and costumes were present on ceremonial occasions.

On feast days, the Master of Ceremonies wore a silver dalmatic with gold galloon trim, a green velvet cloak with a silver brocade collar and tassels, a black velvet hat with three upright plumes, and a saltire badge affixed to his lapel by a blue ribbon. These were worn over a parade costume. The Master also sported a gold Greek cross on his dalmatic and held a staff with a badge of the order on the knob.

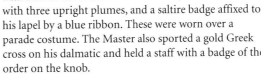

SHRINE FOR "THE EMPEROR'S STATUTES FOR THE ORDERS OF DECORATED RUSSIANS"

This silver and gold rectangular shrine was used for the preservation of "The Emperor's Statutes for the Orders of Decorated Russians." It is one of the rarest historical and aesthetic artifacts from the reign of Czar Paul I. Construction of the shrine was begun in 1785 by a St. Petersburg master named Bergman; it was completed in 1799. The master used stars and symbols of the four Russian orders: St. Andrew the First Called, St. Catherine, St. Alexander Nevsky, and St. Anne. In November of 1798, Paul I announced the founding of the Order of St. John of Jerusalem (the Knights of Malta), which became the highest award in Russia. On August 1, 1799, the Maltese cross with the monogram of Paul I was placed on the chest of the two-headed eagle on the lid of the shrine. The inside of the shrine is lined with blue silk and on the bottom is a pillow of white moiré.

Cloak and Hat of the Master of Ceremonies

Cloak and Hat of the Master of Ceremonies of The Order of Saint Andrew the First Called
1797
Russia
48.8 inches (124 cm) length of coat
4.7 inches (12 cm) height of hat
TK-1691, TK-1573

Shrine for "The Emperor's Statutes for the Orders of Decorated Russians"
1785-1799
Master Bergman
St. Petersburg, Russia
Gold, silver, glass, silk, moiré, casting, embossing, gilding, enamel, mounting, weaving
22.6 x 17.3 x 4.7 inches (57.5 cm x 44 cm x 12 cm)
MR-9793/1-2

Shrine for "The Emperor's Statutes for the Orders of Decorated Russians"

Cane with the Insignia of The Order of Saint Andrew the First Called
Late 18th century
Russia
Wood, bone, silver, gold, enamel, lathe work
37.8 inches (96 cm) height of cane; 1.9 inches (4.7 cm) diameter of knob
DK-1539/1

CANE WITH THE INSIGNIA OF THE ORDER OF SAINT ANDREW THE FIRST CALLED

This cane, made from black wood, was outfitted with four detachable knobs made from bone, each superimposed with symbols of the four principal Russian orders: St. Andrew the First Called (pictured here), St. Catherine, St. Alexander Nevsky, and St. Anne. The cane was made for the Master of Ceremonies for the Order of St. Andrew the First Called. This honorable post at the end of the 18th century was held by Peter Valuev, who played a crucial role in the history of the Kremlin Armory at the turn of the 19th century. Valuev was entrusted with moving the treasures of the Kremlin Museums to Nizny Novgorod in 1812, as Napoleon's armies approached Moscow. After the liberation of Moscow, the treasures were returned to Moscow and placed in the newly relocated Kremlin Armory.

Cane with the Insignia of The Order of Saint Andrew the First Called

Herald's Costume

Seal of The Order of Saint Andrew the First Called

Herald's Staff

HERALD'S COSTUME OF THE ORDER OF SAINT ANDREW THE FIRST CALLED

The heralds played a key role during the order ceremony and during the order's respective feast days. Heralds were appointed by the Czar to administer and maintain the statutes and trappings of the order, and to relay announcements regarding the ceremony proceedings. In accordance with the Czar Paul I's statute of 1797, the herald's costume was to consist of a silver brocade shirt, a green velvet tunic with stars of the order sewn onto the front and back, trousers of silver brocade, and white silk stockings and boots. The costume also included a black velvet hat, a saltire badge, and white gloves. This herald's costume of the Order of St. Andrew the First Called was made in 1797. The original stars on the herald's tunic were removed and replaced with new ones incorporating the two-headed eagle with a cross on its breast.

SEAL OF THE ORDER OF SAINT ANDREW THE FIRST CALLED

The seal of the Order of St. Andrew the First Called was confirmed by Peter the Great at the same time as the order was created. The statute of orders set forth in 1720 contained a detailed description of the seal of the order. In agreement with the statute, the councilor of the Order of St. Andrew the First Called needed to physically possess the order's seal at the moment of the order's bestowal. The seal was carried in the councilor's left hand on a gold cord.

The secretary of the order, who oversaw the paperwork in the office of the Chapter of Imperial Orders, attached the diplomas and official documents with this seal. The Order of St. Andrew the First Called was usually stamped by the hand of the Emperor himself during the decoration ceremony.

The seal here has a black wooden handle and a cylindrical gilded base. On the steel die is an engraved image of the star of St. Andrew the First Called. The rays of the star are entwined with a ribbon with the image of the order at the ends of the ribbon. On the outer edge of the seal is the inscription: "The seal of the Imperial Order St. Andrew the First Called."

HERALD'S STAFF OF THE ORDER OF SAINT ANDREW THE FIRST CALLED

A necessary accessory of the herald was a silver staff topped with the insignia of the order. The preparation of staffs for eight heralds designed for the four Russian orders was executed by the gold master Pierre Teremin. In December 1797, he was paid 425 rubles for each of the two staffs completed for the heralds of St. Andrew the First Called, one of which is featured here. The staff is decorated with gold spheres and gold enamel on the top in the shape of the insignia of the order. The mark of the maker, Master Herman Fredrick Pomo, is engraved on the silver part of the staff.

Herald's Costume of The Order of Saint Andrew the First Called
1797
Tailor: I. Kolb
Glovemaker: I. K. Veber
Russia
Tunic: velvet, silk, galloon, silk thread, sequins, foil, weaving, spangles, embroidery
Gloves: suede, silver galloon and velvet fringe, weaving, braiding
31.5 inches (80 cm) length of tunic
13 inches (33 cm) length of gloves
TK-1658, TK-2561/1-2

Seal of The Order of Saint Andrew the First Called
Second half of the 19th century
St. Petersburg, Russia
Steel, wood, engraving, gilding
3.5 inches (9 cm.) height; 1.7 inches (4.2 cm.) length
OM-2175

Herald's Staff of The Order of Saint Andrew the First Called
1797
Masters Pierre Teremin and Herman Fredrick Pomo
St. Petersburg, Russia
Gold, silver, casting, enamel, gilding
31.1 inches (79 cm) length, 4.2 x 2.4 inches (10.6 cm x 6 cm) dimensions of head
MR-4705/1-2

Cross and Ribbon of the Order of Saint Catherine

Cross and Ribbon of the Order of Saint Alexander Nevsky

Cross and Ribbon of the Order of Saint Catherine
Second half of the 18th century
St. Petersburg, Russia
Gold, silver, gilding, precious stones, enamel, forging, silk moiré, gold and silver thread
Cross: 4.3 inches (11 cm) length; 2.8 inches (7 cm) width
OM-1261/1-2

Cross and Ribbon of the Order of Saint Alexander Nevsky
Late 18th-early 19th century
St. Petersburg, Russia
Cross: gold, glass, silver, enamel, engraving, casting, paint on enamel, silk moiré
Cross: 7.7 inches (19.6 cm) height, 2.8 inches (7.1 cm) width
OM-2311, OM-2312

Star of the Order of Saint Catherine
Second half of the 18th century
St. Petersburg, Russia
Gold, silver, forging, gilding, diamonds
4.3 inches (11 cm) diameter
OM-1264

CROSS AND RIBBON OF THE ORDER OF SAINT CATHERINE

In 1714 Peter I, in honor of his wife Catherine Alexeyevna, confirmed the highest female order of the Russian State—the Order of St. Catherine. At a festive ceremony on November 24, 1714, Peter presented this insignia to Catherine I, who remained the order's sole recipient until 1726. The statute of the order rigidly limited the number of awardees.

The order contained two levels, which dictated the size and decoration of the insignia. The cross of the first level was received by only twelve women besides the czarevnas, but the second level was attained by 92 women, chiefly for distinguished humanitarian work.

In the center of the cross, which has been fashioned with diamonds, is a gold oval medallion with the image of St. Catherine sitting with a white cross and palm leaves in her hands. Between the ends of the cross are the letters "DSFR," an acronym for the Latin phrase "Domine, Salvon Fac Regem"—"God, Save the Czar." On the back of the cross is a rendition of an eagle's nest on a cliff, at the foot of which are two eagles devouring a snake. The cross shown here was the last Order of St. Catherine presented by the Office of Imperial Orders. The ribbon

belonged to Empress Elizabeth Alexeyevna (1779-1826), the wife of Alexander I.

CROSS AND RIBBON OF THE ORDER OF SAINT ALEXANDER NEVSKY

This order was named in honor of Prince Alexander Nevsky, victor over the Swedes in 1240 and the Teutonic Knights in 1242. Peter the Great initiated the award strictly as a military honor. However, when the order was actually instituted on May 21, 1725, by Empress Catherine I, it was intended for both military and civil service. The first twelve Knights of the Order of St. Alexander Nevsky were invested on the day of the marriage of Peter the Great's daughter Anna to Count Karl Friedrich of Holstein-Gottorp.

The Order of Saint Alexander Nevsky had one class, and its insignia consisted of a golden cross, a red moiré ribbon, and a star. The ends of the arms of the cross were made from ruby-colored glass, and between these were two-headed eagles flanking a medallion with a portrait of Alexander Nevsky on a horse with a spear in his hand. The reverse side of the medallion shows a monogram

Star of the Order of Saint Catherine

h the letters "SA" (St. Alexander) beneath a prince's
wn. The cross was worn on a sash from the left
ulder.

e insignia of the order on display here belonged to
zabeth Alexeyevna, wife of Emperor Alexander I, who
ed between 1801 and 1825. During her coronation,
was presented with the insignias of both this order
l the Order of St. Andrew the First Called.

✦

R OF THE ORDER OF SAINT CATHERINE

the center of this eight-pointed star of the Order of
Catherine is a round medallion bordered with a fillet
diamonds; inside the circular frame is an image of a
ss set onto a wheel, a symbol of the martyrdom of St.
therine. In an outer ring of red enamel surrounding
medallion is written the motto "For Love and the
herland" together with an Imperial crown. According
egend, this star once belonged to Catherine the
eat. She was awarded the order when she became
and Duchess, as the wife of the heir to the throne,
er Feodorovich, who would become Emperor Peter

✦

NIC OF A HERALD'S ORDER OF SAINT ALEXANDER NEVSKY

en Emperor Paul I took the throne in 1796, he
ived the system of Russian orders that was used to
ferentiate members of Russian society, in terms of
ir usefulness to the Russian state and to the Emperor
nself. The emperor not only restored the system of
lers but also standardized its usage.

o heralds were present during every order ceremony
per Paul I's decree. The heralds acted as marshals
ring the solemn proceedings. On April 11, 1797, the
iperor appointed the heralds of the Order of St.
exander Nevsky to be collegiate councilor Perepechin
d the court councilor Kazarinov. In June of 1797, two
stumes were made for the pair, one of which is on
play here.

Tunic of a Herald's Order of Saint Alexander Nevsky

STAR OF THE ORDER OF SAINT ALEXANDER NEVSKY

This eight-pointed star of the Order of Saint Alexander
Nevsky was created from open-worked silver. On the
white ground of the central medallion is a monogram
with the letters "SA" (St. Alexander) beneath the prince's
crown. Around the edge of the medallion is a ring of red
enamel with the motto of the Order: "For Work and the
Fatherland." The star was traditionally worn on the left
side of the chest. This star belonged to Emperor
Alexander I.

**Tunic of a Herald's Order of Saint
Alexander Nevsky**
Late 18th century
I. Kolb
St. Petersburg, Russia
Velvet, silk, galloon, fringe, sequins, wire-
ribbon, silver and gold thread, weaving,
embroidery
39.4 inches (100 cm) length
TK-1647

**Star of the Order of Saint Alexander
Nevsky**
First quarter of the 19th century
St. Petersburg, Russia
Silver, gold, base metal, engraving,
forging, gilding, enamel
4.2 inches (10.6 cm) diameter
OM-2324

Star of the Order of Saint Alexander Nevsky

175

Cross and Chain of the Order of Saint John of Jerusalem
1798-1801
Russia
Gold; casting, carving, stamping, enamel
Cross: 3.4 inches (8.6 cm) height, 3.1 inches (7.8 cm) length
Chain: 56.7 inches (144 cm) length
OM-2562, OM-2565

Cross and Ribbon of the Order of Saint John of Jerusalem
Cross: Late 18th century
Attributed to Russia
Gold, casting, enamel, embossing
Cross: 3.9 inches (10 cm) height; 1.7 inches (4.4 cm.) width
Ribbon: 19th century, Russia
Moiré, weaving
Ribbon: 3.7 inches (9.5 cm.) length; 2.8 inches (7.0 cm.) width
13.6 feet x 7.2 feet (408 cm x 218 cm)
TK-2184

CROSS AND CHAIN OF THE ORDER OF SAINT JOHN OF JERUSALEM

This cross was worn on the chest of the Grand Master of the Order of St. John of Jerusalem, the highest rank of the order. The cross belonged to Emperor Paul I, who in 1798 was pronounced Grand Master of the Order. This massive eight-cornered Maltese cross is covered on both sides with white enamel. It is attached by a loop to a gold chain, made from 338 links. After the death of Paul I, the regalia and insignia of the Maltese Order were passed onto his heir, Emperor Alexander I. In 1817 when the activities of the Maltese Order were abolished in Russia, all decorations were given to the Chapter of Imperial Orders.

CROSS AND RIBBON OF THE ORDER OF SAINT JOHN OF JERUSALEM

This insignia is of the ancient European Order of St. John of Jerusalem, also called the Maltese Order; it once belonged to Maria Feodorovna—the wife of Emperor Paul I. She wore the order on a ribbon made of black moiré on her left shoulder.

The Maltese order lost its grandeur at the end of the 18th century during the French Revolution (1789-1794). The order needed a strong protector and found one in the great Russian Emperor. The relationship of Paul to the Maltese Order was not just a romantic one. In 1797 the

Cross and Chain of the Order of Saint John of Jerusalem

Emperor took the title of Protector of the Maltese Order. At that time, the Empress and all the members of the Imperial family were given insignias.

At the beginning of the 19th century, when the Maltese Order was no longer in existence in Russia, the insignia belonging to the widow Empress Maria Feodorovna was given to the Chapter of Imperial Orders. In 1917 this insignia joined the collection at the Kremlin Armory.

Cross and Ribbon of the Order of Saint John of Jerusalem

Maltese Crown of Emperor Paul I
Late 18th-early 19th century
Attributed to Russia
Gold, silver, velvet, silk, casting,
stamping, gilding, enamel, weaving
11.6 inches (29.4 cm) height, 8 x 7.5 x
11.6 inches (20.3 x 19.1 x 29.4 cm)
dimensions of base
MP-9792

Maltese Crown of Emperor Paul I

‌ALTESE CROWN OF EMPEROR PAUL I

‌e Maltese Crown shown here is one of the rarest
‌toric artifacts in the Kremlin Armory. The adoption of
‌s crown as part of the regalia of Imperial Russia
‌ring the five-year reign of Emperor Paul I linked
‌ssia to the Order of St. John of Jerusalem. This famous
‌der of knights was founded in Palestine in the 11th
‌ntury, after the first Crusade. In 1113, the statutes of
‌‍ order were ratified by the Pope, but in 1291, the
‌der left Jerusalem and in 1530 established itself on the
‌editerranean island of Malta, where it acquired its
‌me.

‌‍e first diplomatic links between Russia and the
‌altese Order were established at the end of the 17th
‌ntury. In 1697 Peter the Great's ambassador, B.P.
‌eremetev, was received in Valletta, Malta's capital;
‌ntact was maintained under Catherine the Great, and
‌ok on a new character under Paul I. At this moment,
‌‍ order was in dire need of a guardian. The French

Revolution had dealt Malta a heavy blow; the order lost
all its privileges and rich lands in France. In Czar Paul I,
the Order saw a powerful protector.

In January 1797, Count Litta, the Order's ambassador,
concluded an accord with Russia, and in November of
that year, Paul I became Protector of the Maltese Order.
With the seizure of Malta by Napoleon in June 1798, the
surviving members of the order placed even greater hope
in the patronage of the Russian Emperor, and
consequently, on November 29, 1798, in a ceremony in
the Winter Palace, Paul was made Grand Master of the
Order of Malta. By his decree, the Maltese cross was
introduced into Russia's state emblem and seal. After
Paul's death in 1801, however, the insignia of the order
was removed from the emblem. In 1803 Alexander I
returned the relics of the order to its new Grand Master,
Jean-Baptiste Tommasi, and in 1817 its activities ceased
in Russia altogether.

CHAPTER VIII

The Coronation of the Russian Emperors

The Coronation of the Russian Emperors

by M.V. Martynova

Coronation Procession of Czar Nicholas II and Czarina Alexandra Feodorovna, Moscow Kremlin, May 14, 1896
Illustration

*I*n 1721 Peter the Great adopted the title of "Emperor of All Russia." In the later years of his life, he was gravely worried about the fate of the Russian throne. Peter had no direct male heir, and there was at the time great enmity towards Peter's grandson, who was the son of the executed Czarevich Alexei. For this reason, shortly before his death, Peter decided to crown his second wife, Catherine I (born Marfa Skavronskaya), as Empress and his rightful heir. The coronation took place on May 7, 1724, in the Assumption Cathedral of the Kremlin. The new ceremony did not deviate from the rites of the consecration of the Czar; indeed, the order of events of the coronation largely retained that of the consecration.

Peter had founded the new Russian capital in St. Petersburg, where the royal court now resided. This inevitably led to significant changes in the preparations for the new ceremony. As the coronation festivities approached, the entire court departed St. Petersburg and made their way to Moscow. Before entering the ancient capital, the royal family customarily stopped off in one of the villages just outside of Moscow. This was traditionally the village of Vsesviatskoe, where at the end of the century, the famous Russian architect M. Kazakov built the neo-Gothic Petrovsky Palace.

IN THE PETRINE ERA

The royal entry into Moscow was greeted with military gun salute, the ringing of the bells from the Bell Tower of Ivan the Great in the Kremlin, and the sound of trumpets and kettledrums. The arrival of the royal family was marked by a grand procession in which large numbers took part, including representatives of all the peoples of the mighty Russian Empire. The procession was conducted according to a strictly defined order, which remained virtually unchanged until the end of the 19th century. For coronation ceremonies, triumphal gates were erected of unparalleled decoration; they were funded by the Church, Moscow merchants, the municipal government, and other benefactors. The royal family was graciously greeted by people bearing gifts, singing choirs, and clergymen with crosses.

All along the route of the ceremonial procession, platforms were set up for spectators, the streets were strewn with fir twigs, and valuable carpets of silk and wool were hung from open windows. Fine cloth was often draped from the buildings on Red Square. Amidst this festive milieu the procession wound its way to the Kremlin. Here the Emperor bowed down before the ancient sacred objects, and in the Assumption Cathedral a solemn service of prayer was held for the Empress.

The coronation ceremony in the 18th and 19th centuries, however, contained certain changes from those of the ancient Russian Czars. The strict ceremonial order during Peter's era (often referred to as the Petrine era) was drawn up with the participation of Peter himself, who included several elements adapted from Western European practice. For example, the rights of succession of the sovereign were affirmed not in speeches delivered in the Assumption Cathedral, but in a preparatory manifesto. High-ranking officials and representatives of foreign embassies were informed of the coronation date by the Masters of Ceremonies, while the people were informed on the squares of Moscow by heralds on horseback, to the accompaniment of trumpets and kettledrums.

Other new features were introduced into the outward forms of the coronation ceremony. The traditional journey from the Faceted Palace to the Assumption Cathedral was undertaken by the Emperor on a raised walkway, while onlookers sat on high platforms that had been installed around the Cathedral Square. The decoration of the Assumption Cathedral also took on a more complex and lavish quality. In the center of the church a large dais was set up, surrounded by a balustrade. Above, a magnificent canopy was draped over the arch of the dais, decorated with an embroidered emblem of the Russian Empire—the two-headed eagle—surrounded by the emblems of the chief provinces. The thrones of the Russian Czars of the 16th and 17th centuries were also set upon the dais, in addition to a special table for the coronation regalia. Before the coronation, the regalia were brought from the Winter Palace in St. Petersburg to the Kremlin Armory, which from the beginning of the 18th century had become a state treasury. On the eve of the coronation, the regalia, along with other ancient ceremonial articles, were carried to the Assumption Cathedral.

UNDER A SPLENDID RED CANOPY

The coronation procession was preceded and followed by horse guards. The signal for the processional participants to gather was given by the firing of cannon. The procession was made up of court figures, generals, representatives of the Russian gentry, Russian and foreign merchants, members of the governing Senate, senior clerics, and other high-ranking state officials. The regalia were carried on cushions of gold brocade. In the center of the procession, under a splendid red canopy, walked the Emperor.

The general procedures and program of the coronation largely followed the religious example of the consecration of the Czar, but had several new features. Following the abolition of the Patriarchate by Peter the Great and the establishment of a Holy Synod—an ecclesiastical council which controlled the Church—the Emperor did not sit on his throne alongside a member of the church hierarchy, but sat alone, or with his Empress. The coronation ceremony began with a proclamation by the Emperor of the basic doctrines of the Christian faith, which he read solemnly from a book.

The donning of the ceremonial regalia was accompanied by the reciting of a prayer. In this act, too, there were changes. Peter the Great, who so fervently desired the growth and prosperity of the Russian state, attempted to lend the coronation ceremony an identifiable state character. The life-giving cross was no longer placed on the Czar; the *barmy*, or ceremonial collar, also disappeared, to be replaced by a new coronation cape. Likewise, the ancient crown of the Russian Czars, the Cap of Monomach, was substituted with a Western European-style crown, made of two separate hemispheres separated by an arc. At first, new crowns were usually made for each coronation, but in 1762 the famed St. Petersburg jeweler Jeremiah Poze created a magnificent diamond crown for Catherine the Great. Thereafter, this masterpiece of the jeweler's art was featured in all subsequent coronations, right up to that of the last member of the Romanov dynasty, Nicholas II.

Unlike the consecration of the Czar when the Cap of Monomach was placed on the sovereign's head by elders of the Orthodox church, the coronation—after Catherine I's—was marked by the Emperor himself affixing the crown to his head. Catherine I's coronation was an exception: it was Catherine's husband Peter the Great who crowned her Empress, but in all subsequent coronations the Emperor crowned himself.

Starting with Paul I, son of Catherine the Great, both the Emperor and Empress were crowned at the same time, according to the Byzantine tradition. The Empress knelt before the Emperor, who took the crown from his head, touched it lightly on the head of his wife and placed it back on his own head. The Empress then put on a small coronation crown, which was first made for Maria Feodorovna and was purportedly used at all ensuing coronations.

Beginning in 1742 with the coronation of the Empress Elizabeth Petrovna, daughter of Peter the Great, other articles were added to the coronation regalia; these were the state banner and the state sword, on one side of which was portrayed a two-headed eagle with a slain dragon in its claws, and on the other a griffin with a drawn sword. In 1762, at the coronation of Catherine the Great, a further addition was made: a chain of diamond links. This was the chain of the Order of St. Andrew the First Called, the highest of the Russian orders, established at the end of the 17th century by Peter the Great. Although Peter had proposed that the order be awarded for acts of the highest service to the state, his descendants decided that the heirs to the throne should become Knights of the Order of St. Andrew from birth.

the 18th century, the old custom of
showering the Czar with gold and silver coins
was discontinued, and instead gold and silver
medals were thrown into the crowd during the
procession to the Archangel and Annunciation
cathedrals. In addition, courtiers were
awarded medals specially minted for the
coronation. For several weeks after the
coronation ceremony was over, audiences were
held in the royal palace, where the Emperor
received congratulations and hosted bountiful
banquets. Balls, masquerades, and theatrical
presentations followed one after the other. For
a short time, lavish lightshows and fireworks
turned the ancient capital into a fairytale city.

The rejoicing of the people at the royal
accession to the throne of a new ruler was
expressed in various ways; there were swings
and carousels, jugglers and acrobats, and
many different kinds of refreshments.
Wheeled tables and platforms were set up on
the squares of the city filled with roasted sheep
and oxen, stuffed birds, and pyramids of
kalach, a traditional Russian loaf. Fountains of
wine poured forth, and barrels of beer and
wine were driven about the town.
Commemorative gifts were then distributed
among the people: kerchiefs and tankards
festooned with a portrait of the new Czar or
Czarina were common and afforded the
people a material token by which to remember
the historic ascension of the new sovereign.

*The Coronation of Emperor Nicholas II and
Empress Alexandra Feodorovna, May 14, 1896*
Illustration

Coronation Uniform and Helmet of
Emperor Alexander II
1856
E. D. Bitner
Court Factory of Officer's Accoutrements
St. Petersburg, Russia
Uniform: cloth, wool, silk, brocade, gold
thread, fringe, cord, stones, metal, gold,
silver; weaving, embroidery, embossing,
casting; 33.1 inches (84 cm) length
Helmet: leather, metal, silk, feathers,
weaving, casting, lacquer; 6.9 inches
(17.5 cm) circumference at crown
TK-1988, TK-1558

Coronation Uniform and Helmet of Emperor Alexander II

CORONATION UNIFORM AND HELMET OF EMPEROR ALEXANDER II

On August 26, 1856, the coronation of Alexander II took place in the Assumption Cathedral of the Moscow Kremlin. Alexander was considered one of the grandest rulers ever to take the throne. This is the uniform and helmet that he wore to coronation celebrations. This uniform was made from dark green fabric with gilded buttons and a lining of red wool and silk. The collar, cuffs, and hem of the uniform were embroidered with gold thread and sequins in an oak leaf-pattern. The detachable epaulets were decorated with gold fringe. On the chest of the uniform are stars of the Orders of St. Andrew the First Called and St. Vladimir.

The helmet was crafted from black-lacquered leather an has two peaks. On the front and back of the helmet is th Russian state emblem—the two-headed eagle—done in gilded bronze. A plume of white, black, and red feathers rises from the top of the helmet. A leather chin strap is decorated with metal plates made to resemble serpent scales. Glued to the bottom of the helmet is a printed piece of paper with the symbol of the two-headed eagle under a crown, with the maker's inscription, "Court Factory of Officer's Accoutrements. E.D. Bitner, St. Petersburg."

Coronation Robe of Empress Maria Alexandrovna
1856
Russia
Brocade, silk, fur, gold thread, braiding,
tassels, weaving, embroidery, appliqué
12.3 feet (376 cm) length
TK-2597

Coronation Robe of Empress Maria Alexandrovna

CORONATION ROBE OF EMPRESS MARIA ALEXANDROVNA

Coronation robes in Russia were traditionally made of
smooth gold brocade and trimmed with ermine. New
coronation robes were made for each coronation. Along
with other articles of the regalia, robes were carried by
courtiers on special cushions through the Cathedral
Square into the Assumption Cathedral, where they were
then placed on the Emperor and Empress. After the
coronation ceremony, the robes were stored in the
Armory for preservation. This robe, woven from delicate
gold brocade and decorated with appliquéd two-headed
eagles, was made in 1856 for the coronation of the
Empress Maria Alexandrovna, wife of Alexander II.

Portrait of Emperor Alexander II
Second half of the 19th century
Unknown Artist
Russia
Oil on canvas
40.4 x 28 inches (102.5 x 71 cm)
Zh-1992

Portrait of Emperor Alexander II

PORTRAIT OF EMPEROR ALEXANDER II

This portrait of Emperor Alexander II is a partial copy of the full-sized ceremonial portrait of his father Nicholas I painted by F. Kruger in 1847, when Alexander was still heir to the throne. That same year, a family portrait with Alexander's three brothers and a portrait of Nicholas I were finished for the large dining hall of the Alexandrovsky Palace in Czarskoe Selo, the original royal residence built for Peter the Great, near St. Petersburg. The portrait shown here was the first officially recognized image to be mass-produced for placement in state buildings.

e Crowning of Empress Catherine II in the Assumption Cathedral

HE CROWNING OF EMPRESS CATHERINE II IN THE SSUMPTION CATHEDRAL

he original painting by Stefano Torelli, on which this
nonymous copy was based, was commissioned at the
me of the coronation of the Empress Catherine the
reat, on September 22, 1762. Torelli's paintings were
opular during Catherine's reign. This work is from an
legorical series praising the Empress and her
ccomplishments; Catherine II is featured in her
referred depiction as Minerva, the goddess of wisdom.

he solemn event occurred inside the Assumption
athedral, whose arches, walls and columns are
ecorated with frescoes. The principal characters stand
n a raised dais against the cathedral's west wall, and
nclude the Empress in full coronation dress, the highest

class of dignitaries, and the elders of the Russian church,
with the Metropolitan at their head. The picture's
purpose is to demonstrate the fundamental principle of
Catherine's reign: the divine right of the sovereign.

**The Crowning of Empress Catherine II in
the Assumption Cathedral**
18th century
Unknown Artist (after Stefano Torelli)
Russia
Oil on canvas
58.3 x 69.3 inches (148 x 176 cm)
Zh-1931

Medal Commemorating the Coronation of Alexander II
1850s
V. Alexeyev and R. Hannemann
St. Petersburg Royal Mint
St. Petersburg, Russia
Gold, embossing
2 inches (5.1 cm) diameter
OM-58

Seal of Emperor Alexander II
Second half of 19th century
Master Samuel Arndt
St. Petersburg, Russia
Gold, onyx, gem stones, pearls,
embossing, carving
3.8 inches (9.7 cm) length
OM-2148

Medal Commemorating the Coronation of Alexander II (front view)

Medal Commemorating the Coronation of Alexander II (back view)

MEDAL COMMEMORATING THE CORONATION OF ALEXANDER II

In Russia commemorative medals were not only official memorials but also emblems of state ideology, depictions of the most important events in the history of the Russian state. For coronation ceremonies, special medals of gold and silver were commissioned by the government from the St. Petersburg Royal Mint; these were worn during the official ceremonies attended by members of the Imperial family, Russia's chief dignitaries, and foreign ambassadors.

On August 26, 1856, the coronation day of Alexander II, the Privy Councilor and Minister of Finance, P. F. Brok, presented a golden plate bearing two gold medals,

minted for the occasion, to the mother (Alexandra Feodorovna) and wife (Maria Alexandrovna) of the new Emperor. One of those medals is seen here. The front of the medal bears a half-length profile of the Emperor Alexander II. Beneath the portrait is the inscription "Crowned in Moscow 1856." Around the edge is the name of the medalist, V. Alexeyev. On the reverse side is rendering of the Russian state emblem, with the inscription "God is with us" just above it. Beneath it, along the edge, is the name of the medalist, R. Hannemann. The two medalists who collaborated in the production were renowned artists at the St. Petersburg Royal Mint.

✦

SEAL OF EMPEROR ALEXANDER II

The coronation of a new Czar necessitated the production of a new series of state seals. These included large, medium, and small seal, whose use was strictly regulated by state law. The personal seal of the Emperor was applied in legal matters and in confirming the authenticity of papers, letters, and other documents originating in the sovereign's office. This elegant seal is cut in a stone of rare beauty; the case bears the name of the highly regarded St. Petersburg firm of Nicholls and Plinker.

The seal is made from a single piece of dark brown banded onyx set in a thin gold ornamental band inlaid with small rubies and emeralds. On the stamping surface of the seal is engraved the name "Alexander" in Cyrillic beneath an Imperial crown. The seal's maker, Samuel Arndt, was a master goldsmith responsible for numerous court commissions.

Seal of Emperor Alexander II

HERALD'S COSTUME WITH TUNIC, BESHMET, AND HAT

The first court herald entered into the service of Peter I in 1722. Heralds were given the responsibility of announcing court functions; on coronation day, they announced the proceedings, participated in the coronation procession, and stood near the Emperor's throne.

The unusual cut and design of the ceremonial costume, influenced by both the Middle Ages and Western European court etiquette, remained unchanged until the end of the monarchy in Russia. The robes of the herald consisted of a tunic, also referred to as a *dalmatic* (a robe reaching to the knees with shortened sleeves), a coat with long sleeves called a *beshmet*, pants, boots, gloves, and a hat. The beshmet was worn under the dalmatic. The only variation in design was the color of the outfit. This herald's costume was used for the coronations of Alexander III and Nicholas II. The tunic was constructed from smooth gold fabric made by the Moscow-based Sapozhnikov Firm, one of the finest textile firms in Russia in the 19th and 20th centuries. The opulent velvet hat with gold tassels, galloon and ostrich feathers topped off the herald's costume.

On the front of the tunic is a large two-headed eagle embroidered in gold thread, and on the back is the insignia of the Order of St. Andrew the First Called. The drawing for the state crest was done by the artist A. A. Kozlev.

PROCLAMATION BAG

The Solemn Proclamation of the Day of the Holy Coronation ceremony traditionally began in the Kremlin. After a trumpet salute, an official read aloud the text of the royal proclamation while the herald distributed printed copies from a special bag. The procession then continued to Red Square. Over the next three days, the proclamation ceremony was repeated in various parts of Moscow. The text of the proclamation was reproduced from a handwritten original by the artist V. M. Vasnetsov. In all, around 50,000 copies were distributed.

This bag was made for the coronation of Emperor Alexander III in 1883. It was probably also used in 1896 for the coronation of the last Russian Czar, Nicholas II.

The bag is made of red velvet; it is rectangular in shape and has a long strap. A stunning gilt-bronze two-headed eagle is attached to the bag's front.

Herald's Costume with Tunic, Beshmet, and Hat

Proclamation Bag

Herald's Costume with Tunic, Beshmet, and Hat
1880s
Russia
Tunic: Sapozhnikov Firm, Moscow, Russia, 1883
Gold edging, galloon, fringe, sequins, brocade, silk and gold thread; 32.1 inches (81.5 cm) length
Beshmet: satin, moiré, silk, galloon, cord, weaving, embroidery, braiding; 40.2 inches (102 cm) length
Hat: satin, galloon, feathers, leather, cord, braiding; 4.7 inches (12 cm) circumference at crown
TK-1624, TK-1562, TK-1639

Proclamation Bag
1883
Russia
Velvet, leather, galloon, cord, copper, weaving, embroidery, gilding
Bag: 29.1 x 18.5 inches (74 x 47 cm)
Coat of arms: 15.7 x 13.4 inches (40 x 34 cm)
TK-1285

Two Edge Trimmings from the Coronation Canopy
1727/1826
Russia
Velvet, taffeta, galloon, gold braid and cord; weaving, embroidery, appliqué
7.6 feet x 2 feet (232 x 61 cm)/9.4 feet x 2 feet (285 x 61 cm)
TK-3442/1-2, TK-3443/2

Plafond from the Coronation Canopy
1896
Russia
Velvet, edging, gold and silk threads, silk, sequins, stones, metal, weaving, embroidery, appliqué, casting
4.6 feet x 6.2 feet (140 x 188 cm)
TK-3441/1

THE CORONATION CANOPY

The ceremonial coronation, reworked in Russia in 1723-24 to combine aspects of the ancient ritual with more modern Western European traditions, continued without major changes until 1898. For the next two centuries, the decorative attire created by the best masters and decorators served as the basis for all future Russian coronations. The ceremonial canopies were part of the traditional set of coronation objects and were an ancient symbol of power taken by the Byzantine and the Roman Empires.

In the Russian Empire, large canopies were used inside the Assumption Cathedral of the Moscow Kremlin during the coronation. These velvet canopies were rectangular in shape and attached by chains to the cupola of the church. In the center of the canopy was the crest of Russia, embroidered in gold thread. Along the edge of the frame were attached four velvet trimmings. In the corners were four ostrich feathers and large golden tassels on long ropes.

Two Edge Trimmings from the Coronation Canopy

In the Romanov era, there were three such coronation canopies, all of which are housed in the Kremlin Armory today. The first was created for Peter II's coronation in 1727 and also displayed for the coronation of Alexander I. The canopies were restored before each use. The second canopy was manufactured for the coronation of Nicholas I. The third canopy, shown here, was made in 1896 and used for the coronation of Nicholas II. In the center is the two-headed eagle and on the chest of the eagle is a metal chain of the Order of St. Andrew the First Called.

Two trimmings are exhibited here: one which accompanied the original 1727 canopy, and the other from 1826 which accompanied the canopy used for the coronation of Nicholas I.

Plafond from the Coronation Canopy

COMMEMORATIVE CORONATION TOWEL

This towel is made of white linen and decorated with cross-stitch embroidery, appliqué work, and bobbin lace. The center of the composition features the crest of the Poltavskaya region under an appliquéd crown, with the date 1883. Along the ends of the towel are monograms of Alexander III with a crown, framed in laurel branches, beside which are a pair of two-headed eagles. Two embroidered inscriptions explain that the towel was presented to Emperor Alexander III, upon his coronation in 1883, by members of the gentry from Poltavskaya.

The most noble representatives of the Russian provinces were invited to Moscow to attend the coronation ceremony in the company of the Emperor's retinue. During the celebrations that followed the coronation, the nobles brought the Emperor salted bread on stamped silver or carved wooden dishes. The bread was carried on beautifully designed towels, the inspired handiwork of local seamstresses and lacemakers.

+

SALT CELLAR

This wooden salt cellar is decorated with fanciful ornamentation and a finely detailed carving of the Russian state emblem. It was presented to Nicholas II and Alexandra Feodorovna in Moscow in 1898 by the religious sect of the Old Believers, after the Imperial couple had been presented with the ritualistic bread and salt. Salt cellars were highly valued; originally, this was due to the scarcity and consequent high cost of salt. The traditions surrounding salt cellars were continued in the

19th and early 20th centuries, when particularly beautiful examples were produced. From the second half of the 19th century, wooden and silver salt

cellars were produced in the shape of minutely detailed thrones, with lids that also functioned as the seat of the throne. These were particularly popular in Moscow art, which, in comparison with that of St. Petersburg, was notable for its adherence to Russian folk traditions.

This example from the Kremlin combines the shape of traditional Russian salt cellars with ornamentation based on ancient Russian motifs, a combination which is typical of the Russian Historical movement. Also characteristic is the use of wood, a material much favored in Russian folk art.

+

DISH

This beautiful dish was created by the workshop of Karl Karlovich Sholts, founded in Moscow in the 1870s. Master Sholts created many carved wooden works for prominent individuals and organizations who presented these treasures as gifts to members of the Imperial family. A number of these commissions were carried out in 1903, when Moscow played host to the royal family during the Easter celebration. As was the custom, Emperor Nicholas II and his family were offered bread and salt placed on this very dish. The dish's carved decoration details its history: the bowl is decorated with the monogram of Nicholas II and the inscription: "From the Moscow Guild of Merchants." Carved along the rim are medallions with the state emblem of Russia and the date.

Commemorative Coronation Towel

Commemorative Coronation Towel
1883
Russia
Linen, taffeta, silk thread, lace, weaving, embroidery, appliqué
8.6 feet x 1.9 feet (260 cm x 56 cm)
TK-693

Salt Cellar
1898
Moscow, Russia
Carved wood
5.9 inches (15 cm) height
DK-481

Dish
1903
Workshop of K. K. Sholts
Moscow, Russia
Carved wood
22 inches (56 cm) diameter
DK-352

Salt Cellar

Dish

CHAPTER IX

The Russian Orthodox Church

from the 18th to the 20th Century

The Russian Orthodox Church

from the 18th to the 20th Century

by I.I. Vishnevskaya

The 18th century, which began with the reforms of Peter the Great, ushered in a new era in Russian history, an era in which the Czar reigned supreme, dominating both secular and religious life. Secular culture was valued more highly than ecclesiastical culture, and the idea of "enlightened absolutism" took hold in the second half of the 18th century. Not surprisingly, these developments led to fundamental changes in the relations between the Czar and the Church.

The most significant aspect of this transformation was Peter's abolition of the Patriarchate and the introduction of a governing church body in 1721. The Ecclesiastical College, or Synod, was composed of eleven religious figures of varying rank, and was directly subordinate to the Czar. State supervision of the Synod was exercised by the Chief Procurator, an individual with a military or civilian background.

THE SUPREME JUDGE

The first sitting of the Synod was held after a ceremonial church service on February 14, 1721. Its members took a solemn oath to recognize the sovereign as the "supreme judge of this Ecclesiastical College." Soon afterwards, a three-story stone building was erected for the Synod in St. Petersburg, and its interior decor underlined the secular nature of the new

assembly of church rule. Its central meeting ha featured a portrait of Peter the Great.

Consequently, the Russian Orthodox Church became an apparatus of state and lost its nominal independence from secular power. Local bishops were now essentially state servants, differing from other ranks only in the dress. In the early 19th century, the secular powers continued to intervene in church affair

During the reign of Nicholas I, a system of controls over the Orthodox Church was gradually established, which in all its principal features remained unchanged until 1917. The Czar was the *de facto* and *de jure* head of the Orthodox Church; directly subordinate to him were the Chief Procurator, his assistants, and t Church Synod. The Czar chose his own confessor, who in the Church hierarchy occupied first place after the bishops and was head of the clergy serving in the court and palace churches.

The Church naturally resented its subordinate position to the state, and its disaffection was aggravated by the social and political crises tha gripped Russia in the early 20th century. A campaign was begun to convene a local counci and re-establish the Patriarchate. This council was eventually set up under the interim government on August 15, 1917, by which tim the government had abolished the duties of the Chief Procurator and had established a Minist of the Creed. The Moscow Metropolitan Tikho

as elected chairman of the council, and soon
ter was appointed Patriarch.

espite the broad changes to the legal status of
e Russian church in the early 18th century, the
le of the Orthodox faith as the ideological
undation of the state remained the same as in
e past. Peter the Great's first decree declared
ligion to be "the basis of the prosperity of the
ate, and the strongest support of the monarch's
rone." Events determined by royal
oclamation and government edict were
nderstood by the people to be primarily of a
ligious character. This was no accident:
roughout Russian history, from the time of the
doption of Christianity, religion had permeated
ciety. Russian Emperors, from the time of
icholas I, conducted their affairs on the basis of
Orthodoxy, Autocracy, Nationality," in that
der. This belief system was an outgrowth of the
aditional piety of the Russian people,
rticularly their conception of the monarch as a
zar-batiushka, or paternalistic Czar. To the
ople, the Czar was always the "Sovereign
ointed by God," head of both state and Church.

ussian Emperors customarily demonstrated
eir faith in Orthodoxy during sacred church
rvices and ceremonies. For example, on
hristmas Eve in 1722, Peter the Great sang in
e choir in the Cross Chamber of the former
lace of the Patriarch in Moscow. Contemp-
aries noted Peter's great knowledge of Church
octrine and that he considered the Bible "a
ok exceeding all others in wisdom." Peter's
ughter, the Empress Elizabeth Petrovna, was
rticularly remembered for her godliness.
om Catherine the Great onwards, all the
mpresses of the 18th and 19th centuries were
rict in their observance of the laws of the
ussian Church. This included those who, like
atherine, had been born as Western European
incesses and had converted to the Orthodox
ith in Russia. The Russian Emperors were no
ss committed believers.

RITUALS & SERVICES

Church ritual in the 18th and 19th centuries
maintained the conventions of previous
centuries. Feast day services and traditional
ceremonies such as christenings, marriages, and
funerals adhered to the ecclesiastical canon, but
beginning in the 18th century new decrees were
issued to regulate Church activities. One of these
instituted a mandatory annual confession;
another new element in Church life was the
inclusion in the calendar of "Czar's days," which
commemorated coronations, the name days of
the Czar and Czarina, the births of heirs, and
other events. On these days, church services
would begin with a prayer for the health of the
Czar, then the traditional pealing of the church
bells accompanied by cannon and rifle salutes.

Ceremonial church services were also held to
mark the completion of military campaigns, or
to celebrate the anniversaries of past victories.
After the conclusion of peace with Turkey in
1775, a solemn prayer service was held in the
Kazan Cathedral in St. Petersburg. The main
street from the Winter Palace to the Cathedral
was lined on both sides by two ranks of guards
and artillery regiments. At the moment the
prayer for long life to the sovereign was intoned
three volleys rang out, accompanied by a
cannon salute from the St. Peter and St. Paul
Fortress and the ringing of the church bells. The
ruler at the time, Catherine the Great, was in
Moscow for this celebration, where the main
services were held in the Kremlin's Assumption
Cathedral, long the holiest place in all of Russia.
This event was also marked by the richest of
royal donations to the Kremlin's cathedrals.
These included a stately collection of liturgical
plates, made of gold with brilliant-cut diamonds
and rubies, which the Empress herself placed on
the altar of the Assumption Cathedral.

The last service in Russia to commemorate
military events took place in the Assumption

Detail of *View of Emperor Alexander III inside
the Church of Christ the Savior in Moscow in
1883*

(Facing Page)
Detail of *View of Religious Procession at the
Sanctification of the Church of Christ the
Savior in Moscow in 1883*

Cathedral on August 1914. It was attended in person by Nicholas II, who had come to Moscow specially for the occasion. Pierre Gillard, the former tutor to Nicholas's son Czarevich Alexei, wrote that Nicholas "wanted to follow the example of his forebears in times of trouble, and ask God's blessing on himself and his people." The entire council of the Orthodox Church conducted the service: the Metropolitans of Moscow, St. Petersburg, and Kiev, along with other senior members of the clergy. At the end of the service, members of the royal family paid their respects to the relics of the prelates buried in the cathedral, and to the shrine of Alexei, one of the first Moscow Metropolitans, in the Chudov Monastery of the Kremlin.

The ceremonies dealing with the private life of the royal family such as weddings and christenings took place in the private chapel of the Winter Palace in St. Petersburg. The famous French traveler and man of letters, the Marquis de Custin, wrote a detailed description of the wedding ceremony in 1839 of Count Lichtenberg and the daughter of Nicholas I, the Grand Duchess Maria: "The marriage ceremony was prolonged and magnificent. Every aspect of the Eastern Church served as a symbol, and the magnificence of the church was enhanced by the glitter of the ceremony. The jewelry and precious stones worn by the ladies sparkled magically among the treasures adorning the walls of the cathedral, and it seems almost as if royal opulence was competing with the greatness of God. During the prayers, as one choir answered another, the royal gate was thrown open to reveal priests in gold vestments and headdresses studded with sparkling precious stones."

EASTER: THE FESTIVAL OF FESTIVALS

Easter was the principal festival of Russian Orthodoxy. It was preceded by the forty-day Lenten fast, which culminated in Holy Week. In 1900, after a break of more than half a century, Moscow again became the center of the grandiose Easter celebrations attended by the royal family, who once more observed the Orthodox "Festival of Festivals" in the ancient capital of the Russian state. The arrival of Nicholas II in Moscow was in itself a ceremonial event. When the Imperial train arrived from St Petersberg, the first peal from the great Kremlin Bell Tower rang out, followed by the bells of Moscow's churches.

The first service of Holy Week attended by the royal family in the Assumption Cathedral was the Feast of the Entry into Jerusalem. In a revival of the ritual of two centuries earlier, the Czar left the Palace and was met by a court priest with a cross and holy water, accompanied by singing from the court choir. After the ceremony of the Kissing of the Cross, the Czar took bread and salt from a carved wooden dish carried by the senior standard-bearer of the Assumption Cathedral. The south doors of the cathedral were then thrown open and members of the clergy emerged carrying incense burners, ancient crosses, the altar icon of the Mother of God, a gold cross on a dish, and a vessel containing holy water. The priests were followed by senior representatives of the clergy who were to conduct the service, led by the Moscow Metropolitan Vladimir. After the Metropolitan's welcoming speech, the participants entered the cathedral for the service.

On Monday of Holy Week, the royal couple went to the Mirovarennaya Chamber of the former Palace of the Patriarch in the Kremlin. Here, once every few years, the Boiling of the Chrism (the anointing oil) took place, one of the oldest rituals in the Orthodox Church. Members of the clergy were specially nominated to conduct this ceremony. Metropolitan Vladimir and other clerics wore black velvet chasubles decorated with silver galloon crosses.

immediately before the service, lighted candles were brought to the royal couple. The Metropolitan sprinkled holy water over the hearth, cauldrons, and scented oil. He poured the holy water into the cauldrons, then took the vessels containing wine, butter, and scented oil, blessed each of them and poured them into the cauldrons. He then added pieces of solid fragrant balm from silver plates. On Thursday of Holy Week, the ritual concluded with the solemn ceremony of the Consecration of the Holy Chrism in the Assumption Cathedral.

During Holy Week, the royal couple attended each of the most important services in the Kremlin churches and in the Cathedral of Christ the Savior, which had served as the cathedral of Moscow from the time of its consecration in 1889. The Easter Matins service was held in the Assumption Cathedral. In accordance with ancient custom, two incense burners were placed by the royal door in the church. At nine o'clock in the evening, passages from the Scriptures were read aloud; at midnight the Metropolitan entered the church to conduct the principal service, after which the Procession of the Cross set forth from the church. The procession was headed by the standard bearers, dressed in parade caftans, followed by the choristers of the Synod, then by priests holding the icon of the Mother of God, ancient crosses, the icon of the Resurrection of Christ, and the Gospels. The Metropolitan followed the priests, carrying a gold cross and a three-branched candlestick. The Metropolitan's mitre was adorned with a precious cross of brilliant-cut diamonds, which had been presented to him by the Emperor expressly for this service. The procession wound its way around the church to the west doors, where a solemn hymn was sung. The service ended at two o'clock in the morning.

The Easter celebration was vital to the lives of the royal family. Emperor Nicholas II and Empress Alexandra Feodorovna participated in the services, the procession, and the ensuing ceremony, which continued in the palace. From nine o'clock onwards, processions of festively dressed people entered the Kremlin. By half-past eleven all the Moscow nobility who had been invited to participate were already in their places in the palace, in different halls according to rank, after which the first celebratory cannonade rang out; half an hour later, the chimes of the Savior Tower heralded the dawn of a new day. At the first peal of the Kremlin bells, the most magnificent royal procession began, making its way through the halls of the Great Kremlin Palace towards the Upper Cathedral of the Savior. The Emperor was dressed in the uniform of a Lifeguard of the Preobrazhensky Regiment, with a chain of the Order of St. Andrew the First Called and a ribbon of the Order of St. Alexander Nevsky; the Empress wore a white dress embroidered with gold, with the ribbon of the Order of St. Catherine and the chain of the Order of St. Andrew the First Called. The Easter Matins service finished at half-past three in the morning. In the days that followed, according to tradition, the Empress extended her best wishes to the guests and presented each of them with an Easter egg.

The main Easter services attended by the Emperor in 1900 were held in the Assumption Cathedral, which was still considered by the faithful to be the most important church in Orthodox Russia. The Assumption Cathedral was the site of another defining moment in the history of the Russian Church: on November 21, 1917, the Metropolitan Tikhon was ceremonially enthroned, signifying the return of the Patriarchate in Russia. Of course, by this time, Nicholas II—the last Romanov ruler, whose line could be traced to Mikhail Feodorovich, the first Romanov ruler—had abdicated the throne, and the royal dynasty of the Romanovs was no more.

Mitre of the Archbishop Arseny

MITRE OF THE ARCHBISHOP ARSENY

The gold band that rims this mitre's lower edge contai a stamped inscription denoting that the mitre was presented to the Archbishop Arseny of the Troitse-Sergiev Monastery by Empress Elizabeth Petrovna on November 25, 1744.

The gold-brocade mitre is decorated with enamel pane containing portraits of the three-figured deesis, the guardian angel, St. Zachary, St. Elizabeth, St. Sergius of Radonezh, and St. Nikon. St. Elizabeth was the patron saint of the Empress, while Sergius and Nikon were the founders of the Troitse-Sergiev Monastery. The Holy Trinity is portrayed on a lozenge-shaped panel in the top center of the mitre. The mitre is decorated with sparkling brilliant-cut diamonds, rubies, and smooth, carefully selected pearls. It was clearly the work of the finest court craftsmen. The mitre also includes pearl-embroidered renderings of the two-headed eagle unde a crown, with an orb and scepter in its claws—the state emblem of Russia.

Mitre of the Archbishop Arseny
1744
St. Petersburg, Russia
Brocade, silk, gold, silver, gem stones, pearls, glass, gold thread, weaving, enamel, embossing
8.7 inches (22 cm) height
TK-95

Mantle (Phelon)
1768
Russia
Brocade, corded fabric, galloon, cord, gold, silver, gem stones, pearls, glass; weaving, embroidery, filigree, enamel, carving
63 inches (160 cm) length
TK-2137

MANTLE (PHELON)

The *phelon* (from the Greek word "*phailonion*") was an ancient ecclesiastical garment in the form of a long, broad sleeveless mantle. This phelon was made in 1768 by order of Empress Catherine the Great for the Assumption Cathedral in the Moscow Kremlin. Magnificent gold and silver brocade was used in its preparation and was probably crafted by weavers in Moscow, utilizing French cloth from the mid-18th century. The shoulders of the garment are adorned with large pearls and a multitude of gold studs containing precious stones, which follow the contours of the garment's design.

Mantle (Phelon)

Communion Chalice

Pectoral Icon (Panagia)

Tabernacle

⊃MMUNION CHALICE

∎is gold chalice belonged to one of the splendid sets of ⌐urch wares donated by Catherine the Great to the most ∎portant cathedrals and monasteries in Russia. ∎nfortunately, none of the sets has survived in its ∎tirety. Judging by what has been preserved, however, ∎ese sets were alike in form and artistic decoration. ∎ade in the 1780s and 90s, the sets were the work of the ∎mous St. Petersburg master Ivan Venfeld Bukh, and ∎re wonderful examples of the classical style of Russian ∎plied art. Their finish mixed precious stones with ∎graved gems and reflected the current interests in ∎ssical antiquity and the ancient art of gem-carving. As ∎is communion chalice displays, the combination of ∎ld, carved stones, and diamonds helped to create ∎ssels of rich elegance.

∎CTORAL ICON (PANAGIA)

∎ the second half of the 18th century, pectoral icons, or ∎nagiae, belonging to the highest ranks of the clergy ∎re of particular opulence and beauty. With their ∎undance of diamonds, pearls, and other gems, these ∎ctoral icons were similar to the decorative classical ∎yle favored by the secular nobility. The cool, restrained ∎nge of colors consisting mainly of blue and gray ∎amel, the strength and delicacy of the composition, ∎d the precision of the details contribute to the ∎cellence of this piece. In the center of the pectoral icon ∎ a small half-length enamel portrayal of Christ. A ∎aque in a sumptuous diamond frame is decorated with ∎tertwined ribbons, rosettes, and crosses.

TABERNACLE

Tabernacles (which were used to store the Eucharist) were usually exceedingly expensive to produce and only commissioned by Russia's wealthy monasteries and churches. The tabernacle shown here was made by one of the renowned silver masters at the turn of the 18th century, Alexei Ratkov. He had mastered all the different jeweler's tools and techniques—embossing, niello, casting, carving and gilding—and employed them with great skill during the creation of this tabernacle. The object came to the Kremlin Museums from Viatka, a city in the Urals, and was most likely ordered for the benefit of a local church.

Communion Chalice
1795
Ivan Venfeld Bukh
St. Petersburg, Russia
Gold, silver, diamonds, semi-precious stones, embossing, casting, engraving, filigree, stone carving
12.4 inches (31.5 cm) height
MR-842

Pectoral Icon (*Panagia*)
1787-1792
Russia
Gold, silver, diamonds, pearls, embossing, carving, enamel, gilding
5.8 x 2.7 inches (14.8 cm x 6.8 cm)
MR-568/1-2

Tabernacle
1792
Alexei Ratkov
Moscow, Russia
Silver, embossing, carving, casting, niello, gilding
31.1 inches (79 cm) height
12.0 x 10.7 inches (30.4 cm x 27.1 cm) base
MR-700/1-2

Gospels in Frame
Book: 1698, Moscow
Frame/Binding: 1749, Moscow
Clasp: 1789, Moscow
Gold, silver, gem stones, wood, paper,
embossing, enamel, engraving, gilding
21.2 x 15.4 inches (54 cm x 39 cm)
KN-184

Gospels in Frame (back view)

Gospels in Frame (front view)

GOSPELS IN FRAME

This framed book of the Gospels was created in 1749 in a Moscow church for the widow Catherine Evreinova, possibly in memory of her husband. The book itself, published in 1698, contains 225 pages and four engravings with depictions of the Four Evangelists. The luxurious silver frame is decorated with enamel and precious stones; a total of 387 rubies, emeralds, diamonds, and sapphires were employed in the decoration of the frame. The spine of the book depicts bunches of fruit and a gathering of angels. The two clasp feature images of the Apostles Peter and Paul and were created in 1789 to replace the broken originals. The embossed baroque ornamentation on the frame was popular in Russia in the first half of the 18th century.

ALTAR CROSS

The 1770s were the height of popularity for the Rococo style in the silvermaking shops of Moscow. Masters labored over complicated methods of ornamentation, which often included rendering small masterpieces with relief embossing, painted enamel, and niello. This altar cross is decorated with a depiction of the Crucifixion in the center against a gold background which works stunningly with the gold relief design. On the backside of the cross is an inscription revealing its provenance: it was created in Moscow in 1774 for the Church of St. Nicholas Chudotvorets.

Altar Cross
1774
Master Ivan Savelev
Moscow, Russia
Silver, embossing, niello, carving, flat chasing, gilding
18.1 x 12.6 x 1.4 inches (46 cm x 32 cm x 3.5 cm)
MR-4939

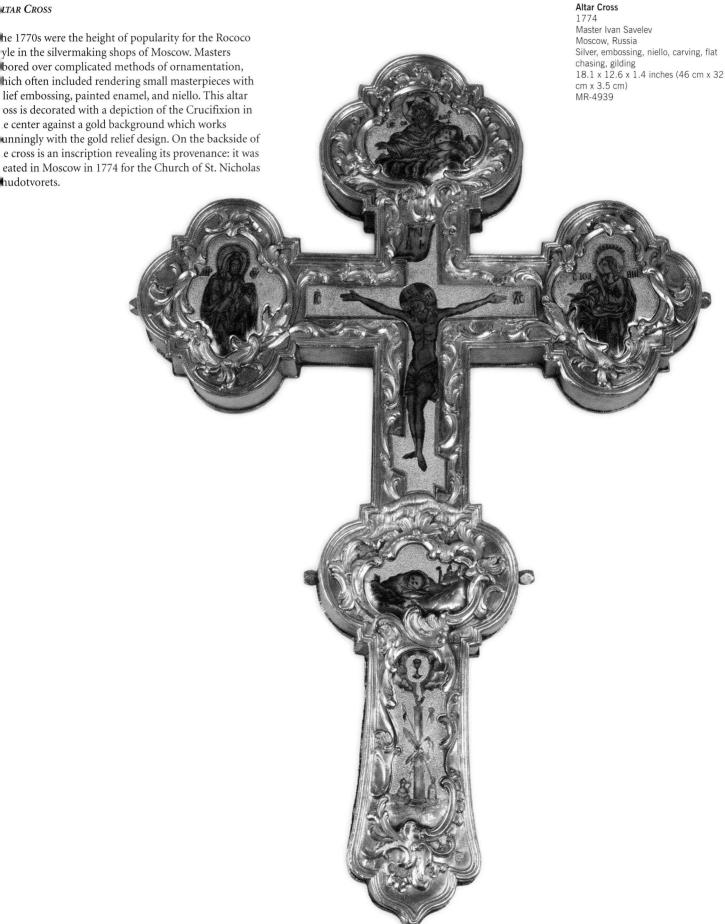

Altar Cross

Sakkos of the Metropolitan Filaret
1856
Moscow, Russia
Two types of brocade, silver and gold
thread, lace, braid, sequins, fringe,
copper, weaving, embroidery, gilding
4.2 feet (128 cm) length

Omofor of the Metropolitan Filaret
1856
Moscow, Russia
Velvet, silver, gold threads, lace, fringe,
weaving, embroidery, gilding
13 feet (396 cm) length, 9.4 inches (24
cm) width
TK-436

Palitsa of the Metropolitan Filaret
1856
Moscow, Russia
Velvet, silver, gold threads, lace, sequins,
fringe, silk ribbon, weaving, embroidery,
gilding
22.4 inches (57 cm) length, 20.5 inches
(52 cm) width
TK-437

Sakkos of the Metropolitan Filaret

Omofor of the Metropolitan Filaret

SAKKOS OF THE METROPOLITAN FILARET

The *sakkos* is the chief ecclesiastical robe of the Russian archbishops; it represented the mantel worn by Christ during his desecration and is considered the garment of salvation. This sakkos is sewn from gold and silver brocade. The highly symbolic parts of the sakkos—the shoulders, apron, cuffs, and hem—are distinguished by long strips of wide gold lace. The edge of the cuffs are sewn with gold braid. It was designed and assembled for the Moscow Metropolitan Filaret for the coronation of Alexander II on August 26, 1856. The Metropolitan Filaret was the head of the Orthodox church for the entire Russian state for over forty years. He played an integral role in the ideological formation of the Russian rulers, and he was known not only for his knowledge of church politics but politics in general.

✦

OMOFOR OF THE METROPOLITAN FILARET

In the Russian Orthodox tradition, the *omofor* is the colorful representation of the archbishops' holy orders and was worn on top of his other vestments. The omofor stood for both the lost sheep and Christ as shepherd, who raised the flock to his shoulders and bore their weight. This omofor was part of the ceremonial robes of the Metropolitan Filaret and was made for him for the coronation of Alexander II. The vestment is sewn out of smooth red velvet and decorated with silver and gold six-pointed stars, and four crosses sewn in gold thread and lace.

PALITSA OF THE METROPOLITAN FILARET

The *palitsa* is one of the seven elements of the archbishops' robes in the Russian Orthodox church. It is generally worn on the right side of the body and attached to a belt with a special hook or to a long white ribbon across the left shoulder. The palitsa symbolized the spiritual sword—the sword of the word of God, with which the archbishops could ward off any act of heresy. This palitsa belonged to the Metropolitan Filaret. It was made from smooth red velvet and decorated with gilded silver six-pointed stars, gold lace, and silver and gold fringe and tassels.

Palitsa of the Metropolitan Filaret

Icon of "The Almighty Savior" in Frame and Shrine

ON OF "THE ALMIGHTY SAVIOR" IN FRAME AND SHRINE

is enshrined icon and frame were created by one of
most famous Russian firms for the creation of church
res, P.I. Olovianishnikov & Sons, founded by Porfiry
novich Olovianishnikov, in Yaroslavl. A second factory
church wares was opened in Moscow in 1848. The
m also maintained a shop in the main shopping mall
St. Petersburg. The head master of the firm was S. I.
shkov who adhered to a style of religious Russian art
sed on traditional Russian folk art and art from the
iddle Ages. He and his firm of craftsmen sought to
ate religious pieces of graceful simplicity, as can be
n in this impeccable example.

✣

NEDICTION CROSS

is luxurious cross was made in 1910 by the famous
m of M. Khlebnikov, which was often commissioned
the Russian court. Altar crosses such as this were used
ring the liturgy and confessions as well as during
ristening and marriage ceremonies held in the Russian
thodox church. This cross is decorated with pockets
ed with enamel and large dark-blue sapphires,
eralds and rubies. The back of the cross is covered in a
otif of white enamel and dark and light-blue flowers.

Benediction cross

**Icon of "The Almighty Savior" in Frame
and Shrine**
Late 19th-early 20th century
Firm of P.I. Olovianishnikov & Sons
Russia
Silver, glass, wood, gesso, tempera,
lacquer, cardboard, brocade, silk, colored
thread, gold thread, embossing, casting,
engraving, filigree, enamel, cloisonné,
painting
12.2 x 10.2 inches (31 cm x 26 cm)
icon in frame
15.7 x 13.4 inches (40 cm x 34 cm)
shrine
MR-12914/1-3

Benediction cross
1910
Firm of M. Khlebnikov
Moscow, Russia
Silver, gem stones, pearl, embossing,
enamel, cloisonné, filigree
12.2 x 5.7 inches (31 cm x 14.5 cm)
MR-1255

RUSSIAN CATALOGUE CONTRIBUTORS

CHIEF EDITOR

A. K. Levykin

SCIENTIFIC DIRECTOR
THE STATE HISTORICAL AND CULTURAL MUSEUM AND PRESERVE OF THE MOSCOW KREMLIN

SECTION EDITORS AND COMPILERS

S. A. Amelekhina
I. A. Bobrovnitskaya
I. I. Vishnevskaya

A. K. Levykin
M. V. Martynova
V. G. Chubinskaya

AUTHORS OF ESSAYS

I. A. Bobrovnitskaya
I. I. Vishnevskaya
A. K. Levykin
M. V. Martynova

O. B. Melnikova
T. N. Muntian
V. M. Nikitina

AUTHORS OF CATALOGUE DESCRIPTIONS

N. E. Abramova
S. A. Amelekhina
I. A. Bobrovnitskaya
I. A. Bogatskaya
I. I. Vishnevskaya
M. V. Vilkova
M. P. Golovanova
I. V. Gorbatova
I. A. Zagorodniaya
S. Ia. Kovarskaya

I. D. Kostina
I. A. Komarov
Z. A. Kodrikova
A. G. Kudriavtseva
L. P. Kirillova
A. K. Levykin
O. I. Mironova
M. V. Martynova
V. A. Morshakova
N. D. Markina

T. N. Muntian
O.B. Melnikova
V. M. Nikitina
A. I. Romanenko
N.A Smirnova
T. V. Samoilova
V. S. Fedotova
V. G. Chubinskaya
E. V. Shakurova
E. A. Iablonskaya

OBJECT PHOTOGRAPHER

V. N. Seregin

Note on Transliteration
Transliteration of the Russian alphabet in the texts throughout this catalogue follows the Library of Congress system, except when the name of an individual or place is more easily identifiable by a familiar English spelling.

Note on Object Captions
The captions for the objects in the exhibition list the name of the object, date, maker, place of origin, medium, dimensions, and the inventory number used by the Kremlin Museums.